AF605924

A Catalog of Identifiable Figure Painters of Ancient Pompeii, Herculaneum, and Stabiae

A Catalog of Identifiable Figure Painters of Ancient Pompeii, Herculaneum, and Stabiae

L. Richardson, jr

The Johns Hopkins University Press
BALTIMORE AND LONDON

Printed in the United States of America on acid-free paper
2 4 6 8 9 5 3 7 1

The Johns Hopkins University Press
2715 North Charles Street
Baltimore, Maryland 21218-4363
www.press.jhu.edu

Library of Congress Cataloging-in-Publication Data
will be found at the end of this book.
A catalog record for this book is available from
the British Library.

ISBN 0-8018-6235-3

Contents

Preface

The catalog presented in this work is described in the title and designed to be a working tool for those seriously interested in the study of ancient Roman painting. Consequently it is selective rather than comprehensive, including, by and large, only pictures that are well enough preserved to permit assured attribution and not more than a fraction of what survives from the sites that were buried by the eruption of Vesuvius in A.D. 79. In some ways it is random, dependent on chance encounters that proved unexpectedly illuminating, but I have also, I believe, at some time systematically scrutinized, with the idea of making attributions, every picture in the galleries of the Museo Nazionale Archeologico in Naples and its storerooms and every adequately preserved apartment in the ruins of the ancient cities.

The references that follow each catalog entry are intended only for purposes of identification; where possible, these are citations of the catalogs of Helbig (H) and Sogliano (S) and the current inventory numbers that appear on labels in the Museo Nazionale. The other citations are of photographic reproductions of the pictures in published works, here given in chronological order and with dates, so the reader will not expect illustration in a book now sixty or more years old to be of the same quality as more recent work. Reproduction, especially of color photography, as well as color photography itself, has advanced by giant strides in the last half-century. There are, however, pictures in the works of Curtius and Rizzo that one cannot find reproduced elsewhere. The best published reproductions of a considerable range and number of ancient pictures are to be found in *Peinture* 1993, Guillaud and Guillaud 1990, Ragghianti 1963, and Maiuri 1953. Although the coverage in *PPM* is very thorough, the photographs of pictures, especially those in the Museo Nazionale Archeologico, are often taken from old collections and are uneven in quality, not infrequently distorting the value of color and line, while those in many recent works are intended more as aides-mémoire than for purposes of study. Sound attribution, however, can never be founded on or tested on the basis of photography alone; it can only be arrived at by close scrutiny of the original and rigorous application of the methods of connoisseurship laid down by G. Morelli in the nineteenth century. Therefore, these citations are intended only for the convenience of the reader and in many cases include reproductions that are of inferior quality.

Furthermore, the citations are not intended as bibliography, nor as a substitute for bibliography. Exemplary bibliographies are now provided at the beginning of each volume of *PPM.* These cover every aspect of the material and are as complete as can be asked for Pompeii and the appearance of important new scholarship focused on it almost monthly. It would be otiose to duplicate these or to offer a selection from them when so little scholarly attention has so far been given to connoisseurship. The interested reader will find citation of such individual contributions as there have been at the appropriate points in the introduction to each painter's work.

I first began to be interested in the contribution that connoisseurship might make to the study of ancient Roman painting in the summer of 1948, while working on a republication of the Casa dei Dioscuri. At that time I was interested only in the surprising number and variety of painters who had worked in that house and their importance as shown by their work elsewhere in the buried cities, but this alerted me to the larger implications of such work. Over the half-century since then I have pursued it intermittently on both sides of the Atlantic, in academic seminars at the American Academy in Rome, at Yale University, and at Duke University, in museums that include Pompeian paintings in their collections, and in the excavations. I have repeatedly received invaluable help from the staffs of these institutions, from my colleagues, and from my students. They are too numerous to mention individually, but to all of them I offer my sincerest thanks. More recently, in the preparation of my efforts for publication I have benefited from the kindness and indulgence of the Department of Classical Studies of Duke University and the Johns Hopkins University Press; to these also I am more than grateful. I am especially indebted to Joanne Allen, who has been responsible for the removal of multiple blemishes from my work.

Abbreviations

Alla ricerca di Iside 1992

R. Cantilena and G. Prisco, eds. *Alla ricerca di Iside: Analisi, studi e restauri dell'Iseo pompeiano nel Museo di Napoli.* Catalog of an exhibition at the Museo Nazionale Archeologico, Naples, inaugurated 15 December 1992.

Allroggen-Bedel 1977

A. Allroggen-Bedel. "Die Wandmalereien aus der villa in Campo Varano (Castellammare di Stabia)." *RömMitt* 84 (1988) 27–89.

Beyen 1938

H. G. Beyen. *Die pompejanische Wanddekoration vom zweiten bis zum vierten Stil.* Vol. 1. The Hague 1938.

BMC 1933

R. P. Hinks. *Catalogue of the Greek, Etruscan, and Roman Paintings and Mosaics in the British Museum.* London 1933.

Brion 1960

M. Brion. *Pompeii and Herculaneum: The Glory and the Grief.* Trans. J. Rosenberg. London 1960.

BullNap

Bullettino Archeologico Napoletano. 7 vols. Naples 1843–63.

Collezioni 1986

R. Pedicini and L. Pedicini, eds. *Le collezioni del Museo Nazionale di*

Napoli, i mosaici, le pitture, gli oggetti di uso quotidiano, gli argenti, le terracotte invetriate, i vetri, i cristalli, gli avori. Rome 1986.

CP

Cronache pompeiane, rivista dell'associazione internazionale "Amici di Pompei." 5 vols. Naples 1975–79.

Curtis 1988

R. I. Curtius, ed. *Studia Pompeiana et Classica in Honor of Wilhelmina F. Jashemski*. 2 vols. New Rochelle, N.Y. 1988.

Curtius 1929

L. Curtius. *Die Wandmalerei Pompejis, ein Einführung in ihr Verständnis.* Leipzig 1929. Reprint. Hildesheim 1960.

DAI

Deutsches Archäologisches Institut.

De Caro 1994

S. De Caro. *Il Museo Archeologico Nazionale di Napoli*. Naples 1994.

de Franciscis 1963

A. de Franciscis. *Il Museo Nazionale di Napoli*. Cava dei Tirreni 1963.

de Franciscis 1978

A. de Franciscis. *Pompeii and Herculaneum: The Buried Cities.* New York 1978.

Elia 1932

O. Elia. *Pitture murali e mosaici nel Museo Nazionale di Napoli*. Rome 1932.

Elia 1957

O. Elia. *Pitture di Stabia*. Naples 1957.

Elia 1961

O. Elia, "Il portico dei triclini del Pagus Maritimus di Pompei." *Bullettino d'arte* 46 (1961) 200–211.

Eschebach 1978

Pompeji: Erlebte antike Welt. Leipzig 1978.

Fröhlich 1991

T. Fröhlich. *Lararien- und Fassadebilder in den Vesuvstädten.* Mainz am Rhein 1991.

Fröhlich 1996

T. Fröhlich. *Casa della Fontana Piccola (VI 8, 23. 24).* Munich 1996.

Gierow 1994

M. S. Gierow. *Casa del Granduca (VII 4, 56), Casa dei Capitelli Figurati (VII 4, 57).* Munich 1994.

Grant 1975

M. Grant. *Eros in Pompeii: The Secret Rooms of the National Museum of Naples.* New York 1975.

Grimal and Kossakowski 1993

P. Grimal. *Pompéi—Demeures secrètes.* Paris 1993. Photographs by E. Kossakowski.

Guillaud and Guillaud 1990

J. Guillaud and M. Guillaud. *Frescoes in the Time of Pompeii.* Paris 1990.

H

W. Helbig. *Wandgemälde der von Vesuv verschütteten Städte Campaniens.* Leipzig 1868.

HBr

P. Herrmann. Continued by R. Herbig. *Denkmäler der Malerei des Altertums.* 3 vols. Munich 1904–50. Plates by F. Bruckmann.

Herbig 1962

R. Herbig. *Nugae Pompeianorum.* Tübingen 1962.

Jashemski 1979

W. F. Jashemski. *The Gardens of Pompeii, Herculaneum, and the Villas Destroyed by Vesuvius.* New Rochelle, N.Y. 1979.

KJ

Kölner Jahrbuch für Vor- und Frühgeschichte.

Kraus and von Matt 1973

T. Kraus and L. von Matt. *Lebendiges Pompeji: Pompeji und Herculaneum, Antlitz und Schicksal zweier antike Städte.* Cologne 1973.

Leach 1988

E. W. Leach. *The Rhetoric of Space: Literary and Artistic Representations of Landscape in Republican and Augustan Rome.* Princeton 1988.

Ling 1991

R. Ling. *Roman Painting.* Cambridge 1991.

London, BM

British Museum, London.

Maiuri 1933

A. Maiuri. *La Casa del Menandro e il suo tesoro di argenteria.* 2 vols. Rome 1933.

Maiuri 1953

A. Maiuri. *Roman Painting.* Lausanne 1953.

Maiuri 1958

A. Maiuri. *Ercolano, i nuovi scavi (1927–1958)*. 2 vols. Rome 1958.

Marcadé 1965

J. Marcadé. *Roma amor.* Geneva 1965.

Marini 1971

G. L. Marini. *Il gabinetto segreto del Museo Nazionale di Napoli*. Turin 1971.

MB

Real Museo di Napoli (Museo Borbonico). 16 vols. Naples 1823–68.

MdPA

Monumenti della pittura antica scoperti in Italia, Sezione terza, La pittura ellenistico-romana.

Mededelingen

Mededelingen van het Nederlands Instituut te Rome.

Michel 1990

D. Michel. *Casa dei Cei (I 6, 15)*. Munich 1990.

MN

Museo Nazionale Archeologico, Naples.

MonAnt

Monumenti antichi pubblicati dall'Accademia dei Lincei.

Neue Forschungen 1975

B. Andreae and H. Kyrieleis, eds. *Neue Forschungen in Pompeji*. Recklinghausen 1975.

New York, MMA

Metropolitan Museum of Art, New York.

NSc

Notizie degli scavi di antichità.

Pagano 1983

M. Pagano. "L'edificio dell'Agro Murecine a Pompei." *Rendiconti della Accademia di Archeologia, Lettere, e Belle Arti di Napoli,* n.s. 58 (1983) 325–61.

Paris, Louvre, MND

Partial inventory of the Musée du Louvre, Paris.

Peinture 1993

G. Cerulli-Irelli, M. Aoyagi, S. De Caro, and U. Pappalardo, eds. *La Peinture de Pompéi.* 2 vols. Paris 1993.

Peters 1963

W. J. T. Peters. *Landscape in Romano-Campanian Painting.* Assen 1963.

Peters 1993

W. J. T. Peters. *La Casa di Marcus Lucretius Fronto a Pompei e le sue pitture.* Amsterdam 1993.

Picard 1970

G. Picard. *Roman Painting.* London 1970.

Pompei 1748–1980

G. Ferrari, ed. *Pompei 1748–1980: I tempi della documentazione.* Rome 1981. Catalog of an exhibition in the Curia Senatus, Foro Romano, Rome, July–September 1981.

Pompeji: Leben und Kunst 1973

Pompeji: Leben und Kunst in den Vesuvstädten. Recklinghausen 1973. Catalog of an exhibition at the Villa Hügel, Essen, 19 April–15 July 1973.

PPM

G. Pugliese Carratelli and I. Baldassarre, eds. *Pompei: Pitture e mosaici.* Istituto della Enciclopedia Italiana. 9 vols. to date. Rome 1990–.

Presuhn 1878

E. Presuhn. *Pompeji: Die neuesten Ausgrabungen von 1874 bis 1878.* Leipzig 1878.

Presuhn 1882

E. Presuhn. *Die pompejanischen Wanddecorationen.* Leipzig 1882.

Ragghianti 1963

C. L. Ragghianti. *Pittori di Pompei.* Milan 1963.

RdSP

Rivista di studi pompeiani. Associazione internazionale "Amici di Pompei." 7 vols. to date. Rome 1987–.

Richardson 1955

L. Richardson, jr. *Pompeii: The Casa dei Dioscuri and Its Painters.* Memoirs of the American Academy in Rome 23. Rome 1955.

Rizzo 1929

G. E. Rizzo. *La pittura ellenistico-romana.* Milan 1929.

RömMitt

Mitteilungen des Deutschen Archäologischen Instituts, Römische Abteilung.

RP

S. Reinach. *Répertoire de peintures grecques et romaines.* Paris 1922. Reprint. Rome 1970.

S

A. Sogliano. "Le pitture murali campane scoperte negli anni 1867–1879." In *Pompei e la regione sotterrata dal Vesuvio nell'anno 79,* 87–243. Naples 1879.

Schefold 1957

K. Schefold. *Die Wände Pompejis, topographisches Verzeichnis.* Berlin 1957.

Schefold 1962

K. Schefold. *Vergessenes Pompeji.* Bern 1962.

Seider 1968

R. Seider. *Römische Malerei.* Königstein im Taunus 1968.

Seiler 1992

F. Seiler. *Casa degli Amorini Dorati (VI 16, 7. 38).* Munich 1992.

Spinazzola 1928

V. Spinazzola. *Le arti decorative in Pompei e nel Museo Nazionale di Napoli.* Milan 1928.

Spinazzola 1953

V. Spinazzola. *Pompei alla luce degli scavi nuovi di Via dell'Abbondanza (anni 1910–1923).* 3 vols. Rome 1953.

Stemmer 1992

K. Stemmer. *Casa dell'Ara Massima (VI 16, 15–17).* Munich 1992.

Stenico 1963

A. Stenico. *Roman and Etruscan Painting.* Compass History of Art. New York 1963.

Strocka 1984

V. M. Strocka. *Casa del Principe di Napoli (VI 15, 7–8).* Berlin 1984.

Strocka 1991

V. M. Strocka. *Casa del Labirinto (VI 11, 8–10).* Munich 1991.

Tran Tam Tinh 1974

Tran Tam Tinh. *Catalogue des peintures romaines (Latium et Campanie) du Musée du Louvre.* Paris 1974.

von Blanckenhagen and Alexander 1990

P. H. von Blanckenhagen and C. Alexander. *The Augustan Villa at Boscotrecase.* Mainz am Rhein 1990.

Ward-Perkins and Claridge 1978

J. B. Ward-Perkins and A. Claridge. *Pompeii A.D. 79.* Catalog of an exhibition at the Museum of Fine Arts, Boston. 2 vols. Boston 1978.

Wojcik 1986

M. R. Wojcik. *La Villa dei Papiri ad Ercolano.* Rome 1986.

Zahn

W. Zahn. *Die schönsten Ornamente und merkwürdigsten Gemälde aus Pompeji, Herculanum und Stabiae.* 3 vols. Berlin 1828–59.

Zevi 1964

F. Zevi. *La casa Reg. IX 5, 18–21 a Pompei e la sua pittura.* Studi miscellanei 5. Rome 1964.

Zevi 1991

F. Zevi, ed. *Pompei I.* Naples 1991.

Zevi 1992

F. Zevi, ed. *Pompei II.* Naples 1992.

A Catalog of Identifiable Figure Painters of Ancient Pompeii, Herculaneum, and Stabiae

Introduction

It is well known that Pompeii was destroyed in an eruption of Vesuvius in late August A.D. 79. Although some people, presumably survivors, returned to the ruined city and tried to eke out an existence there for a short time, probably not more than a few weeks or months, these were most likely only salvagers and treasure hunters who had no intention of staying permanently. The site was then abandoned and soon overgrown with vegetation, and eventually its very name was forgotten. There is no sign that the site was contaminated by occupation later in antiquity. It is only a little less well known that seventeen years before the eruption of Vesuvius, on 5 February A.D. 62, a catastrophic earthquake destroyed about three-quarters of the city, so much of it that none of the buildings surrounding the forum was usable and almost no house left unscathed. Amedeo Maiuri in *L'ultima fase edilizia di Pompei* (Rome 1942) attempted to document the destruction, but he could only indicate its extent in the private houses, where the suturing of cracks and hasty patching together of rooms to make them habitable attest to the frantic efforts of householders with a stringently reduced work force and the pressing demands of public works. When the water supply and municipal government were crippled by the disaster, private citizens must have had to defer to public necessity. One can imagine that earthquake relief and aid would have been forthcoming from Rome, but we know no details about what form it may have taken or how long it may have lasted. At the time of the eruption much still remained to be done in the forum. Although the general food market, the macellum, had been early repaired and repainted, this was done in clearly makeshift form, the tholus of the fishmongers in the center of the court a temporary construction, its roof supported on posts of wood that have disappeared, and the decoration of the walls only painting carried out with little concern for what might be appropriate. The interior of the portico of Eumachia was still in construction, although the elaborate chalcidicum preceding it on the forum had been rebuilt and redecorated, possibly in order to see how this would balance against the new, two-story colonnade being built along the opposite side of the forum. If the basilica near the southwest corner of the forum was functioning at all, it was simply as a roofless enclosure. And work on the temple of Jupiter that dominated the forum at its northern end was still far in the future, the colossal head of the cult statue wrapped in a tarpaulin, the fallen columns cleared away, but with no sign of work on their replacement, and the cult of the Capitoline triad moved to the little temple of Jupiter Meilichios on Strada Stabiana for the time being.

In these circumstances it is hardly surprising to find that most houses in Pompeii were incomplete at the time of the eruption, that many had rooms waiting to be plastered and painted, that even some of the finest houses were still in need of major construction. Most Pompeians had at least some rooms that had been repaired and refurbished, but this had been done a little at a time, only one room perhaps as a beginning, others singly or in small groups at scattered intervals. A house that, like the Casa di Meleagro or the Casa del Menandro, shows extensive consistency of style, evidently the work of a team of decorators working over a comparatively short period, is an anomaly. Even when the whole house is well decorated in the last Pompeian style, one can expect to find striking differences from room to room, suggesting that considerable time elapsed between one room's decoration and another's and that these were the work of very different hands and shops. Even as fine a house as the Casa dei Dioscuri shows great inconsistencies in the various decorations, and although there can have been no lack of money here, one of the dining rooms is still decorated in the Third Style, which we think of as entirely pre-earthquake. One might well imagine on the face of the evidence that a patchwork of decorations, either in the various styles identified by Mau, which are essentially chronologically successive and run from the second century B.C. to the eruption of Vesuvius, as in the Casa dei Quattro Stili and the Domus Sex. Pompei Axiochi, or within the Fourth Style itself and its range of variety, was aesthetically appealing to the Pompeians. Sometimes this differentiation will have been used to define rooms of different purposes, to be sure, but more often it seems to have been a consequence of time and different painters. There are many indications that the Pompeians were conservative in their tastes, that a venerable mansion such as the Casa del Fauno was a prized possession that called for scrupulous maintenance, and that even in the last period of Pompeii the architectural taste looked backward more than forward. Although one does not find deliberate archaizing in the decorations of the Fourth Style, attempts at reproduction of the

Second or First Style, such decorations are sometimes repaired and preserved, and the fine room of a previous generation, even an immediately preceding generation, was often respected or admired. This tendency has proved endlessly puzzling to archaeologists and endlessly perplexing to those trying to date decorations within the Third and Fourth Styles.

The dates of these styles are by no means easy to set even in broad lines. The First Style is at least as old as the earliest great houses in Pompeii, the Casa di Sallustio and the Casa del Fauno, built toward the beginning of the second century B.C., and appears there in full flower. It has been claimed to go back as early as the fourth century, although there is as yet no clear evidence on this point. The Second Style is probably no older than the time of Sulla, and at Pompeii the time of the Sullan colony. We see it in an early example in the Casa delle Nozze d'Argento and in later examples in the Villa dei Misteri and the Villa di Poppea at Oplontis. All these are sumptuous houses, and the preservation of important rooms decorated in this style bears witness to the respect it commanded long after it had been supplanted. If the Casa di Augusto, on the Palatine Hill in Rome, may be taken as a gauge, it continued to be readily available down at least to the beginning of the first century after Christ, since parts of the decoration of that house in a late version of the style must be presumed to date from repairs after a fire of A.D. 3 (Cassius Dio 55.12.4–5).

Decorations transitional between the Second and Third Styles are surprisingly numerous and should perhaps be considered a separate style. They include the Casa di Livia on the Palatine in Rome, the Casa della Farnesina on the right bank of the Tiber in Rome, the building discovered under the Scuderie Reali in the environs of Herculaneum, and the Casa di Obellio Firmo in Pompeii, IX xiv 4. These are all fine buildings of generous proportions, but at least one room in the style in VI Ins. Occ. 41, that from which come panels in the Museo Nazionale in Naples showing a tholus with miniature staffage figures between still lifes of fish and game of heroic scale and with fine detail, was diminutive, a *jeu d'esprit.* These decorations are universally judged to be Augustan, but because they present certain Third Style elements, sometimes strong characteristics, their date in the Augustan age must be relatively late, toward the end of Augustus's life. The Third Style, on the other hand, has been thought to begin as early as the building of the Pyramid of Cestius in Rome, that is, prior to 12 B.C., and to have reached full flower by the time of the decoration of the Villa di Agrippa Postumo at Boscotrecase, perhaps about the turn of the century. This seems unlikely, and none of the dates is very firmly fixed. Vitruvius, writing early in the principate of Augustus, almost certainly before 28 B.C., inveighs against a style of decoration that includes illogical conjunctions and fantastic elements not to be found in nature. Although he enumerates several of these, it is not clear whether he is offended by the inventions of the Third Style or by those of the late Second Style. When he speaks of columns that appear to be canes and reeds supporting excessively heavy superstructures (7.5.3), he seems to be talking about the Third Style. When he speaks of peopled scrolls, centaurs supporting epistyles, and tholi (7.5.5), however, he seems very clearly to be talking about elements characteristic of the Second. It seems best at this point to think that he is especially offended by the transitional style and that it lasted alongside a "purer" Second Style from the time of the second triumvirate down to the time of Tiberius. Improbable as this may seem, it is certainly not impossible, and the number of examples that survives can be seen to support such a thesis.

If the Third Style did not come into full blossom before the accession of Tiberius, it must then have spread very fast and vigorously. There are few houses in Pompeii that one would characterize as Third Style overall, and those there are are relatively modest, with small rooms, relatively few in number. What large rooms there are in this style, the great oecus of the Villa Imperiale, outside the Porta Marina, or that of the Casa del Centauro, seem anomalous, designed without respect to an architectural sequence and experience. The Third Style is hardest of all to understand; in houses where there are suites of rooms or several rooms painted in this style, the Casa di Giasone and the Casa del Frutteto, although aesthetically the individual room may be very clearly differentiated from its neighbors, the differentiation is always subtle and more a matter of mood than one of decorative scheme. The somber room of the Medea and Phaedra of the Casa di Giasone, with its pictures chosen from the repertory of Greek tragedy, is quite unlike the room of the Europa, with its gaiety and light, and that again from the great oecus, from which comes the Encounter of Jason and Pelias now in the Museo Nazionale. The artist of the figure paintings is the same here, but the feeling of the rooms has been calculated: there is real grandeur in the great oecus. In the Casa del Frutteto the strongly Egyptianizing blue cubiculum (8), despite its towering height, has quite a different effect from the similarly proportioned black cubiculum (12), with its strongly stylized trees and bright birds, and this again from the triclinium of mythological landscapes (11). Everything in the Third Style is bright and sharp, the color preponderately red, black, or golden yellow and enlivened with small figures, an isolated animal or human. Large landscape panels illustrate myths by small figures grouped here and there, often in more than one episode or action.

An attempt to classify the various examples of the Third Style in Pompeii and to date these to five periods over the presumed life of the style—20 B.C. to A.D. 45, the third period running from A.D. 1 to 25, the others each of a decade—was offered a few years ago by F. L. Bastet but has met with little acceptance.* Not only were the criteria on which he depended heavily—the treatment of the architectural frame, especially the central aedicula, the use of certain colors, and the introduction of particular decorative motifs—of questionable value but his system required that rooms in the same house with figures that so strongly resemble one another that it would be hard to believe that they could be by different painters be dated at wide remove from one another. The Third Style rooms of the Casa degli Amorini Dorati are a case in point. The shortcomings of the method and the lack of dates that are not open to serious question were pointed out by W. Ehrhardt in his careful review of Bastet's work.† It seems better to think that the style was highly experimental and that it never crystallized into formulae. Certain technical matters, such as the use of cinnabar in the great oecus of the Villa Imperiale, must identify a decoration as early, Augustan and almost certainly before the turn of the century, for Vitruvius already advised strongly against its use in the early twenties. Pictures in which figures are relatively large and more nearly fill the picture field when it is not a landscape are commonly earlier than more miniaturistic ones, as we see from the Villa Imperiale and the Casa di Obellio Firmo; they seem to follow in a tradition seen in the Casa di Augusto in Rome. But the taste for small figures in a landscape we see already in triclinium C of the Villa Imperiale and in the Casa di Livia in Rome side by side with other "curtain style" decorations, in which the upper and lower borders of panels are bowed as though they were fabric stretched and pinned at the corners. These have often been supposed to be a mark of a relatively late Third Style decoration, but they appear in the tablinum of the Casa di Cecilio Giocondo, which is certainly early, and are lacking in the Casa di Lucrezio Frontone, in which the tablinum approaches

* F. L. Bastet, "Proposta per una classificazione del terzo stile pompeiano," *Archeologische Studiën van het Nederlands Instituut te Rome* 4 (The Hague 1979) 1–103.

† W. Ehrhardt, review of "Proposta per una classificazione del terzo stile pompeiano" by F. L. Bastet, *Gnomon* 54 (1982) 577–88.

the Fourth Style in its architectural intervals and heavy upper zone. Any single criterion is probably of small value for dating, but the avoidance of plasticity characteristic of classic Third Style decorations and the use of white ground in the upper zone that contrasts sharply with the lower walls may be taken as marks of the height of the style.

So also for dates: an overlap with the Second Style seems necessary in the light of the Casa di Livia and Casa di Augusto in Rome and another overlap with the Fourth Style. It is almost impossible to decide whether certain simple decorations are Third or Fourth Style. Fourth Style must begin before the earthquake of 5 February A.D. 62, as has been demonstrated by fragments in a sealed deposit under a floor of cocciopesto in a triclinium of the Casa di Ganimede and material from a dump, evidently an important accumulation of building material from buildings damaged by the earthquake, below the city walls behind the Casa di Championnet, VIII ii 1. This dump covered a bath building with a nymphaeum built against the wall. The material was studied and catalogued by Mariette de Vos.* While some of this material is of questionable character and her lists of rooms decorated in the Fourth Style dating from before the earthquake include few examples where the evidence for such a date is compelling, in aggregate the case is convincing; the Fourth Style was certainly already well defined by 62.

Attempts to divide the Fourth Style into periods—Claudian, Neronian, and Vespasianic—seem equally futile. Certain rooms called for less elaborate decoration with less plasticity in the architectural frame; others required richer play for the eye, more figures and deeper perspective. The efforts of Mau, Maiuri, Schefold, Lauter-Bufe, Archer, Strocka, and others to find a rationale in the greater or lesser degree of departure from the principles of the Third Style, or in the reflection of the personality of Nero or Vespasian in the flamboyance of the architectural exuberance and the sobriety of the solid panels with their borders and insets, and to use this as a key to chronology of development in the Fourth Style prove ultimately inadequate. The Fourth Style burst on Pompeii like an explosion; it did not originate there. It was probably the invention of Neronian decorators of the Domus Transitoria and swept the whole of Italy. Its further development cannot be traced. One may suspect that the decorations of the Casa dei Vettii were not complete at the time of the eruption; a room communicating with the great

* M. de Vos, "Primo stile figurato e maturo quarto stile negli scarichi provenienti dalle macerie del terramoto del 62 d. C. a Pompei," *Mededelingen* 39, n.s. 4 (1977) 29–47.

red triclinium (q), which must have been intended to function together with it, was found bare of plaster, which argues that the decoration of q itself must be relatively late. V. M Strocka more recently has offered a scheme of development from the Second to the Fourth Style, with smooth transitions between the styles and key examples for every decade and sometimes shorter intervals, from 30 B.C. to A.D. 60.* However, the figure pictures in the great oecus (A) of the Villa Imperiale of Porta Marina, which he would date at the beginning of the Third Style, 20 to 10 B.C., and the tablinum of the Casa di Cecilio Giocondo, which he would date at its end, in the time of Caligula or the early years of Claudius, are clearly by the same painter, and the only work of this painter that I can find in Pompeii, so they are unlikely to be a half-century apart in date. The decorations of cubicula c and d of the Casa del Salone Nero in Herculaneum, which Barbet would date to the time of Tiberius but Strocka would date no earlier than the early fifties because none of the criteria he uses to date Third Style decorations is present, show very strongly the aesthetic of the Third Style. And his redating of the so-called nymphaeum of the Domus Transitoria to the time of Claudius is hard to accept on the strength of the evidence adduced.

⯈ ⯇

The attribution of pictures from the Campanian cities to particular artists has great potential importance for understanding both the organization and the economics of the decorating industry in antiquity and the taste of the individual patrons. If one finds Fourth Style painters working together in the same house or even in the same room, that may not necessarily mean that they were members of the same shop, since it is evident that rebuilding after the earthquake of 62 went forward by fits and starts and rooms were decorated as they were got ready, with months and even years intervening between the decoration of adjacent rooms. Moreover, a seam around almost every subject painting and still life in Pompeii is indicative that these areas were reserved at the time the general decoration was carried out and that only at some later time did a different artist then paint them. At that time fresh plaster would have been laid in and the picture developed in a mixed medium, part true fresco, part another medium or media overlaid on this. Weeks or even months may have elapsed between the different phases, but I

* V. M. Strocka, "Die römische Wandmalerei von Tiberius bis Nero," *Aventicum V, Pictores per provincias* (Avenches 1987) 29–44.

know of no example of a wall in which these areas were still vacant at the time of the eruption, except possibly the great red triclinium (q) of the Casa dei Vettii, where the excavators decided that the remains of five iron nails around the edges of the void on the north wall meant that the missing central pictures had been painted on wooden panels, or on plaster encased in wooden frames, and let into the walls.* How one should interpret this evidence, however, and the lack of similar observation for the other walls must be open to question since one finds conflicting views recorded that these pictures were removed by salvagers after the eruption and that they crumbled with the carbonization of the wooden panels on which they were painted. In any case, although subject pictures were regularly painted separately from the rest, figures in the architectural frame and in side panels show no area of plaster laid especially to receive them. If they were not painted at the time of the general decoration, they must have been added in a medium suitable for a dry surface. In many examples flaking shows that this was clearly the case. So there must be no prejudice entertained about the relationship of different painters working in different parts of the same room when there is no other supporting evidence. But if the same painters are found working together regularly in the same room, or in a good number of the same houses, that is good evidence of organization in shops. If a man painted only a few pictures that can be identified as his, that is evidence that he was not a resident in one of the Vesuvian cities, and if these are in exceptionally important rooms and of high quality, then he can be presumed to have been brought in especially for this purpose, perhaps from Rome, and to have commanded a substantial fee for his work. On the other hand, if one finds the subject pictures of an important room to be the work of someone who did a great deal of work in these cities but was an artist of only mediocre ability, that does not necessarily mean that the owner of the house was a man of poor taste; it might also be due to a room's being ready for use and requiring decoration when the figure painter, or the caliber of figure painter, that the owner would have chosen was not available, so he settled for journeyman work for the moment, intending to replace it at a later date. One must suppose that there were many anomalous situations in the chaotic years following the earthquake.

A case in point is the so-called Basilica of Herculaneum. This was obviously an important building, given its dedication to the memory of M.

* A. Sogliano, "La Casa dei Vettii a Pompei," *MonAnt* 8 (1898) 339.

Nonius Balbus and his family in addition to its functions in the life of the community. The painters chosen to decorate it presumably would have been chosen with care and have commanded a good fee. And indeed the pictures of the apsidal exedras—Hercules discovering Telephus in Arcadia and Theseus victor over the Minotaur—are among the best that have survived, in both concept and composition. The figures are monumental, carefully drawn and solidly modeled, and although the palette is limited, being heavy with earth colors and with little in the way of rich glazes or even lively light, this might be ascribed to deliberate muting of the painted decorations so as not to detract from the important experience of the complex as a whole. It is therefore interesting to observe that this superior painter did not confine his contribution to the most important subject pictures but also painted the less important groups on the socle beneath them, large-scale groups of Achilles and Chiron and Marsyas and Olympus. Even more surprising is that he also probably painted some of the very minor figures here, staffage figures that populated the architectural intervals between subject pictures or even those introduced in the upper zone, attendants and offerants. He evidently did not regard himself as above such work.

But he did not paint all the figures in this decoration, or even all the subject pictures. A small-scale frieze depicted the labors of Hercules, the expedition of the Argonauts, and possibly other popular myths as well. The surviving fragments show it to have been fine work but not by the Telephus Painter. The figures are of lighter build, sinewy but not statuesque, painted more directly with quick brushwork and fluid lights. The whole approach is different. One might see this as the work of a collaborator but hardly a pupil, an accomplished professional of a different school. Even more surprising is to learn that from this same important building come other subject pictures on a large scale that are distinctly inferior work in every way, an Admetus receiving the oracle of his death and an Infant Hercules strangling the serpents sent to destroy him. Here the drawing, especially of hands, is inept, the expression of faces, when attempted, inadequate, the handling of the medium almost amateurish. How is one to explain this discrepancy, the appearance of excellent work by a skilled craftsman side by side with clumsy hackwork? The Telephus Painter worked in at least two houses in Pompeii, in neither of which is there anything by the Admetus Painter, and in fact the Admetus Painter may have painted nothing else, or almost nothing, in the Vesuvian cities. Was he, then, an outsider brought in along with the Telephus Painter, and accustomed to painting the architectural frame, who just happened to be given an opportunity to show what he could do with a subject picture? That seems unlikely, given the importance of this building. This startling contrast in quality is a phenomenon repeated several times in Pompeii.

One is not interested more than incidentally in trying to reconstruct the *oeuvre* of any of these painters or the dating of the various decorations in which they are found. What is important is whether a painter did a lot of work or only a little, where he worked, and in conjunction with what other painters. I must leave largely to others the further implications of that information.

In making attributions one must follow as strictly as possible the scientific method laid down by Morelli in the last century, the identification of authorship primarily by a close study of forms, especially those forms of the human body that are of lesser importance and apt to be executed formulaically and almost automatically by the painter, such as the ear and foot, but ultimately all the forms and their syntax. Palette can also be important, since a painter always has favorite colors and juxtapositions of color, but palette may also be varied to suit a particular room or condition. Composition will be of little importance in instances where the pictures are in very large part copies of set compositions, either famous masterpieces, which may have been the majority of the models, or popular subjects that had been reduced to a set formula. Both sorts must have been available in copybooks of some kind, collections in which groups of figures suitably posed to convey a familiar narrative moment were shown in color with other groups that might be used as desired to augment a central group, or groups, to fill a larger picture field. Sometimes a composition could be varied by moving the groups around, even sometimes by substituting one group for another, but by and large the basic arrangement and the possibilities it allowed were set. The individual painter had only to add a suitable setting, but in this he could be either highly inventive and develop refined or complex atmosphere or very simple and direct.*

An example or two will illustrate this point adequately. In a well-known picture of the marriage of Mars and Venus in the tablinum of the Casa di M. Lucrezio Frontone, V iv a, the couple is shown with Venus enthroned on a cushioned seat at the left side of the picture, while Mars, wearing a Samnite helmet with side feathers, stands behind her and reaches over her shoulder

* On this point see K. M. Phillips, "Perseus and Andromeda," *AJA* 72 (1968) 1–23.

to caress her breast with his left hand and she restrains him, putting her left hand on his wrist. This group is balanced at the right side of the picture by a pair of seated women who pay no attention to the lovers and look out at the viewer. Their identity is completely mysterious. Midway between these two groups stands a boyish Amor, nude except for a garment draped over his left shoulder and back and caught between his legs to cover his right leg. He holds a bow as though intending to string it. Behind these figures in the foreground a huge marriage bed almost fills the picture field, and behind this in the center stands Mercury (?), with wings sprouting from his forehead, between a pair of women who have no identifying attribute. In the background are a pair of columns and architectural elements in pale colors suggesting a palatial interior. The composition is in perfect balance, an equilateral triangle, the poses and masses of the figures carefully calculated. Another copy of the same composition, with all the same figures but more closely massed and without emphasis on the triangularity of the composition, appears in the tablinum of I vii 19, the annex of the Casa dell'Efebo. But from the tablinum of the Casa di Amore Punito, VII ii 23, comes a picture in which the group of Mars and Venus, throne and all, has been moved to the center of the picture field and is flanked on the left by a woman who kneels with her back to the lovers and searches for something in a large box with a hinged lid and on the right by an infant amorino who flies with straddled legs close to the lovers, looking directly at them, and plays with a rhomb, the strings held in both hands. A votive column rises behind Mars on the axis of the picture, and a few trees and rocks sketched in pale colors suggest a mountain landscape. Clearly the Lucrezio Frontone version is the original composition and this is an invention of the painter to balance better the picture of the punishment of Amor on the wall opposite, however incongruous the elaborate throne in the mountain setting may seem. But the revised version is not unsuccessful as a picture, and it is very interesting that this painter was capable of such manipulation of his material.

Bacchus's discovery of Ariadne on Naxos is a very popular subject in Pompeii, so popular that it has been said that there is scarcely a house in the ancient city without its Ariadne. Usually Ariadne is shown asleep (or dead), half nude, reclining with her head pillowed in the lap of a seated figure with great wings in the lower right corner of the picture. This figure, Sleep or Death, holds a basket and seems to shake a drug from a spray of leaves over the unconscious Ariadne. Bacchus stands to the left, usually nearly filling the left side of the picture field, and gestures toward Ariadne in astonishment, while his thiasus, including Pan and Silenus, follows after him, clambering over rocks and rough terrain stretching back into the distance. Sometimes Amor appears pulling back her drapery to reveal Ariadne to the god, and sometimes this is done by a young satyr. The composition is usually a triangle in which Bacchus forms one side and a sloping line along the members of the thiasus leads down to Sleep and Ariadne. This is the composition of the splendid version of this subject from the Casa del Citarista, I iv 5/25. But the posing of Bacchus is very variable, and the thiasus has figures that can be added or subtracted to suit the size of the picture field. However, what is truly remarkable is that a version of this subject from the Casa dei Capitelli Colorati, VII iv 31/51, shows the composition as a pyramid with Bacchus as a central axis, standing on a slight elevation, and his thiasus arranged around him sloping down to Silenus being helped up over rough ground by a satyr to the left and to the figure of Ariadne, now turned to face the viewer, on the right. One must suppose that the Citarista version, which with variants is the common one in Pompeii, is that suggested by the copybooks. Is the Capitelli Colorati version, then, which is well thought out and solidly structured, one that is suggested as an alternative by the copybooks or a pure invention of an uncommonly clever copyist? Moreover, the group of Ariadne, Somnus, and Amor appears in another important picture from the Casa del Naviglio, VI x 11, transformed into the discovery of Chloris by Zephyrus. Here the group is reversed to fill the lower lefthand corner of the picture and Chloris is turned to face the viewer, while above this group Venus presides over the scene in the role of *pronuba* but seems clearly an adaptation of a model for Omphale in pictures of Hercules drunk and disarmed. Since this picture is unique, it may be an invention to suit a particular request. Despite certain faults in composition, the figures are well drawn and the picture tells its story well. Are we then to suppose that certain models were conceived with multiple uses in mind? a Narcissus that might serve equally well as Cyparissus or Adonis, a Venus riding on a sea centaur that might serve for Thetis or Amphitrite? That does not seem to be the case; most compositions are used only for a single subject, with simpler and more complex versions, but a few groups, such as the staffage figures usually known as Aktae and Horae, do seem to have been conceived with multiple uses in mind.

Pompeian painters, then, were not aiming at faithfulness to an original masterpiece; rather, they were interested in harmony within the particular room in which they were working. One composition having been selected as the chief focus of a room, the other pictures were chosen and adapted to complement it. This was, of course, a complicated business. Much depended on the taste of the householder, who might have very fixed ideas of what he liked or wanted; much also may have depended on the copyist or his copybook and what he could offer in the way of choice. There was more than one composition for a Mars and Venus or an Ariadne abandoned, but we cannot, of course, say whether the copybooks all offered much the same repertory. Presumably they did not.

No Pompeian painter seems ever to have tried to copy another's style. Usually the pictures in a single room are all by the same hand, but when they are not, as, for example, in the oecus south of the atrium of the Casa degli Amorini Dorati, VI xvi 7/38, the contrast in manner is not only obvious but startling. This is not true of the subsidiary figures in side panels and architectural framework, or not so strongly felt. This may in part be due to the lesser figures' having been done by an assistant or pupil of the man who did the major pictures. Here the painter seems always to have given himself almost free rein. This should make the identification of painters much easier, and in many cases it does; a favorite facial type or idiosyncratic way of drawing a hand should emerge repeatedly. But two factors make the task more difficult, one being the poor state of preservation of most Pompeian pictures, the other the mediocrity of most of the painters.

The better preserved a picture is, the easier it is to attribute. Unfortunately, not only have portions of many Pompeian pictures been lost through the fall of plaster, so that corners here and there, a face here or a hand there, are missing, but many pictures have suffered from a complete disappearance of the overpainting, so that what one sees is, in effect, the pentimento, an underpainting in limited palette, chiefly of earth color, over which a finish in glazes and rich pigments would have been laid. And in the process of building the finished picture the artist would have changed and corrected many details, the shape of a finger, the line of a cheek, to conform better to his vision. And some painters are more casual in the pentimento than others, using it as a quick sketch to get the proportions and relationships of the figures right and leaving the shaping of individual features for the overpainting. A good example of this is offered by three pictures from the atrium of the Casa del Poeta Tragico, VI viii 3/5. One picture, Achilles' surrender of Briseis, is essentially complete, only minor portions of the upper left corner having been lost. What survives of the upper left half shows a relatively high finish, but the lower half is almost completely lost, both overpainting and pentimento gone from the left half, while some of the pentimento survives in the right. A companion piece, the Seduction of Zeus by Hera on Mount Ida, has been damaged by a lesion in the plaster that has taken most of Zeus's face and right arm, but otherwise the picture is in remarkably good condition. Its dark palette, rich in dull blues and greens, and finish with extensive use of chiaroscuro and silvery lights make it one of the outstanding treasures of the Museo Nazionale, and it is clear that Achilles' surrender of Briseis must originally have harmonized with it better than it does today. A third picture from the same context, the Embarcation of Helen, has lost its right half, containing the figure of Paris and probably some sailors, and almost all of its overpainting has also been lost, so that now it seems almost a monochrome in sanguine. All these pictures are very clearly by the same painter, as study of the forms of the heads, especially the eyes and mouths, readily shows, but the discrepancies in their preservation, although they were originally located only a few feet from one another, makes attribution more difficult. It is on the study of the forms that we must rely, and whereas this painter was an uncommonly careful workman, so that his pentimento shows his forms very clearly, the pentimento of a painter of different approach might well be far more difficult to read as an index.

The mediocrity of so many Pompeian painters is much more difficult to cope with. A good painter develops an individual style that he is constantly refining. This is true of a copyist as well as an originator, and since most Pompeian painters fall somewhere in the middle between copying and creating, we can expect the good ones to rise like cream to the surface. They do. The Telephus Painter, the Achilles Painter, and the Panthera Painter have well-defined styles, and once one's eye is attuned to their idiosyncrasies, they are easy to spot, even when a picture has suffered considerable damage. But the poorer the painter, the less consistent he is in his forms, mainly because he does not care. He will paint an ear repeatedly with the same set of brushstrokes, but the resemblance between any two of the ears he paints is a matter of chance because of his lack of control over his medium. Sometimes the sheer mass of a mediocre painter's work in the ancient cities can be used to give a definite character to his mediocrity; this is the case, for example, with the Meleagro Painter and the Io Painter. But unless one has such a volume of work, attribution can be very difficult indeed.

For most of the painters in the catalog that follows there are only a few attributions, the pictures in two or three rooms. These attributions seem absolutely certain and should then make others possible, and probably someone with a good eye will be able to augment the number. In some cases it may be possible to merge two or even three of the painters here distinguished into one, although up to the present that has not proved possible. But it still seems clear that a great many of the painters who worked in the Campanian cities are going to be represented by only a small body of work simply because that is all we have; they were not responsible for any considerable number of pictures that have not been attributed. The explanation of this phenomenon has repeatedly delayed and plagued the work of compiling this catalog. It must lie in the way the decorating industry was organized, especially since it is a phenomenon characteristic of the painters of the Third Style as much as of those of the Fourth. These painters cannot have been residents in these cities, or else they would have left far more work there. They must have been itinerant, going from city to city looking for work, getting a few commissions at a time and then moving on.

One can imagine that such painters would appear on market day, the *nundinae,* and set up booths or barrows in the market displaying the range of work they were prepared to execute, possibly in the form of a copybook or books that the potential client could thumb through, and possibly some specimens of work, pictures on panels or pinakes. Probably they were almost always individuals, offering only to do subject and figure paintings, but occasionally there may have been two or three organized as a shop. The householder who had a room or suite that he needed decorated would shop around the market for a painter to suit his taste and bargain for the amount of work to be done. Having collected a few commissions, the painter would stay in a city until he had fulfilled his obligations there, possibly collecting a little more work in the process if he was competent and his clients showed off his work to friends. And then he would move on to the next town and repeat the process. It was not an organization that grew out of the conditions imposed by the earthquake of A.D. 62 but the way things had worked for a long time. One might see the pinakes that are so conspicuous an element in late Second Style decorations as one facet in this business; perhaps originally these painters went from city to city with a collection of landscapes and still lifes in these shuttered frames that they peddled as decorative accents in the markets and added to as they traveled. Out of that trade the undertaking of figure compositions could easily have grown. At what intervals a painter would have returned to a city would, of course, have varied, depending on the likelihood of there being work to do, but one gathers from the relatively rapid changes in fashion that can be observed and the Roman passion for building and remodeling, especially in the first century after Christ, that there was always apt to be work on some scale.

What, then, are we to say about the painters who were fairly clearly established residents of Pompeii, the Iphigenia Painter, the Io Painter, the Adone Ferito Painter, Lucius? Again, it seems clear that these men were not organized in shops but always hired as individuals, that each had his specialties and was hired especially to do these. The decorating industry was essentially a thing apart, but this is a question that must be explored by concentration on it alone.

The purpose of the present study has been chiefly to try to see how figure painting fitted into the economy of Pompeii, whether the best painters worked in conjunction with one another, and if not, in what contexts they do appear, whether they painted only the important pictures in the best rooms, and if so, who painted the rest, whether the best houses were showplaces for these painters' work, and if not, how it functioned in Pompeian life. The results have been a maze of contradictions, both large and small, and much work still needs to be done on sorting out the implications of anomalies. However, it seems clear that while in most large houses a number of painters easily distinguished from one another contributed work, variety as an object was pursued in only a few. Harmony within a room was always desirable, and where two figure painters worked in the same room the division of the work was designed to achieve balance. No example of a gallery in which a deliberate range of works by different artists was displayed is known. And in a given room the large figure pictures are usually the same size and intended to balance one another, all two-figure compositions or all mythological landscapes. Occasionally a single contrasting picture is intended to dominate or give a room focus, such as the Hercules in the garden of the Hesperides in the Casa del Sacerdote Amando, I vii 7, or the Wrestling of Pan and Amor in the white oecus of the Casa dei Vettii, VI xv 1/2, but this is achieved by greater complexity of composition or difference of approach rather than by change of painter. Houses in which there is a clear difference of style in the figure paintings from room to room are rare; the Casa dei Dioscuri, VI ix 6/7, the Casa dei Vettii, VI xv 1/2, and the Casa del Citarista, I iv 5/25, come to mind, and even in these the same painter has done more than one room, albeit in a somewhat different style. Although the Pompeians in the time of the Fourth Style seem to have liked to preserve fine rooms decorated in the earlier styles, as many fine houses show, it was not variety of figure painters that interested them, nor even the individual painter of superior talent, but rather range in the aesthetic of the decoration as a whole. One does not find a fine Third Style picture inserted in a Fourth Style room, nor even a complementary set of Third Style pictures. This makes the discovery of a number of small fine pictures, probably all Third Style, stacked against a wall in a room dependent on the Palestra Grande in Herculaneum especially tantalizing; they were being preserved, but with what eventual disposition in mind is not known.

Although all of the best painters were given important rooms in which to paint the important pictures—the tablinum of a house or the finest oecus or triclinium—no Pompeian painter is known to have painted only important pictures. Even the most accomplished would contribute figures in architecture or in the upper zone of a decoration on occasion. And one fine room with pictures by a superior artist seems to have satisfied most Pompeians. If the tablinum was sumptuously painted with fine figure paintings, then those in the other rooms might be quite ordinary, no matter how important and lavishly decorated they might be otherwise. There are a few exceptions to this rule, the Casa dei Vettii being the obvious one, but the rule holds generally true. The Casa del Menandro, I x 4, a large house of obvious wealth and dignity, has no subject pictures of importance except the portrait from which it gets its name, and that is by a comparatively undistinguished painter. The Casa di Meleagro, VI ix 2, a grand mansion on the fashionable Via di Mercurio, had numerous subject pictures in every room, including the atrium, yet these were all the work of only two painters, neither of whom was very highly skilled. On the other hand, the Casa del Poeta Tragico, VI viii 3/5, a tiny jewel box of a house in which even the humblest cubiculum was elegantly decorated, had magnificent subject pictures in the atrium, an apartment usually rather severely decorated and seldom boasting subject pictures, but only very ordinary pictures in the rest of the rooms. The Casa di Marco Lucrezio, IX iii 5, another lavishly decorated house of unusual architectural refinement, had a magnificent triclinium fenestratum with pictures by two excellent painters but no other pictures that rise above mediocrity. The conclusion that most Pompeians did not care enough about their pictures to want more than a few really good pictures is inescapable.

On the other hand, in a very few houses artists who for the most part produced quite ordinary pictures were able to surpass themselves and paint pictures that almost rise to the level of the best group. In the Casa dei Dioscuri the Meleagro Painter and the Io Painter contributed work that for them was quite extraordinary. In the Casa dei Vettii the Iphigenia Painter was responsible for pictures so good that only after long study could one conclude that these had to be his work. Evidently, in the right surroundings, perhaps under the eye and with the advice of a superior painter in a nearby room, perhaps in response to the importunities of a demanding householder, picture painters were able almost to outdo themselves. And this must make one wonder how often the loss of overpainting, which is so common in these pictures, has made them appear poorer work than they would have been when properly finished.

Attribution of pictures is not at this point scientific; it is not something one can test mathematically or chemically. The best experts disagree about the authorship of certain Renaissance pictures, even very important ones. And Berenson and Beazley changed their minds not infrequently. In dealing with Campanian painting we do not face the difficulties one has with Renaissance art; the painters were clearly not educated through the imitation of earlier masters and copying of masterpieces, nor were they apprenticed to successful artists who ran large workshops with numerous personnel and put to doing glazes and background before they were allowed to work to the master's design. There is no problem here of distinguishing master from pupil or master from collaborator. As in nineteenth- and twentieth-century art, there is no attempt to conceal individuality; on the contrary, it is flaunted and fostered. For this reason it is hard to understand why there is so much disagreement among those who have attempted the attribution of these pictures to individual artists. But for one thing, they are few in number, and for another thing, they do not for the most part adhere rigorously to the method of Morelli, which is the only sound basis for attribution.

The first attempts at attribution of Pompeian pictures to particular artists were random and casual. Paul Herrmann and Reinhard Herbig in their publication of the *Denkmäler der Malerei des Altertums* (HBr) frequently tried to decide whether two pictures of a series or from a single room were by the same hand or different hands. They were conservative and tentative in their decisions and did not try to find other work by the same hand elsewhere. Nor did they argue their attributions with sound method, relying rather on surface similarities and a general impression. But Herrmann had a good eye and had educated it in the years of his study of these pictures, so his attributions are often correct, although they do little to advance our knowledge. When he decides that two pictures from the same room are by different hands, however, he is usually, if not always, wrong.

Wilhelm Klein, in a series of articles written over a period of fifteen years, was the first to try to identify the work of painters throughout the ancient cities.* He believed, however, that all Pompeian pictures could be considered original compositions and that attribution could be made on the basis of repetition of details of dress and architecture. His method was entirely wrongheaded and led him to attribute pictures of completely different character and style to the same painter. He did not hesitate to attribute lost paintings on the basis of nineteenth-century copies in line drawing, as though these were the ancient paintings themselves. His work was completely unscientific, and its flawed approach was aggravated by an insensitive eye; it stands as an object lesson and a warning to students of antiquity.

Christopher Dawson, working only with the mythological landscape paintings, offered a few attributions within that category.† His work is sound, but he did not venture beyond the confines of this limited area. Moreover, he considered compositional similarity a critical element, which is manifestly dangerous; it must be used only with extreme caution when one is dealing with copies, of which the mass of Pompeian pictorial art is composed. But he presented only attributions of which he was very sure, and it is impossible to disagree with his assignments. His eye was sensitive to forms and to the quality of brushwork. It is regrettable that he did not try to do more and to extend his efforts beyond this area.

Mabel M. Gabriel, although herself a painter, was hesitant in her approach to attribution and admitted that she relied on imponderables.‡ Consequently she divided works of the Telephus Painter among three of the painters she proposed to identify, whom she called the Herculaneum Master, the Medea Master, and the Tragic Master. This is a common mistake among attributors and usually easy to correct. But she also blundered badly in attributing the Iphigenia in Tauris from the Casa del Citarista to her Tragic Master; that seems quite absurd, and she does not support the attribution with cogent argument. Since she deals with only thirteen pictures in all, ten of which are here attributed to the Telephus Painter, there is no room for wide disagreement or argument about the others.

Carlo Ragghianti, however, has attributed a great many Campanian pic-

* W. Klein, "Pompejanische Bilderstudien," *ÖJh* 15 (1912) 143–67; 19–20 (1919) 268–95; 23 (1926) 71–115.

† C. M. Dawson, *Romano-Campanian Mythological Landscape Painting,* Yale Classical Studies 9 (New Haven 1944).

‡ M. M. Gabriel, *Masters of Campanian Painting* (New York 1952).

tures to a wide range of more than twenty-five artists.* Unfortunately, although he was a trained art historian, he employed the method of Morelli haphazardly and in cavalier fashion, as many of his names for his painters—Maestro lunare, Maestro bucolico, Maestro visionario—already make plain. He wrote his book on the subject in great haste, completing it in early 1952, although it did not appear from the publisher until 1963, the explanation for this delay being the need to provide adequate illustration, in both color and black and white. But Ragghianti did not revise his text or take any notice of the work on ancient painting done by a number of acute scholars in the interim, claiming that he was not interested in an archaeological approach to the subject, only in an art-critical one. Observing the great discrepancies among copies of the same composition, he espoused the cause of originality and on this shifting sand built his edifice. He should have known better, but he was blinded by juxtapositions in the galleries of the Museo Nazionale in Naples and by his ignorance of the archaeological background. Many of his attributions are unquestionably correct, but they were arrived at more by instinct than by sound method. His book is an object lesson in how not to approach the subject and will be cited in what follows only when one of his attributions seems correct.

Fausto Zevi, in his study of the Casa di Giasone, IX v 18, and its decoration, had to consider a number of Third Style pictures either preserved in the house or removed to the Museo Nazionale in Naples.† His examination of these was detailed and meticulous, and he concluded quite correctly, I believe, that all the pictures of this house had to be by the same hand. But he stopped short of attributing anything else to the same painter.

Maria Theresia Andreae, in her study of a range of the better-preserved hunt panels of Pompeii, objected to Wilhelmina Jashemski's assertion that Lucius must have been the painter of most such pictures in Pompeii.‡ She held that the grounds for such attribution were based on similarities of subject and motif, features that lent themselves to copying and imitation, whereas the only valid basis for attribution is brushwork and the form of details, the method brilliantly developed by Morelli. Consequently she distinguished different manners within large panels and thought she could identify

* C. L. Ragghianti, "Personalità di pittori a Pompei," *Critica d'arte* 1 (1954) 202–38; Ragghianti 1963.

† Zevi 1964.

‡ M. T. Andreae, "Tiermegalographien in pompejanischen Gärten. Die sogenannten Paradeisos Darstellungen," *RdSP* 4 (1990) 45–124, esp. 62.

painters of different sections and find painters of background who were distinct from painters of animals; she concluded that no single painter was responsible for any large number of these hunts. But the parts of Morelli's method dealing with brushwork work best when one is dealing with copies, imitations, forgeries, or pictures produced in large ateliers, where the work of a collaborator may be mistaken for the work of a master. And in Pompeii one has only to consider the enormous range of differences in the various versions of a single composition, Achilles discovered on Scyros or Perseus showing the head of Medusa to Andromeda, to see that the Pompeian painter was never trying to approximate an original but rather always using the composition as the basis for the display of his own particular pictorial style. Consequently in any room in Pompeii the subject pictures are almost always by a single painter and make a harmonious decoration. In attempting to attribute Pompeian pictures one should therefore look not to the niceties of brushwork, for the surface is seldom what it would have been in antiquity and the loss of overpainting will vary greatly even within a relatively small picture, but rather to the vocabulary of forms and their syntax, on which point Morelli was particularly emphatic. Despite the care with which Andreae worked, she is wrong on this point; it is a classic case of the forest and the trees.

This is pretty much where things stand today. The lack of a consensus among those looking for a precise personality to whom to ascribe a Pompeian picture has driven those working in the field to take refuge in examining particular subjects and compositions rather than hands. It is easier and leads readily to discussion of narrative technique and literary value. Or else they turn to Beyen's interest in identification of workshops and the classification of characteristic decorative schemes in the hope of finding a key to the organization of the industry and the relative chronology of decorations. But such an approach is fraught with pitfalls, for it assumes that all or most of the decorations of a house were carried out at the same time, whereas it is more than likely that in Pompeii this was seldom, if ever, the case. Only once we have established the individual personalities of these copyists, what they did individually and how they did it, will we be in a position to talk about collaboration and the larger organization of the work.

The confusion of approaches and lack of any consensus about methodology that prevail today in the study of ancient Roman painting were made abundantly plain at a roundtable discussion on 16 and 17 May 1994 at the Netherlands Institute in Rome on the theme "Mani di pittori e botteghe pittoriche nel mondo romano," a celebration in honor of W. J. T. Peters on the occasion of his seventy-fifth birthday. Most of those scholars known to be actively at work on aspects of ancient painting were invited to participate in this discussion, and sixteen articles based on the contributions were subsequently published as a collection, together with digests of the comments they elicited from other participants and a summary of the proceedings by Daniela Scagliarini Corlàita, of the University of Bologna (*Mededelingen* 54 [1995]). Although many of the contributors cited the method of Morelli and its importance, and although in her summary Scagliarini Corlàita was eloquent in pleading for connoisseurship employing his method, none of the contributors offered anything substantial in the way of such connoisseurship. When they exercised it at all, they contented themselves with casual observation that they did not defend with argument. Umberto Pappalardo quite correctly saw the identity of authorship in the Medea of the Casa dei Dioscuri and the Theseus Victor of the Casa di Gavio Rufo; and Valeria Sampaolo observed that the mythological pictures from the ecclesiasterion of the temple of Isis bear a striking resemblance to others in the newly excavated Casa del Bracciale d'Oro in the treatment of the heads. But that is all. The rest devoted their attentions to the minutiae of decorative details, antiquarian oddities, and technical matters, all subjects of interest but in areas that do not really advance our understanding of either the painters or the tastes of the owners of these houses, the central questions about ancient painting in the Campanian cities.

Catalog

Second Style Painters

The Criptoportico Painters

The Casa del Criptoportico, I vi 2, preserves important remains of several late Second Style decorations, that of the cryptoporticus itself with its series of herms and panels illustrating the Trojan War, that of the splendid yellow oecus (22) off the cryptoporticus with its own series of painted herms and pinakes showing alternately still life and figural scenes, some mythological, some perhaps of initiation, and those of two rooms of an important bath suite. There are in addition the decorations of a triclinium and adjacent cubiculum, including remains of a magnificent megalography in the Casa del Sacello Iliaco, I vi 4, that originally belonged to this house. Unfortunately, in a late period the house was broken up and the east and west wings of the cryptoporticus filled with earth to enlarge the garden, which served to preserve the painted decorations but makes any complete understanding of the architecture of the Second Style building impossible.

The illustrations of the Trojan War are poorly preserved, thanks to their location high on the walls, and even though the individual figures were identified by inscriptions in Greek characters, many of them are mere ghosts and one must guess at what was represented. The best preserved, the battle over the body of Patroclus, Thetis in the forge of Hephaestus, Aeneas rescued from Achilles by Poseidon, and the arrival of Penthesilea and the Amazons, are remarkably consistent in proportions, style, and palette. The figures are small-headed and long-legged, the legs muscular but shapely, the features delicate. The palette is dark, the flesh very dark, and the faces and figures are heavily shadowed against a featureless background that makes everything seem to take place at night. They are almost certainly by the same man who painted the pinakes of the yellow oecus, but he does not seem to have been responsible for either set of herms nor for the figures in the bath suite.

The caryatid herms of the yellow oecus are among the liveliest and most engaging of all Second Style figures. Herms that become pillars below the hips painted in a rosy purplish monochrome, they portray maenads and satyrs who are in sprightly action, carrying a wineskin, offerings, and musical instruments. Their heads are in vigorous play, and their faces are highly expressive. They seem clearly to be the work of the man who painted a similar herm on the north wall of the little atrium of the baths of the Casa del Menandro, I x 4, across the street. Presumably there was originally a series of these herms, but only one survives today, and he has lost his head. The scheme of the decoration, of which only a single panel is preserved, is that of the cryptoporticus, with large orthostats alternating with narrow ones painted with a vertical stenciled pattern above a low socle, the herms set at intervals in front of this and rising with brackets mounted on their heads to carry a cornice. Even the friezes that run above the orthostats are the same: small framed squares of colored marble, interlaced vines, and a narrow golden ovolo. But it is the twist of the torso and lift of the shoulders, the liveliness of the modeling, that confirms the attribution. Above the friezes appears a panel with grotesques parodying the fight of Theseus with the Minotaur. A fragment of the continuation of this is preserved in another part of the room, on the east wall, where the stories of Pasiphaë and Marsyas are parodied, with identifications inscribed in Greek, so apparently it ran all around the room. It may be the work of the painter of the pinakes of the Casa del Criptoportico, but one cannot be sure since so little is preserved and the artist's intention is so different.

Although it is too fragmentary and faint for one to be sure, it seems likely that the man who painted the vista over the central door in the south wall of the frigidarium of the Casa del Criptoportico, a monochrome garden around a baetylus column seen over a looped curtain, a dream garden in shades of gray populated with a collection of fantastic birds, is the same painter who did the original parts of the similar paintings in the rectangular exedra off the southwest corner of the peristyle of the Casa del Menandro later containing a lararium. The many features that the Casa del Criptoportico and the Casa del Menandro have in common strongly suggest that these houses, or at least large parts of them, were decorated by a single team or shop working in the late Second Style. This would not have been the original building period for either house but a refurbishing following extensive architectural modification in the Casa del Criptoportico and probably the construction of at least the bath suite in the Casa del Menandro.

⇢ *Works* ⇠

Criptoportico Painter 1

POMPEII

I vi 2, Casa del Criptoportico

Cryptoporticus

- Battle over the body of Patroclus: Spinazzola 1953, 2.920, fig. 919; *PPM* 1 (1990) 207–8, figs. 23–24.
- Thetis in the forge of Hephaestus: Spinazzola 1953, 2.924, fig. 926; *PPM* 1 (1990) 209, fig. 26.
- Aeneas rescued from Achilles by Poseidon: Spinazzola 1953, 2.936, figs. 942–43; *PPM* 1 (1990) 216, fig. 35.
- Arrival of Penthesilea and the Amazons: Spinazzola 1953, 2.951, fig. 964; Ragghianti 1963, 62; *PPM* 1 (1990) 20, fig. 43.

Yellow oecus (22)

- Pinakes: Spinazzola 1953, 1.505–34, figs. 568, 571, 575, 578, 588, 592; Ragghianti 1963, 53; *PPM* 1 (1990) 258–68, figs. 117, 123, 127, 132; *Peinture* 1993, 1, pls. 2–3, and 2, figs. 5b, 5d.

Criptoportico Painter 2

POMPEII

I vi 2, Casa del Criptoportico

Yellow oecus (22)

- Caryatid herms: Spinazzola 1953, 1.506–24, figs. 569, 572–74, 576–77, 583; Ragghianti 1963, 53, 61; *PPM* 1 (1990) 256–69, figs. 115, 122, 126, 128, 129, 131, 133; *Peinture* 1993, 1, pl. 1.

I x 4, Casa del Menandro

Atrium of the bath suite

- Caryatid herm: Maiuri 1933, fig. 59; *PPM* 2 (1990) 378, fig. 221.

Criptoportico Painter 3

POMPEII

I vi 2, Casa del Criptoportico

Frigidarium of the bath suite

- Fantastic garden: Spinazzola 1953, 1.473, fig. 538; *PPM* 1 (1990), 234, fig. 73.

I x 4, Casa del Menandro

Exedra off the southwest corner of the peristyle

- Fantastic garden: Maiuri 1933, figs. 47–48; *PPM* 2 (1990) 372–74, figs. 210–14.

The Villa dei Misteri Painter

The man who painted the megalographic frieze in the great oecus (5) of the Villa dei Misteri was evidently unassisted in his work. The figures show a notable consistency in proportions, forms, and facial character. And despite the formulaic character of much of the drapery, some weakness in the drawing of such parts as the hands and feet, and a certain failure in the work to convey meaning and emotion in facial expression, it is quite clear that this was a major effort by a more than competent workman. The design of the whole, though better in the east wall than elsewhere, is carefully considered and coherent; the tensions within groups and transitions from group to group are well developed; and the whole work is charged with an authority of craftsmanship that has made it justly the most celebrated of all surviving Pompeian decorations. It is not the finest craftsmanship, and in excellence the individual figures do not rival the work of the Telephus Painter or the Achilles Painter, but the grandeur of the whole is unparalleled elsewhere, and one has only to consider the comparable rooms in the Villa of Fannius Synistor at Boscoreale and the Casa del Sacello Iliaco (or Casa degli Elefanti, I vi 4) to realize how far superior to the run of Second Style painters the man who painted this frieze must have been. One might well imagine that he had been brought from Naples or even Rome, especially if Della Corte is right about the villa's having been an imperial property, and expect to find his work nowhere else in the city.

This is nearly, but not quite, the case; he painted in at least two other rooms in Pompeii, the great oecus in the Casa di Cesio Blando, with its frieze of caryatid herms carrying garlands, and a room in VI Ins. Occ. 41, of which only a few fragments survive. And this fact further complicates the problem of whether he was a native of Pompeii. The Casa di Cesio Blando shows signs of having been a comfortable city house in the days of the Second Style but hardly an elaborate or pretentious one. There was a small private bath, but neither atrium nor peristyle was an apartment of great size or luxury or in any way special.

VI Ins. Occ. 41 is a badly ruined house on the western edge of the city first explored in the eighteenth century, when some important parts of the decoration were removed for the museum. It still preserves, however, remains of late Second Style decorations in all the rooms of the ground floor but one, where the decoration is Third Style. In one of the western rooms, now thought to be either oecus 15 or triclinium 20, although the records assign it to tablinum 6, were collected fragments of painting recomposed to form most of a monumental caryatid figure of a winged female, nude to the waist, carrying a rich garland tied with sashes in great bows that must have swung from this figure to others set at intervals in much the same fashion as those in the Casa di Cesio Blando. Fortunately, the head of this figure is well preserved and is clearly the work of the Villa dei Misteri Painter. So the likelihood that the Villa dei Misteri Painter was of local origin is greatly increased, and one may hope that more work by him will emerge as the excavations continue.

The earmarks of his style are a certain statuesqueness of proportions in the figures, an individual way of showing shadow turning around a curved surface, leaving a fine bright edge to define the form, and certain forms in his heads and hands. The eyes are bright, almost feverish, but deeply ringed with shadow, so that the general expression is one of apprehension or anxiety. The mouths are calm, almost expressionless, with a narrow but well-shaped upper lip and a full, evenly lit underlip. The hands are much simplified, heavier than is usual in Pompeian painting, but not disproportionate. The wrist is apt to be thick and rather solid, its articulation not perfect. The thumb is set very low and usually in strong opposition to the fingers. When they are separated, the fingers are well drawn, but frequently the fingers act together, at which times there is something slightly clumsy and scooplike about the hands. In the feet the heel is almost always excessively sharp, the sole very flat.

⇢ *Works* ⇠

POMPEII

VI Ins. Occ. 41

Oecus 15? or triclinium 20?

- Caryatid herm: *Peinture* 1993, 2, fig. 289; *PPM* 6 (1996) 18–20, figs. 22–24.

VII i 40, Casa di Cesio Blando

Oecus 12, west of the tablinum

- Caryatid herms: Spinazzola 1928, pl. 133; Schefold 1962, pls. 24,

27; *PPM* 6 (1996) 414–26, figs. 72–73, 76–77, 81–82, 85–88, 90, 92.

Environs, Via dei Sepolcri, Villa dei Misteri

Oecus 5

• Megalographic frieze: Rizzo 1929, pls. 11–15; Maiuri 1953, 51–61; Ragghianti 1963, 26, 33, 35, and pls. 14–17; Stenico 1963, pls. 70–73; Picard 1970, 32; Kraus and von Matt 1973, figs. 114, 119–25; de Franciscis 1978, figs. 74–78; Eschebach 1978, figs. 216–18; Guillaud and Guillaud 1990, figs. 147–52, 165; *Peinture* 1993, 1, pls. 108–19, and 2, figs. 354a–f.

Cubiculum 4

• Bacchic figures: Ragghianti 1963, 22; de Franciscis 1978, figs. 79–80; Eschebach 1978, fig. 219; *Peinture* 1993, 1, pls. 106–7, and 2, figs. 353a–b.

Third Style Painters

The Amore Punito Painter

This painter, although exceptionally good among Pompeian artists, especially in the establishment of mood in a picture, has left very few works. It may be that he was not a native Pompeian and spent a comparatively short time there. It may also be that the majority of his work was destroyed in the earthquake of A.D. 62. But such questions cannot be answered unless he can be linked to other artists, and until now he has been found working in collaboration in only one room, a large room, elaborately decorated, in which he painted the single surviving fragment of a subject painting and the amorini that populated the upper zone, while the Villa di Cicerone Painter contributed a frieze of miniaturistic figures between the main and the upper zone. Since the Villa di Cicerone Painter seems to have been something of a specialist in Third Style predelle and friezes and to have painted these parts in rooms where he did nothing else, this evidence is of little importance.

The Amore Punito Painter evidently had a long life and changed and developed in his work to suit the fashions of the times and the taste of his clients. In his surviving works three distinct phases can be marked out, one in which he is still working in the traditions and mannerisms of the Second Style even though he is already a Third Style painter, one in which he works in the classic manner of the Third Style, with small bright figures in large pale landscapes, and one in which, although still in the Third Style, the figures have increased in size and importance, their relationship to their surroundings is more organic, and we see an approach toward the Fourth Style, although crystallization is still some distance off.

His figures, although small in their surroundings, are noticeably tall and slender with the manneristic distortion of the Second Style. The head is small; the average figure is eight heads tall or even a little taller. Sometimes the head is enlarged enough to be in proper, or nearly proper, proportion to the height of the figure, but the delicacy and proportions of the rest of the body make the figures appear tall. The neck is short and slender, the shoulders wide in proportion to the head. In women the waist is elongated, set rather high, and the breasts are very high, so the whole upper torso seems compact, while the belly and hips are elegantly lengthened and widened to give a slightly pear-shaped effect to the torso. In men the upper torso is of nearly normal proportions, except that the shoulders may be rather wide, while the waist is slender and the belly and hips are somewhat shortened and tightened, so the whole torso seems both slender and athletic. The legs of both men and women are elongated, especially the lower legs; the ankles are slim, the feet small and delicately modeled. The arms are long, although not excessively so, heavy rather than muscular in the upper arm, with slender wrists and long, tapering hands.

The heads are broad at the temples with well-domed skulls. Occasionally the arrangement of the hair makes the top of the head seem somewhat flattened in profile, but close examination shows that the underlying structure of the skull is always ample. The forehead is very high, so high that sometimes the hair seems wiglike; generally it is smooth and expressionless and in profile very straight. The nose in full and three-quarters face continues the plane of the forehead; in profile there may be a very slight break between forehead and nose. The nose is apt to be slightly long and always shows a broad, straight ridge, especially broad in full face, that comes to a sharp, square tip. The shadow along the nose is very straight and gives the nose a pinched look except in profile. The wings of the nostrils are generally carefully drawn with the suggestion of a slight sneer. The eyes glare either in worry or in solemn lack of expression, great black pupils under hairline brows. The brow sweeps close to the eye but does not follow its arc exactly; the transition between eyebrow and nose is usually a continuous arc, sometimes sharpened to a corner to give expression. The tail of the brow sweeps well out from the corner of the eye. The lower lid closes a little high over the ball; the white is very bright, the pupil very dark. No distinction is made between iris and pupil, and there is no highlight in the eye. The cheekbone often carries a well-defined rim of light that is one of the hallmarks of this painter. The mouth is apt to be very crisp and usually has a sweet expression, with the suggestion of an absent-minded smile. The upper lip is usually short, the lower full and sensual, the parting indicated by a fine line. The upper lip is always distinct and rather longer than the lower. In full face the lower lip may even seem swollen, but not in profile. The chin is short and firm, shallower and harder in profile than in full face; in full face it sometimes appears to be slightly receding. The cheeks are almost always deeply shadowed in front of the ears, so that the lower jaw seems to taper despite its roundness. The ear is well shaped with a deep lobe and delicate helix, but the interior of the ear is not worked in detail. The hair of the women is parted in the middle and drawn back on either side to a knot at the nape of the neck. It is dressed shallow on the crown of the head, loosely puffed above the temples, and thinly spread along the shoulders. The men's hair, when cropped short, clings fairly close to the skull. It is a mark of this painter that the smooth, slightly curved line of the hair along the forehead is neatly drawn and makes a small point in front of the ear.

The torsos of both men and women are marked by sleekness. The women have broad, strong shoulders drawn in a smooth arch. The neck is just a trifle slender and usually a trifle short, which gives the head impressive weight and dignity. The structure of the chest above the breasts is skillfully suggested; the clavicle never appears, but the base of the throat is generally clearly marked. The high breasts are smoothly domed with conspicuous nipples. The male figures are only more muscular and athletic, but without elaborate emphasis on the surface appearance of these qualities. Their shoulders are broader and squarer with slightly more emphasis on the tendons along the neck, the clavicle, and the depression at the base of the throat. The back is heavier, but smooth. The waist is lower, sharply pulled in, but not exaggerated.

The arms are always of good length, which makes them seem long in comparison with the figures in other Pompeian pictures. Their attachment at the shoulder is smooth and well studied with a slight suggestion of fullness at the armpit. The upper arms of women are smooth, those of men somewhat more muscular. Elbows are not emphasized; when the arm is only slightly bent the outside line does not break at all. The forearm has a slight fullness below the elbow and a regular, gentle taper to the wrist. The wrist is usually slightly thick, not quite sufficiently articulated, rather long. The metacarpus is apt to be much exaggerated, very long and narrow, with the thumb set very low. The fingers are long and thin, so tapering that the last joint is pencil-like, with little creases between them at the base. Their gestures tend to be stiff and angular.

The thighs are relatively short, the shins long and slender. When the knee is bent, the line of the thigh is pulled back to meet that of the shin. The knee is flat and has a pushed-in look. The shin is smooth with a gentle bow. The calf muscle is slender but taut and firm; there is no perceptible tuck under it. The ankles are very slender in both front and back view, the feet tiny and very neatly formed. The toes break distinctly at their joint to the foot and are marked with shadow.

The painter handles drapery very expertly, although he sometimes falls into the trap of surrealist rendering. In a given picture it is easy to distinguish one material from another, and their variety seems almost a deliberate display of technical virtuosity. He is almost as clever in working one stuff over another, or transparent drapery over flesh, as in contrasts, and the range of types of fold, mass, and edge is almost infinite. The garments float, hang, lie, and pull beautifully. The only criticism that can be leveled is that they are occasionally fussily overstudied, in too sharp focus, or in too contrived a contrast. But this is, to be sure, a fault common to most of the better painters of the Third Style.

In the Amore Punito Painter's background landscapes the rocks are piled in more or less conical masses to right and left of center. These are rough and sometimes jagged boulders with steeply sloping sides, and among them are usually balanced and leaning members. From the crevices among them spring small trees, often dead. The trees are almost always small with rather gnarled and twisted trunks, and there is some effort to distinguish different varieties within a picture by variation in the color and brushwork of the foliage. The foreground is kept clear, with the suggestion of unevenness given by light washes and the play of shadows.

The Amore Punito Painter uses a palette and technique of medium intensity and likes to leave considerable areas of his pictures blank. The resulting effect is pale, almost pastel. The flesh of women is usually warm and glowing, pink and white with golden undertones, or cool in gray and ivory. That of men is dark and shining in deep red-brown. Features are emphasized by fine overdrawing, especially in such details as eyebrows and lashes. The shadows on limbs are carefully graded to give roundness, and occasionally edges are sharpened by overdrawing. True hatching is almost absent, but the length and direction of the brushstrokes convey the roundness of throats, shoulders, breasts, and so on. Hair is worked in various ways, but the painter has a fondness for rich chestnut-colored hair and fine coiling curls and tresses. For drapery he shows a liking for dull violet, purple, puce, and brown and a nice balance between dark and light enlivened with touches of bright red or deep, rich yellow. The painting of the flesh and hair is always meticulous and shows signs of patient reworking; that of the drapery is flashy and assured, a set of facile tricks confidently displayed. The colors of the background are almost exclusively gray, green, and tan, so that the landscape in no way competes with the figures for interest, and just around each figure or group of figures there is always an area of light. The brushwork in the landscape is always casual, the pigment worked thin and with large brushes in the rocks and foreground, cursively and vigorously with smaller brushes for trees and foliage. Shadows cast by the figures are pale and hastily, but competently, brushed; they usually run diagonally toward the background and contribute a little, although not a great deal, to the illusion of depth and perspective.

The figures are placed in a line low in the picture field but well above the lower border, filling the middle ground pretty well from one side to the other. The foreground to a height of about one-fifth of the picture is left entirely empty. The figures are grouped singly or in pairs that overlap little or not at all. The pairs themselves are tightly knit, but the relationship between pairs is conveyed by glance and attitude rather than by gesture and composition. What composition there is, is simply a band of figures read from left to right, not a design at all, although some of the groups would certainly work better in another arrangement. The figures are tall, approximately two-fifths of the height of the picture. Beyond the figures more space intervenes, and in the background, near or distant but always faint and shadowy, are enough trees and rocks to suggest a mountain forest. Behind and above these is only blank space.

→ *Works* ←

POMPEII

VII ii 23, Casa di Amore Punito

Tablinum

- Punishment of Cupid: H 826; MN 9257; HBr pl. 1; Curtius 1929, figs. 165–67; Rizzo 1929, pl. 98; de Franciscis 1963, pl. 53; *Collezioni* 1986, 71; Guillaud and Guillaud 1990, fig. 248; Ling 1991, fig. 145; De Caro 1994, 158; *PPM* 6 (1996) 673, fig. 14.
- Mars and Venus: H 325; MN 9249; HBr pl. 3; Curtius 1929, fig. 147; *Collezioni* 1986, 72; Guillaud and Guillaud 1990, figs. 244–45; Ling 1991, fig. 144; De Caro 1994, 157; *PPM* 6 (1996) 675, fig. 16.

VII iv 56, Casa del Granduca di Toscana

Tablinum

- Punishment of Dirce: H 1151; MN 9042; HBr pl. 150; Curtius 1929, fig. 168; *Collezioni* 1986, 81; Ling 1991, fig. 124; De Caro 1994, 156; Gierow 1994, fig. 64; *PPM* 7 (1997) 55, fig. 19.

VII vi 28

Cubiculum 8

- Fragment of mythological subject with seated nude hero and standing draped woman: H 1167; MN 8895; Anderson negative 26740; *PPM* 7 (1997) 192, fig. 13.

• Amorini hunting: H 813; MN 9218 (= MN 9229 = MN 20039); *Collezioni* 1986, 118; Guillaud and Guillaud 1990, figs. 21–22; *PPM* 7 (1997) 195, fig. 17.

• Amorino: H 569 (not described); MN 9165, 9183; Herbig 1962, pl. 45; *PPM* 7 (1997) 193, fig. 15.

Unidentified Building

• Fragmentary genre scene showing two women playing with a goat: H 1434; Paris, Louvre, P.1; Alinari negative 22781; Tran Tam Tinh 1974, 38, fig. 13; Grimal and Kossakowski 1993, 18.

HERCULANEUM

Unidentified Buildings

• Fragment with garlanded head of a woman: H 1963; MN 9094; Brion 1960, fig. 108; Herbig 1962, pl. 27; Ragghianti 1963, pl. 117; *Collezioni* 1986, 65; Guillaud and Guillaud 1990, fig. 62.

• Busts of an actor wearing a mask pushed back on top of his head and a woman with a cithara: H 1441; MN 9079; *Collezioni* 1986, 239; Guillaud and Guillaud 1990, fig. 63.

The Bisogno Painter

In his report dated 21 February 1761 Karl Weber gives an account of a remarkable find of pictures on plaster in the tunnels of Herculaneum under the Masseria di Bisogno, an area later identified as one of the apartments giving onto the Palaestra of Insula Orientalis I and II. Most, if not all, of these were originally nearly square, stacked against a wall of a room with a mosaic pavement, evidently salvaged from an earlier decoration, or decorations, with the intention of preserving them, possibly as a collection. They were all fine Third Style pictures, and the similar size and scale, together with a harmony of palette, suggests that they had been chosen to decorate a single room. However, their authorship is not the same, and they were too many for a single room of ordinary proportions. They included the "Achilles and Patroclus" (H 1389b; MN 9020), the "Player King" (H 1460; MN 9019), the "Dressing of the Bride" (H 1435; MN

9022), a Marsyas and Olympus (H 229; MN 9141), a concert of flute and cithara (H 1462; MN 9021), a lyrist, sometimes thought to represent Achilles and Patroclus (H 1404; MN 9816), and a Perseus freeing Andromeda (H 1188; MN 8993). There were also a number of fragments that could not be composed into identifiable pictures (H 1849; MN 9906). Paderni in his reports dated 21 and 26 February 1761 gives a few more details about this discovery.

Study of these pictures with the object of attribution shows that the "Dressing of the Bride" and the Perseus freeing Andromeda are works of the Principe di Montenegro Painter, originally finer in detail than most of his other work, even though the left half of the Perseus freeing Andromeda has lost its overpainting, so that only the figure of Perseus shows proper finish. The "Player King" is unique, a very distinguished work with elegant simplification of forms, especially in the head and hand of the woman who inscribes the mask, a ready hallmark and not to be found elsewhere at present. The meticulously painted "Achilles and Patroclus," with its tousled, attentive Achilles and discursive Patroclus, one ankle nonchalantly crossed over the other, also seems to be unique.

But the concert of flute and cithara is found in a simpler version by the same painter in a cubiculum of the Casa di Ceio, I vi 15, in Pompeii. Here there are only two figures, the standing citharist and the woman at the left. The surface has been scraped and all detail lost. One can see that the seated woman has long hair gathered at the nape of the neck, and the citharist's instrument is a relatively simple one, but in their volume the figures match closely those in the Herculanean picture, and the forms of the right arm and hand of the seated woman seem to clinch the case for identity of authorship. This man probably also painted the Marsyas and Olympus of the Herculanean group; there is strong similarity of ethos in what is left of the faces of the two flautists, but the Marsyas is too fragmentary for certainty.

→ *Works* ←

POMPEII

I vi 15, Casa di Ceio

Cubiculum c, east of the fauces

- Concert: Spinazzola 1953, 1.268, fig. 294; Michel 1990, fig. 170; *PPM* 1 (1990) 431, fig. 36.

HERCULANEUM

Masseria di Bisogno

- Concert: H 1462; MN 9021; Rizzo 1929, pl. 51; Spinazzola 1953, 1.269, fig. 295; *Collezioni* 1986, 105; *Peinture* 1993, 2, fig. 448.
- Marsyas and Olympus: H 229; MN 9141; Zevi 1964, pl. 22.2.

The Boscotrecase Painter

This painter, after a faltering beginning, became adept at the representation of atmospheric landscapes, but he was always relatively awkward in the representation of human figures, especially in the foreground. Rendering of facial expression did not come easy for him, and his figures are often expressionless and wooden or melodramatically woeful. His earliest subject pictures are probably those in the Casa del Sacerdote Amando in Pompeii, I vii 7, where he was responsible for all the figure paintings, notably three mythological landscapes and a Hercules in the garden of the Hesperides in a triclinium, a picture of Paris introduced to Helen in a cubiculum, and a number of isolated figures of women and amorini in limited palette in side panels. The mythological landscapes show the Fall of Icarus, Galatea and Polyphemus, and Perseus rescuing Andromeda. In all of these the colors in the figures are bright and rather hard with no attempt at chiaroscuro, the lights bright and chalky, the shadows grayed. In the landscapes the ground is dark, a combination of deep-toned blues and greens from which trees with dappled foliage and large puce rocks, often in rounded cloud shapes, emerge dimly. In his figures the faces tend to be elongated with a prominent nose; the arms are long and thin with fingers spread and emphasized, and the feet are shown as rather spatulate and simplified, but with prominent toes. A certain amount of overpainting has been lost in all three, but the gnarled trees and twisted branches with lively foliage are a hallmark of his work. In the Hercules in the garden of the Hesperides the ground is a neutral off-white that contrasts with the darkness of the others, but it is certainly his work, as comparison of the Hesperides with the spectators in the foreground of the Fall of Icarus, as well as the painting of the tree of the golden apples, immediately shows.

He painted the same three mythological landscapes in a room of the Villa di Agrippa Postumo at Boscotrecase in a distinctly superior version and omitting the Hercules in the garden of the Hesperides. The rest of this decoration was, like that of the triclinium of the Casa del Sacerdote Amando, in red and black panels with decorative details of great delicacy and lively color. A number of changes have been introduced, so that Galatea now faces the viewer with her mantle billowing behind and framing her, and a second figure of Polyphemus, hurling a rock at the departing ship of Ulysses, appears behind the seated giant interrupted in playing the syrinx by the sight of Galatea, but the compositions are still substantially the same. The backgrounds are richer and darker, almost nocturnal, and the figures stand out against them in stronger contrast, although the lights are less chalky. This may in part be due to the better preservation of the overpainting. The elongated proportions and forms of the bodies remain unchanged.

The same painter was called upon again to do three large sacral landscapes in the red room next to this, pictures now in the Museo Nazionale in Naples, and three miniature landscapes in the black room adjacent, two of which are now in the Metropolitan Museum of Art in New York. The landscapes of the red room are justly famous, idyllic islands of pale soft color populated with figures in darker color, the views floated against an off-white ground. The subjects are rustic sanctuaries where shepherds loiter and to which worshipers come, while in the background tombs, a long portico, or a walled orchard stretches into the distance, fading away to vegetation and distant mountains.

One shows a golden statue of Cybele enthroned beside a tall column carrying an urn, to which are also tied shields. A goatherd leans against the base of a large vase mounted on a short column to the left, while a group of worshipers approaches, pausing on a bridge at the head of which stands a Priapus herm. A large tree with heavy trunk and branches and dappled foliage that suggests olive makes a background to the central column, while further back is a recession of buildings before distant hills. The painting of the statue of Cybele, with its simplified rectangular face and elongated head, and of the approaching worshipers, rather elongated figures with heavy shoulders and small heads, one much smaller than the others with a head that is a mere dot, is very striking.

A companion piece shows a similar shrine with a pair of statues of female figures standing on a raised base behind a column connected by an architrave surmounted by vessels to a solid wall behind, as though this were a bit of the pronaos of a ruined temple remodeled to make a rustic shrine. Against the base leans a man in a short tunic, his legs crossed, a staff held in both hands in front of him, his head bent as though he were addressing the thin, long-muzzled dog with sickle tail that sits in front of him and raises one paw. Off to the right in the foreground a man with a traveler's boots and staff sits on a knoll in front of a bronze tripod mounted on a base. In the background are buildings, especially a long colonnade seen at a sharp angle, and figures in pale monochrome, but with one side in deep shadow, one of whom seems in a great hurry, his bent legs with thin, tapering calves eloquently sketched. The palette, the treatment of the figures, the foliage, and the architecture leave no doubt that the man who painted the preceding work also painted this piece.

The third member of this trio is equally readily identified. Here the shrine is a triangle of columns built to include a branch of the sacred tree that dominates the composition. Votive offerings, including a large goat's head, are tied to the columns, and low shrubbery comes close around it behind. There are no foreground figures, only a statuary group of three figures with a pair of long torches laid carelessly beside it. But worshipers of the same character as those in the first of this set and a traveler with staff and sticklike lower legs immediately make the authorship obvious. These three landscapes provide us with a rich vocabulary of forms that should be easy to find elsewhere.

In fact, in the black room that was neighbor to this we see this painter's hallmarks in a series of three vignettes, miniatures in bright, glowing polychromy against a black ground. Two of these are in the Metropolitan Museum of Art in New York; one was formerly in the Museo Nazionale in Naples and is known only from a poor photograph. This last would perhaps have been the easiest to attribute, for it showed the hurrying traveler with bent and sticklike legs. It also showed figures with heavy shoulders and dotlike heads, one of whom reclined with bent legs under an awning. But the others are similarly conceived with figures that tend toward monochrome with one side strongly shadowed, heavy shoulders, and dotlike heads. The buildings here are of rather mysterious character, clearly sacred, but two of them towers with porches, and the third vignette is a sacred tree with a syzygium to which a low porchlike addition is appended. Here another figure that is to become familiar appears, a woman in long drapery who bends deeply over an altar, her upper body almost top-heavy in its fullness but highly expressive. The palette is the same as in the red room, with bright pink roofs, golden metal vessels, and trees dappled in shades of green touched on the surface with lights of pale yellow. Only the scale and the restrictions imposed by the scale differentiate these landscapes.

In the more atmospheric manner of the Boscotrecase mythological landscapes this artist painted a Punishment of Dirce in the Casa di Giulio Polibio, IX xiii 1/3. This is identified as his work by the similarity of forms in the nudes, Perseus and Polyphemus in comparison with Amphion and Zethus, especially such details as the long-shanked legs and feet raised on tiptoe, the elongated hands with recurved fingers and underarticulated wrists. Moreover, the simplified depiction of the face and hands of the statue of Bacchus is like that of the statue of Cybele in the Boscotrecase landscape. Once again the figures are rather summarily drawn, but the effect of the picture as a whole is successful. In his less atmospheric mode this painter seems to have been responsible for the mythological landscape known as the Origins of Rome from V iv 13, now in the Museo Nazionale, showing Mars descending from heaven to the sleeping Rhea Silvia and the twins nursed by the she-wolf in the foreground. But so much of the overpainting has been lost that it is impossible to say what the original finish would have been like.

In the Casa del Frutteto, I ix 5, this man painted both the four mythological landscapes and the vignettes of triclinium 11. The vignettes declare their authorship very easily, being very close to his work in the black room of the Villa di Agrippa Postumo in every way, in palette, architecture, trees, and figures. The mythological landscapes, a Diana and Actaeon, a Fall of Icarus, a Punishment of Dirce, and a Duel of Eteocles and Polynices, are poorly preserved but show his characteristic long-shanked figures with strongly shadowed edges, his use of extensive underpainting in golden yellow on a blue ground, and his typical architecture with a low gable and trees with dappled foliage. These pictures are much paler in palette and freer in brushwork than the Boscotrecase pictures and presumably later in date.

Another picture of the same period is the sacro-idyllic landscape of I vii 19, now badly ruined but once showing a cowherd with his dog at a sanctuary composed of a herm and a couple of votive columns together with a low rustic altar before a pine tree with tapering trunk. The authors of *PPM* I are right in observing that the painter of this landscape should be the same as the man who painted the goatherd in the Casa di Giulio Polibio's Punishment of Dirce, and the drawing of the long-muzzled, prick-eared, long-necked dog is strikingly like that of the dog in one of the landscapes of the red room of the Villa di Agrippa Postumo.

Given this repertory of subjects, one might suspect that this painter was responsible for the pictures in the exedra of the bath complex of the Casa del Marinaio, VII xv 1/2, a Perseus and Andromeda, a Punishment of Dirce, a

Polyphemus and Galatea, and a Slaughter of the Niobids. Too little survives of the first three, left in situ, for attribution, but he surely was not the painter of the Slaughter of the Niobids. That was the work of a man I have called the Triclinium Painter. On the other hand, the composition of the Punishment of Dirce, even the placing of the goats and Dirce's scarf, is so like that of the same subject in the Casa di Giulio Polibio as to suggest strongly identity of authorship.

On the basis of his handling of the landscape elements in the sacro-idyllic landscape of I vii 19, one might suggest that our man was responsible for the mythological landscapes of V ii 10, a Fall of Icarus, a Hippolytus worshiping a statue of Diana, a Hercules in the garden of the Hesperides, and a Marsyas, Athena, and the Muses, the story of the flutes. Since only the last was removed to the Museo Nazionale and the others are now known only from drawings, certainty is impossible, but the Marsyas looks like his work, and the composition of the Hercules in the garden of the Hesperides strongly resembles that of the same subject in the Casa del Sacerdote Amando, although here it is treated as a mythological landscape with diminutive figures and strong emphasis on landscape. So also in the Fall of Icarus one notes the posing of Icarus spread-eagled on his back with bent legs and the presence of spectators in a small boat, although they do not gesture, while the perspective makes the flying figures seem too close to the boat and the water. If these were the work of the Boscotrecase Painter, they would have to be very early work of this type.

In the time of the Third Style he also painted a number of figure compositions as well as mythological landscapes. Unfortunately, many mythological landscapes seem to have been lost in the course of time, probably because their large size made them difficult to remove from the walls and their emphasis on landscape at the expense of the narrative element made them less interesting to museum curators. But a few of his subject paintings are well known. Best known is the Aeneas Wounded from the Casa di Sirico, VII i 25/47, in Pompeii. Schefold would date the decoration of the room from which it comes around A.D. 70, but one must doubt this. It is in hopeless disrepair today, and other pictures from it do not survive. The general effect of the decoration is Fourth Style, but the picture itself is clearly Third Style in manner, without development of the background or effects of chiaroscuro. It is very close in every way to the Paris introduced to Helen of the Casa del Sacerdote Amando.

Another picture in the same manner is the Bellerophon harnessing Pegasus from the triclinium of I viii 8, now in the storerooms of Casa Bacco in Pompeii. Here too the ground is essentially neutral, although rocks and clouds have been added to fill the upper left corner of the picture field. The drawing of the hands and the construction of the heads of Aeneas and Bellerophon make the attribution certain. However, the picture of Europa still in place in this triclinium is certainly not by the same hand.

One more picture by this painter is the group of four poets taking part in a contest still in place in VI xvi 36/37. It is in poor condition today, badly blistered and lacking most of its overpainting, but it must certainly be his work. It too is in the Third Style.

In fact, this painter seems to have begun as a painter of architectural vignettes, then branched out into mythological landscapes and figure compositions, and later returned almost exclusively to landscape painting. But at least occasionally in the time of the Fourth Style he seems to have produced other Falls of Icarus. On the pluteus of the peristyle of the Casa dei Gladiatori, V v 3, are the ruins of such a picture, barely legible today but showing familiar elements and our man's architecture and staffage figures. Another small square picture of the same subject in the British Museum also comes from Pompeii; it shows the familiar composition, staffage figures, and gestures. I should judge it a comparatively late product of our painter. Unfortunately, there seems to be no information about its more precise provenience. A third version of the same subject belonging to the last period of his work, also without provenience other than Pompeii, is now in the Museo Nazionale. Here there is no figure of Icarus in the air, only the broken body upon the shore in the foreground, while Daedalus hovers above the familiar little boat. The landscape here is very impressionistically rendered.

Although this painter survived the earthquake of A.D. 62 and was in great demand throughout the time of the Fourth Style in Pompeii, I can find no other subject picture in the Fourth Style to attribute to him. In the Third Style as a landscapist he begins rather stiffly; an elaborate landscape in the peristyle of the Casa di Cerere, I ix 13, is a good example of his early manner. Here one notes the meticulous drawing, with low gables interspersed with occasional trees and shrubs, the emphasis on the verticality of the architecture and on columnar architecture. His fondness for herms, especially Priapus herms, and worshipers is evident, and the whole is populated with characteristic figures. His striding traveler appears at the extreme right. Other good examples of his early manner are a pair of landscapes in triclinium h of I vii 19. Here we see his fondness for oblique angles and architecture against a contrasting ground of vegetation. The figures here are larger, and he paints them with one side in deep shadow, but they show his usual grouping, with one figure much smaller than its companions, often with a dot for a head. His striding traveler appears in the middle of one of these pictures.

In his early period he usually liked to paint miniature landscapes, a slender column or syzygium before a tree with a sketched figure or two, or sometimes without any figures. Good examples of this manner are found in the Casa di Ceio, I vi 15, the Casa di Paquio Proculo, I vii 1, I vii 5, I xvii 2/3, V ii g, V ii i, and the Casa del Triclinio, V ii 4. A variant on this manner in a more complex landscape showing many touches that foreshadow his later manner is offered by a framed landscape in the ala of the Casa del Sacerdote Amando, I vii 7. Here one should note the tower with spreading roof and shadowed windows in the right foreground, the Italic roofs and crenellations of antefixes, and the long portico that closes the scene in the distance. It also shows his figures with dots for heads and a fine striding traveler in the right foreground.

In the time of the Fourth Style he adopted a generally more florid manner, but with variations to suit the size of his panel and the general decoration of the room in which he was working. An excellent example of his range of building types and landscape elements at this time is provided by the panels from peristyle 17 of the Casa del Citarista, I iv 5/25, now in the Museo Nazionale. He likes to paint buildings by the sea, often raised on artificial terraces and approached by bridges, small crescent rowboats, long porticos hung with oscilla with shadows of the columns projected on the wall behind, buildings with a row of trees, often of almost patterned variation, behind them, and statues perched on high isolated bases. The repertory of figures remains constant, although they tend to be drawn more casually, as do his trees; his style becomes fluid and calligraphic.

This painter was responsible for the famous view of a harbor framed by quays that are embellished with a series of statues on lofty columns, MN 9514, and the view of a small seaside temple with a group of statues under a tree to the left and a large tripod to the right, MN 9414, which come from Stabiae and are almost certainly counterparts. Not only are their dimensions and general tonality very similar but in Bayardi's catalog they are numbered 570 and 571. He also did a pair of rectangular views of seaside villas from Stabiae and a series of small, almost monochrome vignettes of rustic sanctuaries in toile de Jouy style in golden yellow highlighted with white and green on a brilliant red ground that probably came from a single room in the Villa di Arianna. These are very simple and delightfully facile work.

Equally important are the landscape vignettes from alternate panels in the portico around the temple of Isis (Tempio di Iside) in Pompeii. Here to his repertory of buildings he has added a number of more exotic types, towers with roofs that are conical or like horned altars, and to his range of figures he has added a spindly-legged fisherman and figures with short cloaks that billow out behind them. His facility is so assured that he often deliberately scribbles in painting water and vegetation. This and the painting of architecture in the background seem to prove that he was also responsible for the views of naumachiae here and in the polychrome exedra of the Casa dei Vettii, VI xv 1/2. Whether he was also responsible for the great Egyptian landscapes of the ecclesiasterion of the temple of Isis is at first a difficult question. Here the color is generally pale, pinks and violets shading into soft warm tans and blues, the architecture seems very carefully studied, and the figures are detailed, but the trees and foliage can be easily recognized as his. In some of these pictures appear statues that have mere dots for heads, and there are other hallmarks of his work, such as the shapes of the votive vessels that are displayed and the way shadows are drawn. Since all this must be post-earthquake, we get a fair notion of his versatility in scale and palette.

Another landscape that is clearly his work comes from Herculaneum; this, although a vignette floated on a white ground, is a framed rectangle and probably comes from a Fourth Style decoration. An early work may be the brown and yellow monochrome from Pompeii, which may have come from a Second Style decoration. No doubt many more landscapes at all three sites are his work and in time will be identified as such. Many of his later landscapes suggest moonlight, buildings with lighted fronts of quick, lively drawing edged with white that are deeply shadowed along their sides and fade into a ground of blues and blacks. Representatives of this manner are numerous in Pompeii; one can find them, for example, in the Casa del Sacello Iliaco, I vi 4, next door in the Fullonica Stephani, I vi 7, in the Casa del Menandro, I x 4, in the Casa degli Amanti, I x 10/11, in the Casa della Fontana Piccola, VI viii 23/24, and in the Casa dei Dioscuri, VI ix 6/7, to name only a few.

But he could also paint bright daylight scenes full of color in his late period, and some of these rank among his best work. A rather ordinary pair can be seen in the Casa della Venere in Conchiglia, II iii 3. Another is in the Castellammare Antiquarium from the Edifizio di San Marco at Stabiae.

More famous is the set of tondi showing bird's-eye views of island villas and sanctuaries now in the Museo Nazionale, while most famous of all is the already mentioned bird's-eye view of a harbor.

In the museum in Naples one is almost overwhelmed by the work of this painter; it seems to leap from every wall, and one asks whether no one else painted landscapes in the Vesuvian cities. Of course there were other landscapists, and their work can be readily identified. Some of the most famous landscapes from the ancient cities are by other artists, the "Paris on Mount Ida" and the "Lost Goat," for example. But the Boscotrecase Painter was prolific, and his work was in great demand. The early excavators recognized his excellence and tended to take all of it that they found for the royal collections. But although most of his work was of very high quality, he was sometimes careless and sometimes almost perfunctory, as in the atrium of the Casa di M. Fabio Amandione, I vii 2/3. In his later work he seems to have liked to paint more broadly, with coarser brushes and stronger contrasts of light and shadow, his palette tending to dark greens and blues, but even then he was capable of meticulous work, work with exquisitely drawn foregrounds and subtly rendered lights and distances.

→ *Works* ←

→ *Subject Pictures in the Third Style, Especially Mythological Landscapes* ←

POMPEII

I vii 7, Casa del Sacerdote Amando

Triclinium b

- Fall of Icarus: Rizzo 1929, pl. 167; *MdPA,* 1938 (Maiuri), pl. 1.2; *PPM* 1 (1990) 594–97, figs. 10–13; *Peinture* 1993, 1, fig. 10.
- Perseus and Andromeda: Rizzo 1929, pl. 166; *MdPA,* 1938 (Maiuri), pl. B; Kraus and von Matt 1973, 250; *PPM* 1 (1990) 602–5, figs. 19–23; von Blanckenhagen and Alexander 1990, pl. 57; *Peinture* 1993, 1, fig. 9.
- Polyphemus and Galatea: Rizzo 1929, pl. 165; *MdPA,* 1938 (Maiuri), pl. 1.1; *PPM* 1 (1990) 598–600, figs. 14–17; von Blanckenhagen and Alexander 1990, pls. 58–59; *Peinture* 1993, 1, pl. 13.
- Hercules and the Hesperides: Rizzo 1929, pl. 95; *MdPA,* 1938

(Maiuri), pl. A; *PPM* 1 (1990) 590–92, figs. 5–7; *Peinture* 1993, 1, pl. 12.

Cubiculum c

- Paris introduced to Helen: Rizzo 1929, pl. 96; *MdPA,* 1938 (Maiuri), pl. C; *PPM* 1 (1990) 609, fig. 31.

I viii 8

Triclinium 10

- Bellerophon harnessing Pegasus: Pompeii Antiquarium 20878; *RdSP* 3 (1989) 107, fig. 2.

I ix 5, Casa del Frutteto

Triclinium 11

- Diana and Actaeon: *RömMitt* 75 (1968), pl. 40; *PPM* 2 (1990) 52–58, figs. 74–80; *Peinture* 1993, 2, fig. 54c.
- Duel of Eteocles and Polynices: *RömMitt* 75 (1968), pl. 41; *PPM* 2 (1990) 74–79, figs. 98–103.
- Fall of Icarus: *RömMitt* 75 (1968), pl. 38; *PPM* 2 (1990) 88–92, figs. 112–16; *Peinture* 1993, 2, fig. 54b.
- Punishment of Dirce: *PPM* 2 (1990) 111–12, figs. 137–38.

V ii 10

Cubiculum q

- Marsyas, Athena, and the Muses: MN s.n.; HBr pl. 154; *PPM* 3 (1991) 842, fig. 22.

V iv 13

Triclinium R

- Origins of Rome: MN s.n.; HBr pl. 155; Rizzo 1929, pl. 195.1; *PPM* 3 (1991) 1064–66, figs. 4–7.

V v 3, Casa dei Gladiatori

Peristyle, pluteus interior

- Fall of Icarus: *RömMitt* 75 (1968), pl. 39.1; *PPM* 3 (1991) 1072, fig. 6.

VI xiii 2, Casa del Gruppo dei Vasi di Vetro

Triclinium 20

- Medea and the Peliads: S 553; MN 111477; Maiuri 1953, 45; *Collezioni* 1986, 92 and p. 55; *PPM* 5 (1994) 155, fig. 23; De Caro 1994, 161.

VI xvi 36/37

Room H

- Contest of four poets: *NSc* 1908, 366, fig. 3; *PPM* 5 (1994) 991, fig. 16.

VII i 25/47, Casa di Sirico

Triclinium 8 (triclinium fenestratum)

• Aeneas Wounded: H 1383; MN 9009; Rizzo 1929, pl. 195.2; *Collezioni* 1986, 209 and p. 63; Guillaud and Guillaud 1990, fig. 283; *Peinture* 1993, 1, fig. 73; De Caro 1994, 264; *PPM* 6 (1996) 245, fig. 35.

IX xiii 1/3, Casa di Giulio Polibio

Triclinium EE

• Punishment of Dirce: *RömMitt* 93 (1986), pls. 53, 54.1, and color plate; Leach 1988, fig. 24; *Peinture* 1993, 1, fig. 101, and 2, fig. 343.

BOSCOTRECASE

Villa di Agrippa Postumo

Mythological room 19

• Polyphemus and Galatea: New York, MMA 20.192.17; Guillaud and Guillaud 1990, fig. 233; von Blanckenhagen and Alexander 1990, pls. 42, 44–45.

• Perseus and Andromeda: New York, MMA 20.192.16; Guillaud and Guillaud 1990, figs. 234–35; von Blanckenhagen and Alexander 1990, pls. 43, 46–47.

→ *Subject Pictures in the Fourth Style* ←

POMPEII

Unidentified Buildings

• Fall of Icarus: London, BM; *BMC* 1933, pl. 12; *RömMitt* 75 (1968), pl. 39.2.

• Fall of Icarus: H 1209; MN 9506; Brion 1960, fig. 112; *RömMitt* 75 (1968), pl. 32.2; *Collezioni* 1986, 171.

→ *Landscapes in the Second Style* ←

POMPEII

Unidentified Building

• Monochrome landscape of sacro-idyllic character: MN 9493; Rizzo 1929, pl. 173.2; Guillaud and Guillaud 1990, fig. 258.

⇢ *Landscapes in the Third Style (Early to Middle)* ⇠

POMPEII

I vi 15, Casa di Ceio

Fauces

• Landscape: Michel 1990, fig. 80; *PPM* 1 (1990) 415, fig. 8.

I vii 1, Casa di Paquio Proculo

Peristyle

• Landscapes: *PPM* 1 (1990) 531, figs. 80–81.

I vii 19, Annex of the Casa dell'Efebo

Triclinium b

• Framed landscapes: *PPM* 1 (1990) 759, figs. 16–17.

I ix 5, Casa del Frutteto

Triclinium 11

• Landscapes: *PPM* 2 (1990) 62, fig. 84 (= *Peinture* 1993, 1, fig. 16); 66, fig. 88; 68, fig. 90; 71, fig. 94; 96, fig. 120; 100, fig. 124.

I ix 13, Casa di Cerere

Peristyle

• Large landscape: *Mededelingen* 38, n.s. 3 (1976), pl. 53; *PPM* 2 (1990) 216, fig. 68.

I xii 8

Cubiculum 12

• Landscape: *PPM* 2 (1990) 774–77, figs. 20–23, and 780, fig. 27.

I xvii 2/3

Triclinium 4

• Landscape: *PPM* 2 (1990) 1035, fig. 11.

V ii g

Cubiculum b

• Landscapes: *PPM* 3 (1991) 642–44, figs. 1–3.

V ii i, Casa delle Nozze d'Argento

Peristyle

• Landscapes: *PPM* 3 (1991) 720–21, figs. 89, 91.

V ii 4, Casa del Triclinio

Cubiculum u

• Landscapes: *PPM* 3 (1991) 820–21, figs, 53, 55.

→ *Landscapes in the Late Third Style* ←

POMPEII

I vii 19, Annex of the Casa dell'Efebo

Cubiculum f

- Large landscape with cowherd: *PPM* 1 (1990) 782, fig. 54; *Peinture* 1993, 1, fig. 13.

BOSCOTRECASE

Villa di Agrippa Postumo

Red room 16

- Landscape with a statue of Cybele: MN 147501; Rizzo 1929, pl. 172; Kraus and von Matt 1973, 296; *Collezioni* 1986, 48 and p. 42; Guillaud and Guillaud 1990, fig. 232; von Blanckenhagen and Alexander 1990, pls. 24–25.
- Landscape with a large tripod: MN 147502; Rizzo 1929, pl. 173.1; von Blanckenhagen and Alexander 1990, pls. 31, 32.2, 33.
- Landscape with a rustic temple: MN 147503; *Collezioni* 1986, 49; von Blanckenhagen and Alexander 1990, pls. 30, 32.1.

Black room 15

- Landscape vignette: New York, MMA 20.192.1; Guillaud and Guillaud 1990, fig. 217; von Blanckenhagen and Alexander 1990, pl. 1.
- Landscape vignette: New York, MMA 20.192.10; Guillaud and Guillaud 1990, fig. 216; von Blanckenhagen and Alexander 1990, pl. 13.2.
- Landscape vignette: MN (lost); von Blanckenhagen and Alexander 1990, pl. 13.1.

→ *Landscapes in the Early Fourth Style* ←

POMPEII

I iv 5/25, Casa del Citarista

Peristyle 17

- Frieze of villa landscapes: MN 9496, 9608, 9610; *Collezioni* 1986, 316; Guillaud and Guillaud 1990, figs. 85, 249.

VIII vii 28, Tempio di Iside

Portico surrounding the temple

- Landscapes in vignettes and panels:

  MN 8517; *Alla ricerca di Iside* 1992, 1.22, fig. p. 45; *PPM* 8 (1998) 772, fig. 63.

  MN 8518; *Alla ricerca di Iside* 1992, 1.43, pl. 6.1; ; *PPM* 8 (1998) 744, fig. 15.

  MN 8520; *Alla ricerca di Iside* 1992, 1.24, fig. p. 108; *PPM* 8 (1998) 773, fig. 65.

  MN 8528; *Alla ricerca di Iside* 1992, 1.27, pl. 5.5; *PPM* 8 (1998) 776, fig. 69.

  MN 8539; *Alla ricerca di Iside* 1992, 1.10, pls. 4.1, 4.3; *PPM* 8 (1998) 764, fig. 50.

  MN 8577; *Alla ricerca di Iside* 1992, 1.51, pl. 3.3; *PPM* 8 (1998) 749, fig. 23.

  MN 8607; *Alla ricerca di Iside* 1992, 1.2, pls. 4.2, 6.3, 6.4; *PPM* 8 (1998) 756, fig. 37.

  MN 9425; *Alla ricerca di Iside* 1992, 1.11, pl. 7.2; *PPM* 8 (1998) 765, fig. 52.

  MN 9444; *Alla ricerca di Iside* 1992, 1.15, fig. p. 42; *PPM* 8 (1998) 763, fig. 49.

  MN 9475; HBr pl. 174.1; Rizzo 1929, pl. 176; *Collezioni* 1986, 302; Guillaud and Guillaud 1990, fig. 256; *Alla ricerca di Iside* 1992, 1.40, fig. p. 49; *PPM* 8 (1998) 741, fig. 11.

  MN 9490; *Alla ricerca di Iside* 1992, 1.50, pl. 3.4; *PPM* 8 (1998) 742, fig. 13.

  MN 9495; *Alla ricerca di Iside* 1992, 1.48, fig. p. 51; *PPM* 8 (1998) 747, fig. 21.

  MN 9505; *Alla ricerca di Iside* 1992, 1.45, pl. 6.2; *PPM* 8 (1998) 745, fig. 17.

  MN 9515; *Alla ricerca di Iside* 1992, 1.7, fig. p. 112; *PPM* 8 (1998) 760, fig. 42.

  MN 9771; *Alla ricerca di Iside* 1992, 1.56, fig. p. 104.

  MN s.n.; *Alla ricerca di Iside* 1992, 1.28, fig. p. 46; *PPM* 8 (1998) 777, fig. 71.

- Naumachiae (H 1576, 1577):

  MN 8519; *Alla ricerca di Iside* 1992, 1.44, fig. p. 51; *PPM* 8 (1998) 744, fig. 16.

MN 8527; *Alla ricerca di Iside* 1992, 1.29, fig. p. 48; *PPM* 8 (1998) 778, fig. 73.

MN 8529; *Alla ricerca di Iside* 1992, 1.25, pl. 5.2; *PPM* 8 (1998) 774, fig. 66.

MN 8530; *Alla ricerca di Iside* 1992, 1.23, pl. 5.1; *PPM* 8 (1998) 773, fig. 64.

MN 8541; *Alla ricerca di Iside* 1992, 1.20, fig. p. 44; *PPM* 8 (1998) 771, fig. 61.

MN 8552; *Alla ricerca di Iside* 1992, 1.41, pl. 5.4; *PPM* 8 (1998) 743, fig. 14.

MN 8554; *Alla ricerca di Iside* 1992, 1.39, pl. 5.3; *PPM* 8 (1998) 741, fig. 10.

MN 8590; *Alla ricerca di Iside* 1992, 1.47, fig. p. 51; *PPM* 8 (1998) 746, fig. 19.

Ecclesiasterion

- Landscape with syzygium and ibis: H 1571b; MN 8575; *MdPA,* 1941 (Elia), 31, pl. 1; *Alla ricerca di Iside* 1992, 1.62, pl. 9, fig. p. 117; *PPM* 8 (1998) 824, fig. 187.
- Landscape with tholus and statue: H 1571e; MN 1265; *MdPA,* 1941 (Elia), 32, pl. 2; *Alla ricerca di Iside* 1992, 1.66, pl. 11; *PPM* 8 (1998) 840, fig. 211.
- Landscape with syzygium with curtain: H 1571a; MN 8558; *MdPA,* 1941 (Elia), 35–36; *Alla ricerca di Iside* 1992, 1.67, pl. 12; *PPM* 8 (1998) 841, fig. 213.
- Landscape with sarcophagus of Osiris: H 1571d; MN 8570; *MdPA,* 1941 (Elia), 33–34; *Alla ricerca di Iside* 1992, 1.68, pl. 13; *PPM* 8 (1998) 836, fig. 205.
- Landscape with island sacellum: H 1571c; MN 8574; *MdPA,* 1941 (Elia), 31–32; *Alla ricerca di Iside* 1992, 1.70, pl. 15; *PPM* 8 (1998) 826, fig. 189.

Unidentified Buildings

- Landscape: MN 9487; HBr pl. 175.1; Grant 1975, 54; *Collezioni* 1986, 301 and p. 68.
- Landscape: MN 9509; HBr pl. 174.2.
- Landscape from a house on Via della Fortuna: Pompeii Antiquarium; Rizzo 1929, pl. 175.1; Spinazzola 1953, 2.845, fig. 831.

HERCULANEUM

Unidentified Building

- Landscape: MN 9513; *Collezioni* 1986, 312.

STABIAE

Villa di Arianna (Villa della Venditrice di Amori, Villa di Varano)

Cubiculum 26 (Weber)

- Toile di Jouy landscapes:
  MN 9396; HBr pl. 200; *RömMitt* 84 (1977), pl. 6.3.
  MN 9397; *RömMitt* 84 (1977), pl. 7.2.
  MN 9398; *RömMitt* 84 (1977), pl. 9.2.
  MN 9401; HBr pl. 201; *RömMitt* 84 (1977), pl. 7.4; Guillaud and Guillaud 1990, fig. 219.
  MN 9402; *RömMitt* 84 (1977), pl. 8.1.
  MN 9403; HBr pl. 201; *RömMitt* 84 (1977), pl. 6.3; Guillaud and Guillaud 1990, fig. 218.
  MN 9405; *RömMitt* 84 (1977), pl. 9.1.
  MN 9407; HBr pl. 200; *RömMitt* 84 (1977), pl. 8.2.
  MN 9459; *RömMitt* 84 (1977), pl. 7.1.

Edifizio di San Marco

- Landscapes:
  MN 9408; HBr pls. 164.3 and 164.4.
  MN 9409: *Collezioni* 1986, 311.
  MN 9479; *RömMitt* 26 (1911), pl. 8.1 (companion to MN 9480).
  MN 9480; Ragghianti 1963, pl. 84.1; *Collezioni* 1986, 319; Guillaud and Guillaud 1990, fig. 254.
  MN 9511; *Collezioni* 1986, 306; Guillaud and Guillaud 1990, fig. 251.

⯈ *Landscapes in the Middle Fourth Style* ⯇

POMPEII

I x 4, Casa del Menandro

Triclinium 18

- Landscape: *PPM* 2 (1990) 351, fig. 177.

VI xv 1/2, Casa dei Vettii

Peristyle

- Toile de Jouy landscape: Grant 1975, 45; *PPM* 5 (1994) 508, fig. 68.

Triclinium p (polychrome exedra)

- Naumachiae: Schefold 1962, pls. 92, 93; Eschebach 1978, fig. 153; *RdSP* 3 (1989) 136–37, figs. 2–5; Grimal and Kossakowski 1993, pl. 64; *Peinture* 1993, 1, pls. 67, 69; *PPM* 5 (1994) 537, fig. 117, and 541, fig. 122.

VI xv 7, Casa del Principe di Napoli

Exedra m

- Landscapes: Strocka 1984, figs. 161–62; *PPM* 5 (1994) 674, fig. 37.

VI xvi 7/38, Casa degli Amorini Dorati

Peristyle, west wall

- Landscapes: Seiler 1992, figs. 256, 257; *PPM* 5 (1994) 753, figs. 73, 74.

HERCULANEUM

Environs, Villa dei Papiri

- Landscape: MN 9399; *Collezioni* 1986, 304; Wojcik 1986, pl. 9.
- Landscape: MN 9447; *Collezioni* 1986, 40.
- Landscape: MN 9499; *Collezioni* 1986, 307; Wojcik 1986, pl. 15.

STABIAE

Villa di Arianna (Villa della Venditrice di Amori, Villa di Varano)

Diaeta west of summer triclinium (room E)

- Landscape: MN 9392; *RömMitt* 84 (1977), pl. 45.1.
- Landscape: MN 9421; *RömMitt* 84 (1977), pl. 45.2.
- Landscape: MN 9424; *RömMitt* 84 (1977), pl. 45.3.
- Landscape: MN 9431; *RömMitt* 84 (1977), pl. 46.1.

UNCERTAIN CAMPANIAN PROVENIENCE

- Landscapes: MN 9510; *Collezioni* 1986, 305.

➔ *Landscapes in the Late Fourth Style* ➔

POMPEII

I vi 4, Casa del Sacello Iliaco (Casa degli Elefanti)

Triclinium c

- Landscape: *PPM* 1 (1990) 290, fig. 13.

I vi 7, Fullonica Stephani

Oecus g

- Landscapes: *PPM* 1 (1990) 342, fig. 17; 348, figs. 30, 31.

I vii 2/3, Casa di M. Fabio Amandione

Atrium

- Landscape: *PPM* 1 (1990) 559, fig. 10, and 565, fig. 18; *Peinture* 1993, 1, fig. 8.

I x 10/11, Casa degli Amanti

Atrium

- Landscape in tondo: *PPM* 2 (1990) 443, fig. 13; *Peinture* 1993, 1, fig. 21.

Cubiculum d

- Square landscape: *PPM* 2 (1990) 461, fig. 34.

II iii 3, Casa della Venere in Conchiglia

Peristyle

- Landscapes: *PPM* 3 (1991) 134–35, figs. 33, 35.

VI viii 23/24, Casa della Fontana Piccola

Ala 7

- Landscapes: *PPM* 4 (1993) 634, figs. 19, 20; Fröhlich 19 96, figs. 148–49.

VI ix 6/7, Casa dei Dioscuri

Cubiculum 35

- Landscape: *PPM* 4 (1993) 879, fig. 38.

Unidentified Buildings

- Landscape: MN 9488; HBr pl. 171.1; Maiuri 1953, 122; *Collezioni* 1986, 310; Guillaud and Guillaud 1990, fig. 3.
- Landscape: MN 9484; *Collezioni* 1986, 320.

HERCULANEUM

Environs, Villa dei Papiri

- Landscape: MN 9458; *Collezioni* 1986, 303 and p. 68; Wojcik 1986, pl. 19 (identified as MN 9467).

Unidentified Buildings

- Landscape: MN 9419; Herbig 1962, fig. 56; Ward-Perkins and Claridge 1978, 24 and 160, no. 111; *Collezioni* 1986, 59.
- Landscapes: MN 9436, 9438; Maiuri 1953, 121; *Collezioni* 1986, 308, 309.

BOSCOREALE

Villa in Contrada Giuliana

Room B

- Maritime landscape: Paris, Louvre, MND 313; Tran Tam Tinh 1974, 50, fig. 30.
- Maritime landscape: Paris, Louvre, MND 314; Tran Tam Tinh 1974, 50, fig. 31.
- Maritime landscape: London, BM; Rizzo 1929, pl. 168; *BMC* 1933, pl. 5.

STABIAE

Edifizio di San Marco

- Landscape: Castellammare Antiquarium; Picard 1970, 83, fig. 57; de Franciscis 1978, 186.

Unidentified Buildings

- Harbor landscape: MN 9514; Maiuri 1953, 123; Ragghianti 1963, pl. 83; Stenico 1963, pl. 121; *Collezioni* 1986, 317 and p. 74; Guillaud and Guillaud 1990, fig. 324; *Peinture* 1993, 1, fig. 159; De Caro 1994, 195.
- Seaside sanctuary with tripod: MN 9414; Rizzo 1929, pl. 174.1; Ragghianti 1963, pl. 82; Stenico 1963, pl. 120; *Peinture* 1993, 1, fig. 161.

UNCERTAIN CAMPANIAN PROVENIENCE

- Landscape: MN 9503; *Collezioni* 1986, 313.
- Landscape: MN 9672 (no publication known).

The Cassandra Painter

The work of this painter closely resembles that of the Giasone Painter but is broader, less miniaturistic, in approach and of a softer texture. The painter may have been a pupil of the Giasone Painter. His characteristics are a strong preliminary drawing in very dark color, commonly black, over which he builds forms in lighter but still relatively dark pigments; doll-like figures, well proportioned, in very static poses, as if frozen in tableaux; and a muted palette that favors grays and dull violets with very dark flesh for the male figures. His legs and feet are well drawn with well-observed knees; his hands tend to be clumsy, and his arms, weak. His children tend to look like reduced adults. He furnishes his background more than the Giasone Painter and brings it more into play with the action of the figures but still leaves a lot of unencumbered blank space.

→ *Works* ←

POMPEII

I ii 28, Casa della Grata Metallica

Triclinium i, south of the peristyle

- Cassandra in prophecy: S 560; MN 111476; HBr pl. 179; *Collezioni* 1986, 78; *PPM* 1 (1990) 63, fig. 12.

IX ii 16, Casa di Panthera

Triclinium c

- Hercules and Nessus: S 501; HBr text 1.203, fig. 59.

The Cecilio Giocondo Painter

The subject pictures of the tablinum of the Casa di Cecilio Giocondo, V i 26, the two central mythological compositions of Iphigenia in Tauris, on the north wall, now removed to the Museo Nazionale, and the Return of the corpse of Hector (?), on the south, and the paired busts of satyrs and maenads and a maenad carrying an amorino in the side panels, are the work of a single painter with a highly individual style marked by a strongly triangular face with sweeping eyebrows, a strong unification of forehead and nose ridge in a single plane, and a small, very full-lipped mouth commonly slightly out of alignment with the axis of the face. Another identifying trait is fingers in which the first joint is abnormally small but rounded. The artist is a good colorist, and his soft blues and yellows shimmer, quite unlike the enameled quality of much Third Style painting. While his drawing is often faulty, his shading and modeling give an effective softness and plasticity to his figures that is also unusual for the Third Style. His style is so marked that one would expect to find it always easy to identify.

We find it in the great cinnabar red oecus of the Villa Imperiale of the Porta Marina, where he painted three subject pictures but not the genre panels of the frieze or the tiny figures of the predelle. His subjects are the Fall of Icarus, Theseus victor over the Minotaur, and Theseus abandoning Ariadne, the last two compositions familiar from other copies, the first, the best preserved of the three, a hybrid invention in which a hovering Daedalus wears the billowing costume of a Victoria and an Akte who looks sorrowfully down at the corpse of Icarus lying on the beach is one of the loveliest figures in all ancient painting. That these are his work is obvious in the triangular faces, the sweeping eyebrows, the mouths out of alignment, all his hallmarks. I have been unable to find any other work by him. I believe that the other pictures attributed to him by Caroline E. Dexter in *The Casa di Cecilio Giocondo in Pompeii* (Ann Arbor: University Microfilms, 1975), 127–30, are by an entirely different painter, the Amore Punito Painter.

➔ *Works* ➔

POMPEII

V i 26, Casa di Cecilio Giocondo

Tablinum

- Iphigenia in Tauris: S 583; MN 111439; HBr pl. 118; Curtius 1929, 246–47, figs. 144–45; Ragghianti 1963, 87; Stenico 1963, fig. 101; *Collezioni* 1986, 87 and p. 51; Guillaud and Guillaud 1990, title page; *PPM* 3 (1991) 589, fig. 23; *Peinture* 1993, 2, fig. 141b.
- Return of the corpse of Hector (?): S 579; *PPM* 3 (1991) 597, fig. 40b.
- Maenad carrying an amorino: S 208; MN 110591; HBr pl. 239; Elia 1932, 112, fig. 40; Brion 1960, fig. 99; *Collezioni* 1986, 85; *PPM* 3 (1991) 589, fig. 25.
- Satyr and maenad: S 236; MN 110590; HBr pl. 239.2; Brion 1960, fig. 103; *Collezioni* 1986, 86; Guillaud and Guillaud 1990, fig. 70; *PPM* 3 (1991) 589, fig. 24; De Caro 1994, 159.
- Satyr and maenad: S 233; Schefold 1962, pl. 45.2; *PPM* 3 (1991) 600, fig. 49; Grimal and Kossakowski 1993, fig. 43.
- Satyr and maenad: S 234; *PPM* 3 (1991) 602, fig. 53; Grimal and Kossakowski 1993, fig. 72.

Environs, Porta Marina, Villa Imperiale

Great cinnabar red oecus

- Fall of Icarus: *RömMitt* 75 (1968), pls. 27, 29.2; Kraus and von Matt 1973, figs. 128–29; *Peinture* 1993, 2, fig. 364.

- Theseus victor over the Minotaur: Kraus and von Matt 1973, fig. 286; Ling 1991, 120, fig. 121; *Peinture* 1993, 2, fig. 361.
- Theseus abandoning Ariadne: *Peinture* 1993, 2, fig. 358.

The Centauro Painter

The comparative rarity of work by this painter in Pompeii, together with the importance and high quality of what is preserved, may be taken as indication that he was an artist of at least local celebrity and probably not a native Pompeian. However, it must be remembered that grand rooms in the Third Style are relatively uncommon and that few Third Style painters are represented by any considerable number of pictures. Although the Centauro Painter has easily recognizable virtues, he has also equivalent, if less conspicuous, faults.

In proportion his heads are large and well shaped, those of men apt to be just noticeably larger than those of women. The torsos tend to be slightly elongated. The shoulders, especially those of men, are broad and muscular. The upper torso is relatively short and heavy, the waist slightly high but not strongly marked. The buttocks are heavy and rounded. Men's arms are generally of good proportions, sometimes light and short, a defect commoner in the arms of women. The hands are well shaped and tend to be small. The legs are well studied, strong but not overly muscled, the feet large.

The heads have a well-domed skull in full face but are distinctly flattened on top in profile. The face is generous and classical with a wide and generally high forehead and a heavy but well-shaped jaw. The eyes are wide-set, large and almond-shaped, under calm, thin eyebrows in a regular arch. Their thinness makes the brows seem strange for men. They are not infrequently elongated and drawn parallel with the corner of the eye. The upper lid is apt to be heavy, the lashes along it thick and dark. The lower lid is sometimes drawn high on the ball, especially in profile, but in full face the white of the ball often appears under the iris. There is almost never a highlight in the iris, so the eyes have a vacant and dreamy expression, especially when the lower lid is not drawn high. In profile they bulge and stare. The noses are broad, the bridge of the nose continuing the plane of the forehead in women but apt to be slightly aquiline in men. The tip of the nose is crisp but not sharply pointed. At the nostrils the nose is broad and flaring, and the wings of the nostrils are often fleshy and carefully drawn. The crease of the cheek at the nostrils is almost always indicated by a shadow. The upper lip is apt to be in light shadow, full and well shaped; the lower is touched with light, often along its whole length (especially in profile), and usually seems slightly pouting. The upper lip is apt to be short, the mouth small but not tight. In full face the lips generally appear slightly parted because of deepening of the shadow along their meeting. The chin is long and firm, usually well formed. There is usually the suggestion of a slight cleft and a good shadow below the lower lip. The cheeks are full but firm, but there is almost always a soft fleshiness under the jaw, one of the hallmarks of this painter. The ears are well placed, apt to be long and narrow. The lobe is pronounced, the helix narrow and shapely, but the interior of the ear varies greatly from figure to figure. The hair of young men is generally thicker and longer than that in other Pompeian paintings and only slightly curling. It is brushed back from the forehead and generally relatively thin around the ears. High on the nape of the neck it ends in short ducktails. The hair of women is closely crinkled but dressed simply and without emphasis.

The men's shoulders are broad and muscular, the necks strong but not thick. The cords of the throat are indicated but not emphasized. The clavicle is distinct and characteristic, a high, shallow V below which the chest seems deep and ample. The shoulders are well rounded, but when the arm is in play the deltoid seems short and twists somewhat too far back. The breasts are full and muscular, even a trifle heavy, the nipples small but clearly indicated. The linea alba is shown as a groove, uncertain in the vicinity of the clavicle, deep and clear between the breasts and over the stomach. The volume of the rib cage is well realized both at rest and in action, sometimes slightly overdrawn, as in the figure of Nessus. The waist is a bit high, the belly a bit heavy, the belly fold faint and carelessly indicated. The hip bulge is usually indicated, but without emphasis. The backs of men are broad and rather fleshy with very heavy shoulders. There is little play of muscles in the shoulders or around the ribs, but the line of the spine is deep and clear, as are the shoulder blades. The heaviness of the upper back tapers sharply to the waist, from which the buttocks shelve sharply out. No nude torso of a woman is shown in the surviving works; from the draped torsos we see that the shoulders are regularly much narrower than those of men, sloping and rounded, the breasts high and firm but not sharply pointed, the waist slender.

The arms of the men are on the whole well formed, the upper arm strong, the elbow slightly pointed and bony, the lower arm rounded below the elbow and tapering to a slender wrist. The articulation of the wrist varies in quality but is seldom expert, being generally too abrupt when the hand is bent and in play and underemphasized when it is not. The hands themselves also vary in form, but usually the metacarpus is rather long, the fingers long and tapering. The artist takes great pains with the hands, but there is always a slight awkwardness about them, usually more in their posing than in the drawing. When a hand is relaxed, the painter has a trick of showing it with the index and middle fingers spread wide apart so the third finger covers the ring finger. The taper of the fingers is sometimes exaggerated at the tip. The hands and arms of women are almost always conspicuously light in comparison with those of men, but in their basic forms they are similar to those of the men.

The legs of this painter's figures often seem long and slender in proportion to the torsos, although actually they are seldom far out of proportion. The thighs are smooth, tapering regularly to a light, rather sharp knee. The formation of the bent knee is marked by a tendency to project the line of the front of the thigh beyond that of the shin, making the knee jut slightly. In neither bent nor standing legs is the knee studied with care. The calf is smooth and somewhat simplified, the bow of the shin indicated but not emphasized, the tuck of the calf muscle almost always drawn in, sometimes with slight exaggeration. The ankles are thick but clear, the feet large but not so well drawn as the hands. In feet where the muscles should be in play the pull of these is insufficiently studied; in others the study of form and light is negligent.

The only child in the preserved works is drawn with a nice sense of the difference between children's anatomy and adults'. The animals are equally good, although the exigencies of space and subject cause the artist to draw them small in comparison to the figures. While he seems unable to draw the horses in the Hercules and Nessus with expert foreshortening, his attempt achieves a certain measure of success. The forms of the animals are somewhat simplified, but with the purpose of subordinating them to the human figures rather than from a lack of understanding. The hooves and knees of the centaur, for example, are precise in their delineation.

The drapery of the Centauro Painter, while not so expertly worked as the other parts of his pictures, is nicely differentiated in weight and texture. He shows some preference for broad and simple treatment (the mantle of Atalanta, the chiton of Deianira), slashed folds of dark edged with a narrow line of light. This pattern, which he shares with certain other painters of the Third Style, he handles less confidently than they do and with less success; while avoiding their oversharp effect and surrealistic finish, his use of the formula falls into a shorthand. The folds do not bunch or cling, but remain flat and uninteresting. So also in his handling of veils and transparent drapery, while he shows their crushed and clinging lines and the forms below emerging through them, they still do not convince. The folds are too sharp and thin, too little differentiated; the sleeves cling too tight. He is at his best in the heavy woolen cloaks of men, which seem to have real weight and substance, and in heavy overgarments, where simplified rendering best expresses the folds. In other details he is also skillful; his painting of sandals and of a straw hat *(causia)* may be cited as examples of careful observation and facility.

There is little to observe about the Centauro Painter's treatment of objects and background. We may note that in his backgrounds he likes to paint several sorts of foliage, carefully distinguishing one from another and achieving his effects by extremely lively brushwork, that he likes simple forms of architecture simply expressed, and that he keeps his foreground carefully clear, relying on the play of the shadows cast by his figures to keep the foreground from vacancy and monotony.

He prefers a palette of clear colors, essentially low in key but enlivened by sharper, brighter hues in the finish of the foreground figures and their drapery. Thus, the figures are laid in in cool grays and pale browns and finished with strong, warm red-browns, yellows, and blacks. The base color is laid flat; he then gives the forms definition by working over this with lighter and darker tones, partly in broad striped brushwork, partly in loose but skillful oblique hatching. The shadows along the side of the figure away from the light are apt to seem too dark, overemphasized and streaky, while the shadows along the lighted limbs are feathery. The final finish is crisp and brilliant; in this the painter makes full use of overdrawing in several colors to emphasize forms and edges, while shadows and lights are picked out by light, loose hatching in relatively pure tone. Among the painter's idiosyncrasies should be noted a reflected light on the underside of the chin and a relatively strong light on the cheekbone. In contrast to his careful working of flesh, the drapery is slashed in quickly with rather broad brushes and few colors; here white, grayed purple, gray, and rich dark red predominate. The background brushwork is free and neat but cursive, so that forms seem pale and shadowy. That in the foreground is broad and simple, darkened a little at the corners and lightened a little near the important figures.

✧ *Works* ✧

POMPEII

VI ix 3/5, Casa del Centauro

"Tablinum" 26

- Hercules and Nessus: H 1146; MN 9001; HBr pls. V, 147; Rizzo 1929, pl. B; Ragghianti 1963, pl. 50; Kraus and von Matt 1973, fig. 264; *Collezioni* 1986, 83; Guillaud and Guillaud 1990, fig. 280; *PPM* 4 (1993) 854, fig. 68.
- Meleager and Atalanta: H 1165; MN 8980; HBr pl. 223; *Collezioni* 1986, 82; *PPM* 4 (1993) 852, fig. 66.

VII iii 29, Casa di Spurio Messore

Room t, west of the peristyle, next to the tablinum

- Scene of purification: S 616; MN 120086; HBr pl. 176; *PPM* 6 (1996) 921, fig. 36.
- Amazonomachy: S 548; MN 120085; HBr pl. 177; *PPM* 6 (1996) 919, fig. 34.

IX ii 16, Casa di Panthera

Atrium d

- Bellerophon before Proetus: S 521; MN 115399; HBr pl. 204; *Collezioni* 1986, 77.

The Cinque Scheletri Painter

This painter, a Third Style painter of only moderate ability, seems to have liked a nearly square picture field and filled it with proportionately large figures in rather crowded compositions. In this he approaches the Fourth Style, as he does also in his interest in a setting painted in colors nearly as strong as those of his figures. He shares certain characteristics with the Cecilio Giocondo Painter and may have been his pupil. His tall, lanky figures are poorly drawn; the arms and legs are stiffly and awkwardly posed. The thigh is regularly too long, the lower leg much too short. He has trouble drawing hands and often hides them to avoid having to draw them, but does so awkwardly.

His heads are blocky, broad-cheeked and lantern-jawed. Men's hair is short and bristles in feathery tufts; women's is often pushed too high on the forehead and above the ears. The painting of the ears is a hallmark; they are always very small but conspicuous and misplaced, either too high or too low and often too far back. The other features tend to seem small and crowded.

→ *Works* ←

POMPEII

VI x 2, Casa dei Cinque Scheletri

Triclinium 6

- Paris and Helen: H 1310; MN 9002; *PPM* 4 (1993) 1039, fig. 17.
- Cassandra in prophecy: H 1391b; MN 8999; HBr pl. 180; *Collezioni* 1986, 90; *PPM* 4 (1993) 1040, fig. 18.
- Ulysses and Penelope: H 1331; MN 9107; HBr pl. 55; Curtius 1929, 235, fig. 136; *Collezioni* 1986, 91; *PPM* 4 (1993) 1041, fig. 19.

VII ii 25, Casa delle Quadrighe

Triclinium n

- Forge of Vulcan: H 259; MN 9531; *Collezioni* 1986, 165; *PPM* 6 (1996) 713, fig. 56.

VIII iii 24, Casa di Apolline e Coronide

Triclinium 6

- Apollo and Coronis (or Daphne): H 213; HBr pl. 133.2; *PPM* 8 (1998) 422, fig. 7.

IX ix d (18), Casa di Sulpicio Rufo (Casa del Maiale, Casa del Porco)

Cubiculum l

- Hunter resting: Schefold 1962, pl. 45.1.

Triclinium c, west of the atrium

- Architectural landscape with figures: Beyen 1938, fig. 131b; Schefold 1962, pl. 47.3.
- Architectural landscape with statues: Beyen 1938, fig. 132b; Schefold 1962, pl. 46.

The Citarista Painter

A Third Style painter of very marked style, very popular and well suited to the rather astringent restrictions of that style in its full flower, the Citarista Painter liked to work with isolated figures in static poses against a neutral ground, usually off-white, where landscape could be suggested by a pale tree or a temple façade, but the figures stand out in sharp relief. When necessary he would introduce screen walls to emphasize the figures. The figures are tall with broad shoulders and hips but disproportionately small heads. They tend to stand or sit very firmly with just a suggestion of contrapposto when standing and nearly equally distributed weight when seated; the outline tends to be tightly closed. The upper arm is usually held tight to the body, but the hand is not infrequently large and in play. This painter's drapery falls heavy around the body, neither fluttering nor clinging; veils tend to be pulled rather tight. Feet often disappear under the skirt; when shown they are small, often neatly shod. The painter's most striking characteristic is the drawing of the facial features, which tend to be cramped into an ovoid outline, the forehead and the ridge of the short, straight nose a single plane, rather conspicuously flat, the small, dark, beady eyes glowing under low, thin eyebrows. The abstracted intensity of their stare is often arresting. The mouth is always very small and tight with what often seems a dissatisfied expression. The complexion of men is always exaggeratedly dark.

The painter is named for his work in the Casa del Citarista, I iv 5/25, where he painted large subject pictures in two of the large reception rooms, a Judgment of Paris in room 21 (MN 120033), now unfortunately faded to the point that its lower third is almost illegible, and a Leda, or Nemesis, in room 20 (MN 120034). The latter is from a room that was otherwise Fourth Style in its decoration and may be regarded as a survival from an earlier decoration. Both pictures are uncommonly ambitious and complex; this artist usually preferred to work with more intimate subjects.

The Judgment of Paris is set in a rather cluttered walled sanctuary behind which appears rather ragged foliage. There are a large globular vase mounted on a column, a statue at about half life size mounted on a high pillar, and an altar with scrolled bolsters at either end. Paris sits at the right in conversation with Mercury, who puts his right foot on the base upon which Paris sits and leans forward. Mercury wears a cloak, a winged petasus, and winged sandals. Paris wears the Phrygian cap but is otherwise nude except for a cloak that falls behind him and over his right thigh. The three goddesses are ranged before him, Athena nearest, a monumental draped figure with her helmet and shield beside her. Juno sits on the altar, a regal figure with a long scepter steadied by her raised left hand. Venus stands to the left, fully draped and wrapped in an enveloping mantle that also covers her head. She stands in profile and lifts her left hand pensively to her chin. The figures seem a bit lost in the space provided; there is a deep empty foreground and a feeling of vastness to the sky above the precinct wall, thanks to the meagerness of the vegetation. The attribution of this picture to this painter is based on the treatment of the drapery, the shallow crowded profiles of Venus and Mercury, and the poses of the figures, especially the seated ones with raised elbows.

In a small chamber, room 23, opening behind room 21, this artist painted a pair of two-figure compositions. On the south wall is one of a white-bearded citharist, garlanded, seated on a high klismos in profile to the left, who turns his upper body to face the viewer, pausing in his playing, and a statuesque young female lyrist crowned with laurel who stands in profile at the right. They seem to have been interrupted in a performance; he holds his plectrum, and she presses the strings of her lyre with thumb and forefinger. Both have very small eyes under rather heavy eyebrows, and their principal facial features are crowded along the axis of the nose, although the head is of good proportion. The subject has been interpreted as a concert or contest between Pindar and Corinna. The condition of the picture is poor but better than that of its companion. That both are by the same hand is apparent from pose, proportions, palette, and the drawing of hands and profiles.

On the north wall is a squarish panel showing an aged Oriental monarch in a Phrygian cap and long drapery seated on a backless stool facing a beardless individual in a tight-sleeved garment and trousers under a long embroidered tunic. This second figure, perhaps a messenger, wears a broad band around his head and carries a long, slender spear or staff; he gestures toward the king with his open right hand as though pleading with him. Just behind them stretches a long white building with high windows. The subject has been variously interpreted, but no interpretation is thoroughly satisfying. The picture is now in very poor condition but was photographed while still fairly legible.

The third picture in this room is rather different, a very youthful Apollo, nude except for a mantle falling behind him and draped over his right knee and left forearm, who stands resting his left arm on a cithara propped on a low square base while with his right hand he plays with his thick, curling hair. A tripod mounted on a base to the left identifies the god, and branches to the right complete the setting. This picture is barely recognizable today.

The picture of Pindar and Corinna is one of several copies of the same composition. These are found in V ii 4 (*PPM* 3 [1991] 820, fig. 52), VI xiv 38 (S 644; Schefold 1962, pl. 55.1; *PPM* 5 [1994] 380, fig. 7), VI xiv 43 (H 1379; *PPM* 5 [1994] 463, fig. 70), VII i 25/47 (H 1378), where there was also a copy of the companion picture of an Oriental monarch (H 1388b), VII iii 29 (*PPM* 6 [1996] 927, fig. 46), and IX ix 12 (19). They are all in Third Style decorations, but except for that from the Casa degli Scienziati, VI xiv 43, removed to the Museo Nazionale in Naples (MN 9269), all are in very poor condition today. Another, from the Villa of N. Popidius Florus at Boscotrecase, is recorded in a photograph belonging to the German Archaeological Institute in Rome (DAI 68.4810; *PPM* 1 [1990] 162, fig. 72). What remains are still to be seen suggest that these are all the work of the same man.

In the Casa degli Scienziati copy there is a third figure, flanking Corinna, identified as Myrtis, and the musicians are shown on either side of a slender baetylus column. Only the center of a large panel was cut out for removal to the museum, but it declares its authorship immediately, and we see how the painter could adjust his composition to the needs of a client. The palette is somewhat softer here, but the forms remain constant.

Another work of his in the same vein is the Third Style picture of Apollo instructing a citharist (one of the Muses?) while another woman leaning on a low pillar listens (H 217; Spinazzola 1953, 1.274, fig. 302). This comes from VI Ins. Occ. 19–26 and is now in the British Museum. Nothing seems to be known about possible companion pieces. Another copy of the same composition in the Casa di Ceio, although in poor condition, seems to be by the same painter (Spinazzola 1953, 1.273, fig. 301; Michel 1990, fig. 242), as are also the minor figures in the decoration of the same room (Michel 1990, figs. 229, 233, 235).

Somewhat more ambitious works by the same painter are the illustrations of the *Aeneid* from the atrium complex of the Casa di Laocoonte, VI xiv 28–31. That from the south wall of the atrium itself, which unfortunately has lost perhaps a third or even half of its left side, shows Laocoon and one son struggling with the serpents, while the other son lies dead in the foreground (S 581; MN 111210). The sacrificial bull charges to the right behind Laocoon, and off to the right is a group of four astonished Trojans. Although as a rare illustration of Vergil's epic the picture has always drawn attention, its damaged state has prevented frequent reproduction. From the north wall of the tablinum comes an illustration of Aeneas's encounter with Polyphemus, the Cyclops standing with his sheep and goats at the lower left, the ship of Aeneas in the middle, and Aeneas with a group of companions to the right (S 603; MN 111211). The Trojan hero lifts his right hand in astonishment and half turns away. The figure of Polyphemus has been damaged, the lower body largely flaked, or scraped, away, and much has been lost at the top of the picture, but otherwise it survives in fair condition. That these two pictures are by the same hand is shown by their palette and composition and confirmed by examination of the heads of the minor figures in both. The painter builds his major figures in strong, bright colors and firm edges, while he only sketches in background elements and tends to leave staffage figures drawn in pale earth colors or dark silhouette. But the impassive head of Laocoon and the abstracted stare with which he faces his doom are very close in concept and structure to the head of Pindar, and Aeneas and his companions are in every way close relations of the figures in the Judgment of Paris. The case for attribution is a very strong one.

In triclinium m of I ii 6, an unpretentious house down the Strada Stabiana from the Casa del Citarista, this painter painted a large Theft of the Palladium, now in the Museo Nazionale (MN 109751). This is his most ambitious work and among the best preserved. At the left a bearded Ulysses holds the Palladium; he is accompanied by a dark young man dressed in an animal skin drawn over his head in a hood (Diomedes), a woman who must be Helen, and an androgynous figure labeled Aithra. These stare in amazement while Cassandra in wild transport is seized from behind by a Trojan labeled Hyperbates in trousers and a short, full cloak. The action is set in a temple precinct, the temple façade, altar, offering table, and a tripod on a high base being conspicuous in the background before a backdrop of pale green trees. Votive columns in the foreground on either side frame the scene. The identification of the figures by inscriptions in Greek characters under their feet is rather unusual but not unique. The heads of Ulysses and Helen are typical of this painter, while the profile of Aithra strongly resembles that of one of Aeneas's companions in the picture of Aeneas and Polyphemus.

Finally the Rape of Europa in triclinium 10 of I viii 8 may be an unusual work of our man, the figures more active than he usually likes, although not more so than Cassandra, the drapery more agitated and varied. But the drawing of facial features runs close to his standard, especially in the eyes and mouths, and the resemblance of the figure at the extreme right to the Cassandra of the Theft of the Palladium is very strong.

⇢ *Works* ⇠

POMPEII

I ii 6

Triclinium m, south of the peristyle

- Theft of the Palladium: S 580; MN 109751; HBr pl. 149; *Collezioni* 1986, 66; *PPM* 1 (1990) 15, fig. 18.

I iv 5/25, Casa del Citarista

Room 21, east of the middle peristyle

- Judgment of Paris: H 1286; MN 120033; HBr pl. 113; *Collezioni* 1986, 64; *PPM* 1 (1990) 155, fig. 64.

Room 20, east of the middle peristyle

- Leda, or Nemesis: H 152; MN 120034; HBr pl. 111; *PPM* 1 (1990) 152, fig. 60.

Cubiculum 23, east of room 21

- Pindar and Corinna: H 1378b; *PPM* 1 (1990) 161, fig. 71.
- Oriental monarch and messenger (?): H 1388; Schefold 1962, pl. 54.4; *PPM* 1 (1990) 157, fig. 66.

I viii 8

Triclinium 10, north of the peristyle

- Rape of Europa: *PPM* 1 (1990) 821, fig. 31; *Peinture* 1993, 1, pl. 22.

VI xiv 28–31, Casa di Laocoonte

Atrium

- Death of Laocoon: S 581; MN 111210; *Collezioni* 1986, 84; *PPM* 5 (1994) 354, fig. 17.

Tablinum k

- Aeneas's encounter with Polyphemus: S 603; MN 111211; HBr pl. 206; *PPM* 5 (1994) 359, fig. 23.

VI xiv 43, Casa degli Scienziati

Room 19, north of the peristyle

- Pindar and Corinna: H 1379; MN 9269; Schefold 1962, pl. 57.2; *PPM* 5 (1994) 463, fig. 70.

VI Ins. Occ. (xvii) 19–26 Casa di Polibio

Music lesson: London, BM; H 217; *BMC* 1933, 26 and pl. 10; Spinazzola 1953, 1.274, fig. 302.

BOSCOTRECASE

Villa of N. Popidius Florus

Triclinium 4

- Pindar and Corinna: *PPM* 1 (1990) 162, fig. 72.

The Giasone Painter

The figures of the Giasone Painter are for the most part short and slight, diminutive, doll-like figures dwarfed by the size of the picture in which they appear and the landscape or architectural volume of their setting. Their heads are likely to be disproportionately large, some figures being only about six heads tall. But occasionally the artist overcorrects this fault and paints a figure eight heads tall. The heads are blocky and long-faced, the necks disproportionately short and apt to be willowy. The shoulders are broad and square, the torsos long with thick waists and heavy hips. The arms and legs are light, the hands and feet tiny and delicate in their drawing. The arms are sometimes of proper length but never of proper weight. More often they are short as well as light.

The heads are blocky, the skull only slightly domed, the face broad at the cheekbones and heavy-jawed. The forehead is usually low and wide, the eyes wide-set, large and calmly staring. The eyebrows swing in a low expressionless arc; beneath them the eyes are very wide and seem to bulge. The white is very prominent, especially toward the outer corner, the iris dark and shown as nearly a complete circle. Each eye has a tiny highlight, almost a pinpoint. The upper lid is always carefully drawn and usually touched with light; the lower is frequently rimmed with shadow, giving the face a more or less haggard expression. In full and three-quarters face the ridge of the nose seems to continue the plane of the forehead; in profile the forehead bulges slightly and there is a break between it and the nose. The nose almost always has a sharp, prominent tip touched with a bright highlight; in profile it may have an almost pert look. Otherwise the nose is straight and thin, rather short, with a tight, pinched look about the nostrils. The mouth is small but with relatively full lips and apt to be pulled down slightly at the corners, so that it has a sour expression that is emphasized by a pouting lower lip. Occasionally the mouth is slightly off-axis. The chin is small and hard, but the broad face is almost always somewhat lantern-jawed. The ears are generally set a bit high, and while they are delicately drawn and of good size and shape, they are somewhat simplified. They are also apt to be somewhat pointed and flaring. The hair of men (and of women when it is dressed high) grows in an arc from ear to ear, leaving the back of the neck surprisingly bare. The women's hair is usually parted to the left of center; the part is clearly marked, and when seen from the front it runs through the hair from front to back. The hair always seems somewhat thin and sparse and is worn close to the head in any of a number of ways.

Few of the torsos of this painter are nude, so description of their forms must be general. The shoulders are broad and level, although there is careful observation of the bow and pull of the tendons of the neck. The line of the clavicle is nearly straight. The chest is deep with ample breasts. The breasts of women are conical but never emphasized. The linea alba is deeply marked on men. The waist is well placed but always distinctly fleshy. The navel is placed somewhat low; the hips are broad. The hip bulge is well marked, even exaggerated, in nude males; the groin is apt to be overdrawn.

The arms are generally short and light, and their attachment to the shoulder is usually faulty, so there is little sense of muscular continuity. The upper arms are apt to be smooth and shapeless cylinders, the forearms given a little more character by a gentle swelling below the elbow and an even taper to the wrist. The elbow is always played down, sometimes barely articulated. When the arm is sharply bent the elbow is pointed. The wrist is generally well marked and well understood but somewhat thick. Occasionally the painter has trouble drawing a hand in some position (for example, when locked about a knee) and the attempt may be extremely awkward, but for the most part his hands are successful, and he is careful to distinguish men's hands from women's. The attention lavished on the hands makes them often rather conspicuous in his pictures.

Like the arms, the Giasone Painter's legs are somewhat too smooth and regular. The thigh is on the whole well formed but appears a trifle short and tense. The bent knee is flattened, the line of the thigh being pulled back to meet the line of the shin. The calf is well drawn with a well-bowed shin and no perceptible tuck under the calf muscle. The feet are very small, which tends to make the ankles appear thick, but the drawing of the ankles and feet is almost as nice as that of the hands. Nude feet are apt to seem a little short, thick through the instep, and flat, but the drawing of the toes and the footgear, of which this painter is especially fond, is superior for Pompeii.

The drapery has an overly crisp, sculptural, almost surrealistic quality. In drawing, the differences between one stuff and another are well distinguished, but in painting such distinction tends to disappear, partly because of the painter's fondness for brilliant color in these parts. In the drawing the cloaks fall in heavy locked folds, the himations in long flat folds, or else they are folded in bunched and slightly crushed masses. The chitons and tunics are softly bloused. In the painting all folds have neatly rounded edges, the shadowed channels drawn in smooth dark lines, the lighted margins in equally smooth brilliant rods. In a few cases there seems to be a definite attempt to convey the sheen of silk or linen, or the richness of soft wool, but by and large this is lost under a display of technical proficiency that gives wool and linen alike a smooth, almost lacquered brilliance. This hard, carved quality of the drapery is a characteristic of the work of the Giasone Painter that is also seen in the work of a few other Third Style painters, notably the Amore Punito Painter, but it is especially conspicuous in the work of the Giasone Painter.

→ *Works* ←

POMPEII

I vii 19, Annex of the Casa dell'Efebo

Exedra e

- Hercules and Nessus: *PPM* 1 (1990) 777, fig. 49.

VI xiv 20, Casa di Orfeo

Cubiculum r

- Amorino: *PPM* 5 (1994) 302, fig. 62.

VI xvi 7/38, Casa degli Amorini Dorati

Tablinum

- Paris and Helen: HBr pl. 77.2; Seiler 1992, figs. 162, 164; *PPM* 5 (1994) 738, fig. 42.

Exedra G, east of the peristyle

- Encounter of Jason and Pelias: HBr pl. 76; Zevi 1964, pl. 23.2; Eschebach 1978, fig. 183; Seiler 1992, fig. 173; *Peinture* 1993, 1, pl. 74; *PPM* 5 (1994) 779, fig. 123.
- Unexplained mythological subject: HBr pl. 77.1; Seiler 1992, fig. 184; *Peinture* 1993, 1, pl. 73; *PPM* 5 (1994) 782, fig. 127.

VI Ins. Occ. (xvii) 42, Casa del Bracciale d'Oro

Triclinium 31

- Square field framing busts of two women and a man: *PPM* 6 (1996) 141, fig. 182.
- Genre scene with a poet holding a wreath and a woman with a writing tablet: *PPM* 6 (1996) 145, fig. 187.

IX v 18, Casa di Giasone

Cubiculum g

- Rape of Europa: S 79; MN 111475; HBr pl. 68; Rizzo 1929, pl. 99; Curtius 1929, pl. 4; Zevi 1964, pl. 17; *Collezioni* 1986, 69; De Caro 1994, 154.

• Concert of satyr and nymphs: S 196; MN 11473; HBr pl. 69; Rizzo 1929, pl. 100; Maiuri 1953, 119; Zevi 1964, pls. 18, 22.1; Picard 1970, pl. 38; Kraus and von Matt 1973, fig. 300 (detail); *Collezioni* 1986, 68; Guillaud and Guillaud 1990, fig. 243; De Caro 1994, 153.

• Hercules and Nessus: S 502; MN 11474; HBr pl. 70; Zevi 1964, pl. 19.1; *Collezioni* 1986, 70.

Cubiculum c

• Paris and Helen: S 569; MN 114320; HBr pl. 71; Zevi 1964, pl. 20.2; *Collezioni* 1986, 74.

• Phaedra and her nurse: S 541; MN 114322; HBr pl. 72; Zevi 1964, pl. 20.1; *Collezioni* 1986, 75.

• Medea and her children: S 555; MN 114321; HBr pl. 73; Ragghianti 1963, 98; Zevi 1964, pl. 19.2; *Collezioni* 1986, 75.

Oecus d

• Unexplained mythological subject: S 627; MN 111471; HBr pl. 74.1; Zevi 1964, pl. 15.2; *Collezioni* 1986, 73.

• Encounter of Jason and Pelias: S 551; MN 111436; HBr pl. 75; Rizzo 1929, pl. 101; Zevi 1964, pls. 16, 21.2; Picard 1970, pl. 37; *Collezioni* 1986, 67; De Caro 1994, 155.

The Lucrezio Frontone Painter

In the tablinum of the Casa di M. Lucrezio Frontone, V iv a, are two small but well-preserved subject pictures. They are slightly wider than high and composed in variations of the familiar triangular composition of many Third Style pictures, but there is no likelihood that they were originally planned as a pair. On the south wall is a Triumph of Bacchus, the god reclining with his consort, Ariadne, on a couch mounted on what we must suppose is a wagon drawn by a pair of oxen. The painter was clearly unequal to the demands of representing this complicated equipage, and the couch seems rather to stand on an elevation behind the animals. The divine couple is attended by members of the thiasus, a bacchante, nude except for a floating scarf and slippers, who dances and clashes a pair of cymbals, and a second, more sedate one behind her to the right; Silenus mounted on his donkey but clearly having difficulty maintaining his seat; and a nude satyr wearing a wreath of pine who plays a pair of long slender flutes to the left.

The ground and background merge, a pearly gray streaked with shadows only in the foreground. The three groups that are the apices of the triangular composition are clearly distinct, but the triangle is not equilateral and the outstretched arm of Bacchus makes a further disbalance.

On the north wall opposite we find preparations for the wedding of Venus and Mars, the wedding bed with dark coverlets filling almost the whole width of the picture behind the principals. These are Venus, enthroned and bejeweled, to the left, over whom Mars leans from behind, laying his left hand on her breast, while she lifts her left hand to restrain him. He wears a flamboyant crested helmet, and his bare sunburnt shoulder makes a background for Venus's head. Opposite these on the right side of the picture sit a pair of unidentified women, essentially Akte figures, on a low cubical base. They look out at the viewer and seem almost disinterested bystanders. Between these two groups a boyish Amor in contrapposto gazes at the divine couple and prepares to string his bow, while above him, behind the wedding bed, appear Mercury and a pair of women, who also gaze at Mars and Venus with some slight suggestion of apprehension. The background focuses the perspective, a pair of stout pale columns supporting an architrave that recedes to a central doorway flanked by pilasters. The composition is known in another example by the Triptolemus Painter that is quite different in ethos.

That these two pictures are by the same hand is shown by the broad, blocky heads of several figures, forehead and nose ridge in a single plane, small eyes with hairline eyebrows, tight mouth with compressed lips, and sweeping, squarish jaw. Women's hair is crinkly, parted at the center of the forehead, puffed out slightly at the temples, and drawn behind the ears, bound up and bloused out behind or streaming in loose ringlets. The ear is almost always very pink and meticulously studied. Women's arms are rather thin and wooden, their hands very small with tiny, but sometimes elongated, fingers. The hands are well painted and have a great variety of character and pose. The metacarpus is generally long and usually sturdy; the fingers are slender, not excessively long, and taper elegantly at the tip. The artist has a fondness for showing the hand half open with the fingers held together. Male figures are well muscled and well proportioned except for their small hands and tiny feet. The feet are always exaggeratedly small with a rather thick instep and slender ankle with a well-articulated ankle bone. The artist likes to paint feet and elaborate shoes and sandals, but the sole of a shoe is apt to be slightly out of drawing. Drapery tends to be stiff, often with a sculptural appearance, even when free; skirts cling to the legs. One should observe the patterns of folds at shoulder and waist and the way in which patterns are picked out in overpainting with fine cursive lines. The palette is bright and rather intense, with strong yellows, greens, blues, and violets set off by a pale ground in soft tans and pearly grays. There is a good bit of hatching, especially to render the coats of animals, and a good bit of overdrawing with fine brushes to pick out features, edges, and drapery.

In a cubiculum south of the atrium of this house the same painter was responsible for two square compositions, a simple composition of Ariadne delivering the magic thread to Theseus and a more elaborate Toilet of Venus, in which the seated goddess examines herself in a shield held by Amor and Psyche while two of the Graces attend her, one busy arranging her hair. The picture is poorly preserved, having entirely lost its surface, but in this context the vocabulary of forms and palette make the attribution a certainty. The other picture is fairly well preserved despite flaking that has damaged both faces, and the forms of Theseus's nude body and carefully drawn hands and the treatment of Ariadne's drapery run true to this painter's style.

In the atrium of the Casa dei Quadretti Teatrali, I vi 11, this painter painted a series of at least five scenes from comedy and tragedy, two- and three-figure groups in bright color against a neutral ground. Two of these were found badly damaged when they were excavated; of one only a corner showing the bearded head and back of a banker or *leno* (slave dealer) of comedy survived. But both are enough to show traits of our painter, his outline, a rather chiseled profile, his way of handling drapery. The other three were found in excellent condition, and although they have suffered with the passage of time since then, they still declare their authorship very plainly. The best preserved of these shows a slave of comedy with a young hetaira and a young man in long clothes and shoes who must be her lover, for he puts his hand on her shoulder as though to reassure her. Hands, feet, and drapery here all run true to the Lucrezio Frontone Painter's forms. Another shows a scene from tragedy, an aged man with a white beard and hair who carries a pedum reclining at the right, while a woman in a high tragic mask and her elderly male attendant turn away from him, apparently in distress. Again, the drawing of the hands of all three and the treatment of the drapery betray the authorship. The third shows another scene from comedy, a bald man with white beard who wears the long clothes of a gentleman sitting on a stool, while a young man, presumably his son, stands beside him and stretches out his right hand as though pleading with him. At the same time he turns away toward a diminutive figure in dark dress who is cut by the frame of the picture. Enough is preserved to assure the attribution; the younger man's eloquent right hand alone might be enough.

In the Casa dei Quattro Stili, I viii 17, this painter was responsible for the Daedalus fastening his wings to Icarus and a large picture in the tablinum that may represent Hercules freeing Theseus in the Underworld. The first is only a fragment, the upper half of the picture completely lost; what remains is mostly underpainting, but it still shows the Lucrezio Frontone Painter's handling of his medium and his technique with drapery. The Hercules is complete, but again the overpainting of most of the foreground, including the figures of Hercules, Theseus, and Pirithous (if this interpretation is correct), is gone, while Proserpina is damaged, and only the Akte figure reclining in the center background is reasonably well preserved. Once again we must rely on the painter's handling of the medium for the attribution, but the chiseled profiles of Proserpina and Theseus support this, as does the handling of the drapery of the Akte and Proserpina. The loss of so much of this picture, once a major work, must be regarded as a tragedy.

In I xi 15/9, in a picture that was stolen from the excavations in 1977, this painter produced a second copy of the Toilet of Venus of the Casa di M. Lucrezio Frontone, adding a seated Mars to replace one of the attendants. The lovers sit facing one another, Mars, nude, to the left, Venus, half-nude, to the right against a neutral background. An attendant behind Venus assists her in dressing her hair, while a diminutive servant girl holds up a large round shield to serve as a looking glass. The profile of Mars, his proportions, and the closeness of the figure of Venus to the similar composition in the Casa di M. Lucrezio Frontone serve to identify the painter. He was also responsible for the rather disappointing Theseus abandoning Ariadne on an adjacent wall, now ruined by the theft of the figure of Ariadne. This was the familiar treatment of the subject, with Athena appearing overhead (though here she was transformed into a member of the thiasus of Bacchus), except that Ariadne lay obliquely, close to the gangplank, facing the viewer, her eyes open. The attribution is based on the profile of the sailor assisting Theseus in embarking, the drawing of his left hand, and the drawing of Ariadne's features and square jaw. The third picture in this room is a fragment of a seated figure, probably a woman, but the subject cannot be identified. It too was the work of the Lucrezio Frontone painter.

And in the next insula, in a small cubiculum in I xii 3, the Caupona di Soterico, this painter produced another version of the Theseus receiving

Ariadne's thread, here designed to fill a large panel but without change in the posing of the figures. Although it is much ruined and the faces of both figures are unrecognizable, the design and closeness in every way to the copy in the Casa di M. Lucrezio Frontone make the attribution a certainty.

Another picture that is the work of our man is the group of three nymphs, including one who rests her left elbow on an overturned jar, from Herculaneum, now in the Museo Nazionale. Here the palette has been limited, and the green background mottled with foliage is a further departure from his usual manner, but the square-jawed heads, small eyes under low arched brows, and tight mouths are characteristic of our man, and the drawing of the hands of all three figures is unmistakable. So also is the working of the drapery.

He seems also to have been the painter of a small but well-preserved picture of a bacchante seated contemplating a nude kneeling child with a pedum and a basket against a background of simplified architecture in the Casa del Colonnato Tuscanico, VI 17/26. This is very close in its finish to the pictures of the Casa di M. Lucrezio Frontone in Pompeii. There is, then, every likelihood that he painted the badly ruined companion piece showing two women in conversation, one seated, resting her chin pensively on her right hand, the other standing. These are pictures in the frieze zone; unfortunately the pictures of the main zone are illegible.

Asked to set these pictures in chronological order, I should divide this painter's work into only two groups: a later period represented by the pictures of the Casa di M. Lucrezio Frontone, those of the atrium of the Casa dei Quadretti Teatrali, and those in and from Herculaneum; and an earlier period represented by the others, the pictures of the Casa dei Quattro Stili, I xi 15/9, and I xii 3.

✧ *Works* ✧

POMPEII

I vi 11, Casa dei Quadretti Teatrali (Casa dei Calavi)

Atrium

- Scene from comedy with slave and lovers: *NSc* 1929, pl. 24; Rizzo 1929, pl. 147; Maiuri 1953, 95; de Franciscis 1978, fig. 50; *PPM* 1 (1990) 380, fig. 33; *Peinture* 1993, 1, pl. 8.
- Scene from tragedy with an old man: *NSc* 1929, pl. 23; *PPM* 1 (1990) 376, fig. 26.

• Scene from comedy with a bald man and a youth: *NSc* 1929, pl. 31; *PPM* 1 (1990) 373, fig. 21.
• Fragmentary scene from comedy: *PPM* 1 (1990) 373, fig. 22.
• Fragmentary scene from tragedy: *PPM* 1 (1990) 381, fig. 35.

I viii 17, Casa dei Quattro Stili
Tablinum
• Daedalus and Icarus: *PPM* 1 (1990) 866, fig. 35.
• Hercules in the Underworld (?): *PPM* 1 (1990) 869, fig. 39.

I xi 15/9, Casa del Primo Piano
Cubiculum 14
• Toilet of Venus: *PPM* 2 (1990) 637, fig. 32.
• Theseus abandoning Ariadne: *PPM* 2 (1990) 638, fig. 33.

I xii 3, Caupona di Soterico
Cubiculum 3
• Theseus receiving Ariadne's thread: *PPM* 2 (1990) 718–19, figs. 21–22.

V iv a, Casa di M. Lucrezio Frontone
Tablinum
• Wedding of Mars and Venus: HBr pl. 157; Maiuri 1953, 78; Ragghianti 1963, 93; Picard 1970, fig. 45; *PPM* 3 (1991) 1018, fig. 94; *Peinture* 1993, 1, pl. 46; Peters 1993, 285, pl. 10.
• Triumph of Bacchus: HBr pl. 158; Ragghianti 1963, 91 (detail); Picard 1970, fig. 44; *PPM* 3 (1991) 1013, fig. 85; Peters 1993, 285, pl. 11.
Cubiculum 5
• Theseus receiving Ariadne's thread: HBr pl. 159; *PPM* 3 (1991) 992, fig. 50; Peters 1993, 284, pl. 8.
• Toilet of Venus: *PPM* 3 (1991) 997, fig. 60; Peters 1993, 284, pl. 9.

HERCULANEUM

VI 17/26, Casa del Colonnato Tuscanico
• Bacchante and child: *MdPA,* 1974 (Manni), pl. 7.1; *Peinture* 1993, 1, pl. 142.
• Conversation of women: *MdPA,* 1974 (Manni), pl. 7.2.

Unidentified House
• Three nymphs in conversation: H 1017; MN 9387; HBr pl. 213; Ragghianti 1963, 97; *Collezioni* 1986, 108.

The Neoptolemus Painter

One of the oddest Third Style painters is the man who painted the Murder of Neoptolemus, the only surviving picture in the triclinium off the southwest corner of the atrium of the Casa di M. Lucrezio Frontone, V iv a. In this picture Neoptolemus, nude except for a short cloak and high boots, kneels on his left knee on an altar before the temple of Apollo at Delphi, identified by a large tripod at the upper left, while Orestes, to the right, seizes his hair with his left hand and is about to drive the sword in his right into Neoptolemus's chest. Pylades is at the left and seems to goad Neoptolemus with a light spear, while Hermione, fallen to the ground on her left knee, draws her drapery defensively over her head with her right hand but continues to clutch a tray of offerings with her left. Another pale, cloaked figure behind Pylades aims a spear at Neoptolemus's back and seems to hold a bow in his outstretched left hand. Neoptolemus and Hermione are of more or less normal proportions, although Neoptolemus has a very long right leg. Orestes is slightly elongated, and Pylades is diminutive, barely coming to Neoptolemus's shoulder blade. He is, however, carefully drawn and of a ruddy sunburnt brown, while Neoptolemus has the pallor of a woman and Orestes is an ashy brownish gray. Hermione is also gray, but paler than Orestes. There is no explanation for this extraordinary range of flesh colors. Neoptolemus has an anguished, frightened expression with wild eyes and open mouth. Orestes and Hermione show no emotion at all; their tiny mouths and shadow-ringed eyes are impassive and masklike. There is no chiaroscuro, and the drapery is mannered, the edges of the billowing cloaks of Neoptolemus and Pylades falling in regular zigzags that echo one another, while the rippled hem of Hermione's garment is like corrugation. The picture resembles a theatrical tableau, and this is underscored by the flatness of the background.

The masklike faces of Orestes and Hermione occur again in the isolated figures of the triclinium off the northeast corner of the atrium of the Casa di Ceio, I vi 15, a Bacchus teasing a panther with a bunch of grapes and a young woman holding a long torch horizontally in both hands. Bacchus, nude except for a cloak kilted about his waist and high boots, stands against a few sketched landscape elements; the young woman has only a ground line. Both figures are elongated and have grayish brown skin and reddish hair in the palette typical of this painter. He seems to have painted nothing else in this house.

→ *Works* ←

POMPEII

I vi 15, Casa di Ceio

Triclinium e

- Bacchus: Michel 1990, figs. 191, 196; *PPM* 1 (1990) 447, fig. 61; *Peinture* 1993, 1, pl. 10.
- Torchbearer: Michel 1990, fig. 202; *PPM* 1 (1990) 453, fig. 68.

V iv a, Casa di M. Lucrezio Frontone

Triclinium 4

- Murder of Neoptolemus: *PPM* 3 (1991) 986, fig. 40; *Peinture* 1993, 2, fig. 162; Peters 1993, 288, pl. 14.

The Obellio Firmo Painter

In the oecus and connecting cubiculum south of the peristyle of the Casa di Obellio Firmo, IX xiv 4, a large subject picture of a group of three women making a sacrifice at a tomb is identified by Spinazzola as Electra at the tomb of Agamemnon. Elsewhere in this room are a single statuesque figure of a woman mounted on a console glimpsed through a doorway, a small sketchy picture of Venus in the frieze zone, and large female heads mounted on scrollwork bases in grisaille in the dado. In the adjoining cubiculum are pinakes showing a seated woman with a huge round tympanum under her right arm who gestures with her lifted left hand toward an open door and a standing woman about to make an offering on a tiny altar. All the figures, including the heads in the dado, are much elongated and have very long, square-jawed faces and broad shoulders. Their hands, when shown, are large, and their arms, heavy. They have a calm intensity, and even those of the pinakes look out at the viewer; they seem self-absorbed, their brows level, their expressions almost fierce.

Almost directly across the Via di Nola, in the Casa dei Gladiatori, V v 3, is a handsome triclinium decorated in the Third Style with an outer section of black ground embellished with female herms who hold garlands from which float broad ribbons in the main zone and large female heads mounted on scrollwork bases or tiny wings in the upper zone. The inner section, where the couches were disposed, has a white ground decoration and is embellished with a scattering of small figures, sacrificants and dancers in the main zone, herms with swallowtail drapery, archaizing winged figures, and other architectural inventions in the upper zone. In the center of the short north wall was a large landscape of a rustic sanctuary, evidently without worshipers, that is now in poor condition. It is all very mannered and delicate, much of the detail spidery, in bright, clear colors. The effect is bizarre and rather frivolous, the opposite of that in the oecus of the Casa di Obellio Firmo, but the figure painter is clearly the same. The long, square-jawed, solemn faces of the large isolated heads in the upper zone are easily identified as nearly identical with those in the dado of the oecus of the Casa di Obellio Firmo, and the smaller figures in full face are simply smaller versions of these.

❖ *Works* ❖

POMPEII

V v 3, Casa dei Gladiatori

Triclinium n, at the northeast corner or the peristyle

- Herms, isolated heads, and small figures: Schefold 1962, pls. 7.1, 36–37; *PPM* 3 (1991) 1082–93, figs. 29–52.

IX xiv 4, Casa di Obellio Firmo

Oecus south of the peristyle

- Genre scenes, pinakes, isolated heads in the dado: Spinazzola 1953, 1.350–54, figs. 397–400, 402; Schefold 1962, pls. 28–31; Kraus and von Matt 1973, fig. 81; Eschebach 1978, fig. 128; *Peinture* 1993, 1, pls. 102–4.

Cubiculum adjoining the oecus south of the peristyle

- Pinakes: Spinazzola 1953, 1.354–57, figs. 401, 403–5; Schefold 1962, pl. 32.

The Principe di Montenegro Painter

The painting style of the Principe di Montenegro Painter bears a general resemblance to that of the Lucrezio Frontone Painter, close enough to suggest that they studied under the same master. But the Lucrezio Frontone Painter is easily and in every way the superior workman; the Principe di Montenegro Painter barely rises above mediocrity even in his most ambitious pictures, and the bulk of his work is far below the high standard of the surviving examples of the Third Style. He seems to have been simply a journeyman decorator.

His surviving work is divided into two categories, large vertical panels that are more or less filled with figures and groups scattered over the whole of the available surface and small horizontal panels filled with a single group. He has no command of the recession of space; his figures all stand in a single plane. And he has no ability at compositional relationships, a weakness of which he seems to have been unaware. The figures are painted in a rather heavy palette, too dark and tending too much to yellow and red in the flesh of male figures, too chalky in the flesh of women. The ground is light and misty in grayed violets, blues, and tans. Only a few of his compositions are known in other copies, in which case his version is conscientious but never the best. It appears that he followed his originals closely, but without imagination, and he depended heavily on a pattern book. Unfortunately, little of his work remains in situ, and the houses where it was found are in very poor repair today, so there is no opportunity to study his relation to a shop or other painters; in view of the poor quality of his work, it seems unlikely that he worked alone.

The earmarks of this painter's style are easily recognized. The heads are long and narrow with an odd fullness and softness to the oval jaw, as if the chin were held pulled back. The facial expression is one of abstraction and worry and tends to be understated. The eyes are small under thin, slightly raised brows; only the upper lid is distinctly marked. Nose and ear are elongated, the nose usually hooked, the ear set high and poorly studied, but with a distinct lobe tight against the jaw. The forehead is always excessively high, and the hair fits over it in a cap, often with the suggestion of a wig. The neck is usually distinctly long. The arms are almost always short and light, but the hands are of good size, although poorly drawn. The fingers tend to taper excessively and when carefully drawn terminate in nipplelike tips. The gestures are somehow loose and ineffectual, as if the hand were incapable of closing and grasping. Legs are well drawn but somewhat oversimplified and usually stiffish in their movement; the drawing of the knee as an extension of the thigh is characteristic. The feet are apt to be a trifle small but are well drawn, with a characteristically heavy and protuberant heel, light instep, and short toes. The drapery within a picture is usually of several types, carefully and relatively skillfully distinguished. The painter is fond of adding lines and patches of shadow in several gradations to the figures in finishing his pictures; although he observes the rule of the light source, he works its intensity in the reverse of logic, the darkest shadows falling on the most important figures, a device by which he sets these off. His lights tend to be patchy, especially in the faces.

All this painter's pictures, except one of Io watched by Argus, are assigned by Ragghianti to his "Maestro Ellenico" (Ragghianti 1963, 55–57), to whom are also assigned pictures I consider to have been done by the Lucrezio Frontone Painter, the Bisogno Painter, the Villa di Cicerone Painter, and others (see also also W. Wohlmayr, "Der hellenische Meister in Herkulaneum," *KJ* 24 [1991] 43–49).

⇢ *Works* ⇠

POMPEII

VII Ins. Occ. 15, Scavo del Principe di Montenegro

Oecus next to the tablinum

- Hercules and Omphale: H 1137; MN 9000; Rizzo 1929, pls. 19, 119.1; Stenico 1963, 108 (detail); *Collezioni* 1986, 79; Guillaud and Guillaud 1990, fig. 241 (detail).
- Perseus freeing Andromeda: H 1189; MN 8997; Curtius 1929, 256, fig. 153; *Collezioni* 1986, 80.

IX ix 17 (14)

Triclinium l

- Io watched by Argus: HBr text 1.68, fig. 18; Curtius 1929, 260, fig. 156.

HERCULANEUM

Unidentified Buildings

- "Dressing of the Bride": H 1435; MN 9022; Rizzo 1929, pl. 49; Curtius 1929, 269, fig. 160; Ragghianti 1963, 73 (detail) and pl. 22; *Collezioni* 1986, 106; Guillaud and Guillaud 1990, fig. 240.
- Perseus freeing Andromeda: H 1187; MN 8993; Maiuri 1953, 79; Stenico 1963, 97; Ling 1991, 131, fig. 135.

The Triptolemus Painter

In a large reception room of the house of the baker T. Genialis, IX iii 19–20, is a picture showing the dispatch of Triptolemus by Ceres in a car drawn by dragons. The picture is unique in Pompeii, poorly composed, dominated in the upper right quadrant by the figure of Triptolemus about to spring into the car. He is nude except for a short cloak about his shoulders that flies back with his action, his right leg bent and right arm lifted. Balancing him is Ceres, who fills the lower left quadrant, a seated figure with a long scepter resting her head against her right hand. Behind her stands a young woman with short dark hair, and at the bottom right, seen from the back, reclines a wreathed woman with nude torso who carries a cornucopia in the crook of her left arm. Although the picture has suffered and the figure of Ceres is faint, the dark figure of Triptolemus is reasonably clear, as is the character of his long oval head with heavy-lidded eyes and lantern jaw. The oval shape of the head is shared by Ceres and the Akte and contrasts with the broad face of the young woman behind Ceres.

We find this man's work again in the tablinum of the little atrium house that is an annex of the Casa dell'Efebo, I vii 19, where he painted a Wedding of Mars and Venus in the composition familiar from the tablinum of the Casa di M. Lucrezio Frontone, V iv a (Peinture 1993, 1, pl. 20), and a Rape of Hylas in the composition best known from the copy from the Casa delle Forme di Creta, VII iv 62, now in the Museo Nazionale (Rizzo 1929, pl. 129). Here a nymph has been added to the right of Hylas and the nymph at his feet omitted, bringing the composition into better balance. The pair of staffage figures at the upper right has been omitted, and poses and costumes have been somewhat altered, but there can be no mistaking the subject and the common source of the two pictures. A mythological landscape treatment of the same subject in IX vii 16 shows much the same central group in miniature with a place divinity reclining under a large pine tree in the middle distance (*Peinture* 1993, 1, fig. 96). This may represent the original composition most faithfully. The Casa dell'Efebo copy has lost almost all its overpainting and is blurred; facial features have almost entirely disappeared. But the consonance between it and the Mars and Venus opposite in proportions and the general vocabulary of forms makes its authorship clear. In the Mars and Venus the long oval faces of the two principals contrasting with the broad ones of Mercury and his companion, the peculiarly small eyes with heavy lids that seem to squint, and the slightly pursed, dissatisfied mouths identify the painter.

The only other work I can attribute to him is a large picture of Orpheus playing the lyre surrounded by the Muses and Hercules in the Casa di Epidio Sabino, IX i 22. This is in very poor condition, its upper half completely destroyed and what is left faded, but the way Hercules' back is painted and his drapery gathers around his hips, the palette, and the way what survives is worked convince me that this must be his work. The attribution can, of course, be only tentative.

⯈ *Works* ⯇

POMPEII

I vii 19, Annex of the Casa dell'Efebo

Tablinum

- Wedding of Mars and Venus: *PPM* 1 (1990) 767, fig. 28; *Peinture* 1993, 1, pl. 20.
- Rape of Hylas: *PPM* 1 (1990) 768, fig. 29; *Peinture* 1993, 2, fig. 38a.

IX i 22, Casa di Epidio Sabino

Room t

- Orpheus with Hercules and the Muses: H 893; Schefold 1962, pl. 61; *PPM* 8 (1998) 1034–36, figs. 136–38.

IX iii 19

Triclinium

- Triptolemus dispatched by Ceres: S 99; Schefold 1962, pl. 60.

The Villa di Cicerone Painter

Early in the excavations of Pompeii a number of miniature figures were cut from a Third Style decoration of a suite of two rooms in the so-called Villa di Cicerone, outside the Porta di Ercolano along the Via dei Sepolcri. The rooms were decorated *en suite* and were clearly important reception rooms. The figures were women dancers, mostly single but at least once a pair, many of them carrying musical instruments and attributes of Bacchus and Venus, shown floating in light billowing veils in the center of large black panels; Bacchic groups of centaurs and centauresses with riders or companions; and satyrs colored bright red and green, who strut and dance along rods hung with garlands that bounded the tops of the panels. These were all very varied in pose, dress, and ethos, some frenzied, others almost sedate, but all proportionately tall with small heads and often large hands. From the moment of their discovery they were recognized as exceptionally evocative and charming. They are painted in relatively heavy impasto, the brushwork rather free and allowed to show plainly, the hands and feet rather roughly blocked out but expressive in their gestures. There is considerable overdrawing with fine brushes to add detail, especially in the faces. These are clearly the work of an assured and skillful painter of unusual competence; his figures are not drawn from a stock repertory and do not appear elsewhere, and his command of his medium and such technical matters as foreshortening is impressive. The fluidity of his style is uncommon for the Third Style, where one expects a crisp outline and precise detail, and his fondness for crushed gauzy drapery, smooth oval faces, and textured pelts should make his work easy to identify elsewhere.

We find it in the miniature frieze of Bacchic subjects on a black ground from what must have been an especially splendid room, parts of which are now in the Museo Nazionale in Naples. This too was one of the early finds in Pompeii, discovered in April 1762 in a room in VII vi 28. The pieces recovered show scenes of worship in which both men and women take part, but mostly women. They appear singly, only once in a group of two, but with suggestions of interaction, are both seated and standing, and carry baskets and boxes, torches and thyrsi. Two male figures in short kilts with pine crowns, who may be satyrs, drag along goats, evidently for sacrifice, and there are altars and small images of Priapus. The effect is solemn and mysterious, but the figures are painted in the fluid impasto of the Villa di Cicerone figures, and their hands and facial features declare their authorship. However, the large picture that ornamented the central aedicula in the main zone, of which only a detached fragment survived at the time of excavation (H 1167; MN 8895), was by a completely different hand, that I identify as the Amore Punito Painter.

The Villa di Cicerone Painter also worked at Stabiae in the Villa di Arianna, where he produced the famous picture known as the Venditrice di Amori and the four individual figures of women known as Primavera, Leda, Medea, and Penelope. The first of these betrays its authorship in many ways, although it has lost much of its overpainting, and the faces of the women seated and standing at the left side of the picture have been further damaged. Yet the handling of pigment in fluid impasto, the proportions of the figures, and the character of the hand and face of the woman with the cage of amorini seem good indications. The individual figures are at somewhat larger scale and better preserved. Here the poses of the hands, especially those of the Primavera and Penelope, the building of forms, and the overdrawing, especially in the faces, like that of the dancers from the Villa di Cicerone, support the attribution. These, however, are the only pictures by this artist that I have been able to discover.

✦ *Works* ✦

POMPEII

VII vi 28

Cubiculum 8

- Panels with a frieze of Bacchic subject: H 569; MN 9165, 9183; Herbig 1962, pls. 35–41, 44, 47–49; *Collezioni* 1986, 53–54 and p. 43; Guillaud and Guillaud 1990, figs. 226 (detail), 298; *PPM* 7 (1997) 193, figs. 14–15.

Environs, Via dei Sepolcri, Villa di Cicerone

- Dancers: H 487, 1904, 1923, 1939 (= MN 9295); H 484, 1906, 1907, 1921, 1928, 1931, 1937 (= MN 9297); HBr pls. 88–92, 101, 102; Ragghianti 1963, figs. 20–21; *Collezioni* 1986, 126–27; Guillaud and Guillaud 1990, figs. 27, 29–34 (= MN 9297).
- Satyrs: H 442; MN 9118, 9119, 9121, 9163; HBr pls. 95–100; *Collezioni* 1986, 123–25; Guillaud and Guillaud 1990, figs. 26, 28; De Caro 1994, 170–71.
- Centaur groups: H 499–502; MN 9133; HBr pls. 93–94; Curtius 1929, 50; Rizzo 1929, pl. 24.2; Ragghianti 1963, fig. 199; Seider 1968, 50–52; Kraus and von Matt 1973, 307–8; *Collezioni* 1986, 128; De Caro 1994, 170–71.

STABIAE

Villa di Arianna (Villa della Venditrice di Amori, Villa di Varano)

- Primavera: H 1856; MN 8834; HBr pl. 195; Rizzo 1929, pl. 136; Curtius 1929, pl. 6; Maiuri 1953, 83; Elia 1957, 62; Brion 1960, fig. 30; Seider 1968, 41; *Collezioni* 1986, 111; Guillaud and Guillaud 1990, figs. 15, 18; De Caro 1994, 169.
- Penelope (or Diana): H 239; MN 9243; HBr pl. 198; Maiuri 1953, 82; Elia 1957, 63; *Collezioni* 1986, 112; Guillaud and Guillaud 1990, fig. 17.

• Leda: H 150; MN 9546; HBr pl. 196; *Collezioni* 1986, 113; Guillaud and Guillaud 1990, fig. 14.
• Medea: H 1265; MN 8978; HBr pl. 197; Ragghianti 1963, fig. 19; *Collezioni* 1986, 110; Guillaud and Guillaud 1990, fig. 16.
• Vendor of amorini: H 824; MN 9180; HBr pl. 199; Rizzo 1929, pl. 138; Elia 1957, pl. 43; *Pompeji: Leben und Kunst* 1973, 217.

Fourth Style Painters

The Achilles Painter

This painter was first identified, and his characteristics described, in my work on the Casa dei Dioscuri (Richardson 1955, 135–39). The attributions made to him there still seem to me correct, but to these a few can now be added. He ranks with the Telephus Painter and the Player King Painter as one of the finest among Pompeian copyists, and he was responsible for the principal pictures in three of the most splendid Fourth Style rooms in the city, one in a villa of Stabiae, and very little else. On the basis of the small number of his pictures available today, and because of their variety, it is impossible to make very firm statements about his style. More than any other of these ancient painters, he seems to have had the ability to adapt his compositions in scale and atmosphere to the architecture and purpose of the room in which he was working. Thus, in the tablinum of the Casa dei Dioscuri the figures are in vigorous action that calls attention to them and large enough to dominate their extraordinarily rich surroundings but not so large as to crowd or confuse the composition. In the triclinium fenestratum of the Casa di Marco Lucrezio the figures are very nearly the size of a Second Style megalography, but their relatively quiet composition keeps them from overwhelming the room. And this harmony is more than just care in the choice of models; the composition of his Bacchus discovering Ariadne from the Casa del Citarista, for example, although made up in large part of stock figures and groups, is in its totality very likely the painter's own invention since it falls into none of the familiar formulae of the Fourth Style and, although a very charming picture, is not without a few awkwardnesses. Bacchus is exaggerated in scale, and the path of approach of the thiasus in the background is not clear. The indications are, then, that we are dealing with an unusually talented and unusually mercurial workman, one able and accustomed to doing more than stock commissions and probably one who, if he did not himself set the tone of a room or choose the subjects for its pictures, was in any case hired to lift the decoration above run-of-the-mill Fourth Style. Since the houses in which he worked were few and all uncommonly richly decorated, we must presume that he hailed from Naples or Rome.

The characteristics by which his work is most clearly marked are certain peculiar forms in the heads and hands. The head is generally decidedly elongated with full fleshy cheeks and a chin that is squarish in shape but at the same time soft, with a tendency to be double. The eyes are overdrawn, short and very wide, with thin brows, and they often have a pained and surprised expression. The ball bulges; the lower lid often falls away from the ball unnaturally toward the outer corner. The corners, both inner and outer, are sharply creased. The mouths are small with full curling lips and, because of the quality of the shadow along their parting, generally appear to be slightly open. The hands are well drawn, the fingers usually stand well apart, and the thumb is set low and turned somewhat out. Thumb and fingers curl back distinctively at their tips. Although the wrist is sometimes too thick and soft, the action of the muscles in the hand and wrist is well understood, and there is a suggestion that this artist liked to paint hands, for he works them conspicuously into his pictures and lights them dramatically. The indentation in the line of the arm at the elbow is not infrequently overemphasized. He seems fond of painting drapery as well, especially crushed and floating drapery in soft colors with fluttering edges and lapped folds over shoulders. He is also fond of painting a distinctive wiry S-curl in finishing the hair of his figures.

→ *Works* ←

POMPEII

I iv 5/25, Casa del Citarista

Exedra 35, east of the south peristyle

- Iphigenia in Tauris: H 1333; MN 9111; HBr pls. 115–16; Rizzo 1929, pls. 77–78; Richardson 1955, pls. 34, 38.2–3; *Collezioni* 1986, 88; *PPM* 1 (1990) 134–35, figs. 31–32; *Peinture* 1993, 2, fig. 2.
- Bacchus discovering Ariadne: H 1239; MN 9286; HBr pl. 114; Rizzo 1929, pl. 110; Richardson 1955, pl. 35; *Collezioni* 1986, 160; *PPM* 1 (1990) 137, fig. 35; *Peinture* 1993, 2, fig. 3.

VI ix 6/7, Casa dei Dioscuri

Tablinum

- Achilles discovered on Scyros: H 1297; MN 9110; HBr pl. 5; Rizzo 1929, pl. 57; Maiuri 1953, 73; Richardson 1955, pls. 32, 38.1; de Franciscis 1963, pl. 41; Ragghianti 1963, 108 (detail);

Collezioni 1986, 205; *Peinture* 1993, 2, fig. 190b; *PPM* 4 (1993) 908, fig. 88.
- Achilles and Agamemnon: H 1307; MN 9104; HBr pl. 125; Rizzo 1929, pl. 56; Richardson 1955, pl. 33; Stenico 1963, 90; *PPM* 4 (1993) 903, fig. 82

IX iii 5, Casa di Marco Lucrezio

Triclinium 16 (triclinium fenestratum)
- Hercules and Omphale: H 1140; MN 8992; HBr pls. III, 59–60; Rizzo 1929, pls. 73–74; Richardson 1955, pl. 36; *Collezioni* 1986, 185; Guillaud and Guillaud 1990, figs. 48, 64; *Peinture* 1993, 2, fig. 313b; De Caro 1994, 180.
- Triumph of the infant Bacchus: H 379; MN 9285; HBr pl. 61.
- Bacchus dedicating a trophy: H 565; HBr pls. 62–63; Richardson 1955, pl. 37.

Unidentified Building
- Amazon: H 1248; MN 9368; Ragghianti 1963, 113; *Collezioni* 1986, 146; Guillaud and Guillaud 1990, fig. 65.
- Amazon: H 1248; MN 9365; *Collezioni* 1986, 147.

STABIAE

Villa di Arianna (Villa della Venditrice di Amori, Villa di Varano)

Atrium
- Floating satyr and maenad: H 513; MN 9136; *RömMitt* 84 (1977), pl. 51.2.

Villa di Carmiano

Triclinium 8
- Neptune abducting Amymone: Castellammare Antiquarium 3685: Picard 1968, fig. 60; *Peinture* 1993, 1, pl. 174.
- Acis and Galatea (?): Castellammare Antiquarium 3687; *Peinture* 1993, 1, pl. 175.

The Admetus Painter

This painter, a man of small talent but a very distinctive style, was responsible for at least two, probably three, paintings from the "Basilica" of Herculaneum and a small rectangular picture showing two busts, possibly mistress and servant but probably not portraits. It is hard to explain why he should have been chosen to do large panels in the "Basilica," since he is quite clearly an inferior painter. And the choice is harder to understand because there he was working side by side with the Telephus Painter, one of the most accomplished of all the Campanian painters, a man who had probably been brought from Naples or Rome on commission to do the major pictures in that public building. But the walls of Campania abound in just this sort of enigma, and a range of explanations is, of course, possible. Perhaps when the "Basilica" has been completely excavated there will be some clarification of this question.

The idiosyncrasies by which the work of the Admetus Painter can be most readily identified are forms in the heads and hands. The heads tend to be strongly spherical and have very broad, smooth jaws but abnormally small, tight mouths. In profile there is a distinctive softness under the jaw, and the lips appear overdrawn. The ear is almost always set much too low and is peculiarly simplified with a much thickened helix; it is always completely exposed. The eyes are small and often set at a slant, the outer corner below the inner, and not infrequently the shadow along the lower lid has the look of makeup. The neck is usually unnaturally heavy. Hands and feet are small, sometimes ludicrously so. Where it is shown, the palm is unnaturally shallow and somewhat puffy; the fingers tend to be sausagelike and look as though they could be flexed only with difficulty; clearly this painter had trouble with them. In the drapery the surface tends to be unusually streaky with long folds and hanging V-folds that do not interlock.

⇢ *Works* ⇠

HERCULANEUM

"Basilica"

- Admetus receiving the oracle: H 1157; MN 9027; HBr pl. 84; Rizzo 1929, pl. 84; *Collezioni* 1986, 197.
- Infant Hercules strangling the serpents: H 1123; MN 9012; HBr pl. 83; de Franciscis 1963, pl. 43; *Collezioni* 1986, 183.

Unidentified Building, almost certainly the "Basilica"

- Contest of Venus and Hesperus: H 970; MN 9239; HBr pl. 146.

Unidentified Building

- Young girl with diptych and attendant: H 1425; MN 9074; *RP* 260.13; *KJ* 24 (1991) 168, fig. 3.

The Adone Ferito Painter

The picture from which this painter receives his name is a large composition covering the garden wall of a small peristyle in a relatively modest house on the Via di Mercurio, VI vii 18. It shows Adonis, nude except for a mantle draped behind him and over his left forearm and right thigh, seated, presumably on a rock, and leaning back against Venus, who sits fully draped at a somewhat higher level and leans forward toward him to put her arm behind his back and support his right arm. His left thigh is being bandaged by an amorino, and a large basin of water stands before him. Five more amorini surround the couple, and an enigmatic female figure wearing a long, tight-sleeved chiton and a mitra or turban that almost completely conceals her hair sits on a rock a little away and contemplates the scene in sorrow, her chin propped on her left hand. The picture is flanked by pairs of musicians at smaller scale, clearly to be read as sculptural groups, Achilles and Chiron to the right, Chiron holding a small lyre, a similar group, the parts below the waist lost, to the left. To the right of this a second large panel containing an illusionistic garden vista with a statue of a sleeping satyr in the foreground (*PPM* 4 [1993] 430, fig. 41, and 432, fig. 43) contrasts with the mythological picture, which is remarkable for its complexity, its uniqueness, and the relatively poor quality of its execution. It provides, however, a repertory of this painter's forms.

There is a general elongation of the proportions of the figures. The heads are smaller than natural in the manneristic distortion favored in the Flavian period, the face usually heart-shaped with a rather sharply pointed chin but sometimes given an elongated appearance by a high and bushy arrangement of the hair. The torsos are elongated but not attenuated, with broad shoulders and heavy hips and high breasts and waists. The arms are proportionately slender, the hands large and usually elongated, especially in the metacarpus. The legs are long, usually extremely long in the calf, less markedly so in the thigh, but sometimes the thigh is very long as well. The knees are apt to be prominent. The feet are almost without exception very long and narrow and the most striking idiosyncrasy of this painter.

The forehead is always low and broad, the eyes wide-set, large, with staring pupils. A deep shadow under the upper lid and at the inner corner gives them a slightly haggard and dreamy, unfocused look, which may be emphasized by a second shadow along the lower lid. Toward the outer corner the lower lid frequently drops slightly to emphasize the stare. The nose is proportionately almost always very prominent, thick and straight, almost always somewhat jutting, with a sharp tip. The mouth is usually small, slightly creased and dimpled at the corners. Sometimes these creases are emphasized. The lips generally appear somewhat pressed together. The upper lip is narrow with an even shadow along it; the lower lip is touched with a bright highlight that makes it seem thick and frequently pouting. The cheekbones are not usually marked; when they are, they are high, close under the eye. But usually the cheeks are smooth but not fleshy. The shadow along the cheek usually has no definite edge, which sometimes gives the face an unwashed appearance. The jaw is wide, sometimes exceptionally so; its width is in awkward contrast to the pouting mouth. The hair is worn high, generally only moderately thick on the crown and well puffed out at the sides. The hair of women is usually dressed in close waves (a version of the "melon coiffure") or in a roll along the brow and a knot at the nape of the neck. The ears are set at an unnatural angle to the head, tilted back from the vertical, but small and inconspicuous.

The necks are of good proportion, neither long nor short, but apt to be just slender enough to seem graceful. The shoulders are broad and level but not muscular. The attachment of the arm is generally somewhat faulty, especially when the arm is held across the body. The joint is too weak and slender, and there is no muscular continuity from shoulder to upper arm. The linea alba is generally only faintly marked and sometimes not marked at all. The volume and shape of the rib cage and breasts are well understood, but not so those of the belly and groin, which are always conspicuously flaccid.

The light, even flimsy arms have little shape along their length and taper sharply to almost excessively thin wrists. The hands are large, almost always muscular and spreading for the men, delicate and elongated for the women. In the men's the thumb tends to be short and stout, the fingers thick at the base, sharply tapering at the tips, the nails sometimes added like a row of nipples, a peculiarity that can sometimes be used as an easy indication of authorship. When relaxed the fingers have a little the look of small sausages. Between the fingers at the base are little forked creases. The women's hands have always a deep metacarpus, often an exaggeratedly slender one, and the strongly tapering fingers and nipplelike nails of the men's. The muscular action of the hands is only poorly conveyed, the joints of the fingers being seldom articulated. However, attention is lavished on the drawing of the hands, and attention is called to them by their size and a certain eloquence of gesture. In a clenched hand the knuckle of the last finger protrudes beyond the rest.

The thighs are smooth, usually very short, the knees prominent and somewhat bony. The structure of the knee is, on the whole, well understood, but there is often a tendency to elongate the joint. The calves are long and slender, without clearly marked muscles, the ankles thick. The feet are always very large and very long. The instep is thick and long, the heel well shaped, although sometimes too prominent and somewhat too round, the toes long, with the same meticulous drawing as the fingers, even to the nails. When the foot is relaxed the great toe stands well out from the rest and is cocked up. In profile, especially when the foot is crossed over its mate, it is sometimes of extraordinary length.

The painter's command of drapery is poor, almost elementary. No attempt is made to distinguish textures, and in the folds there is a strong preference for straight, free folds and shallow V-folds, even when looped folds or crushed masses seem required. This is particularly noticeable in drapery between the knees of figures. Occasionally the painter attempts a zigzag edge or a crushed heap, but never with success.

His understanding of perspective is elementary, so that successive planes within a picture tend to shift and tilt disturbingly. He seems to have been conscious of this defect and consequently tried to avoid perspective. The horizon line is usually just below the center of the picture, but it is not strictly observed. The painter is clever with some objects, such as basins and statuary, but clumsy at rendering others, particularly those in which texture is important, such as rocks and water. Often he covers, or attempts to cover, this weakness by cursive, expressionistic brushwork or simplification and schematization.

The palette of this painter is generally muted and low in key; he never permits himself the luxury of bright, clear reds, blues, or greens but always grays these colors. His drawing is in dull red, fine and expressive, but broad and simple in its lines. Flesh is laid in with warm yellows and browns for the men, lighter grayed browns for the women, the brushwork swift and sure but the pigment worked moderately thick. There is no prevalent direction in this work, but the strokes are curved to follow approximately the contours of the body. Lights and darks are laid in with hatching, the lights worked denser than the darks and lights along edges laid over them when necessary. This final finish is apt to be very broadly handled and not graded into the texture of the rest. However, there is no appreciable effect of overdrawing in this man's work. The lights tend to be very chalky, the darks dull. Drapery is usually dull rose, dull blue, or grayed green. The backgrounds are dark and murky, a darkness from which forms emerge, the foregrounds only a little better lit. So the whole effect is somewhat theatrical, the figures alone brilliantly lit and shaded, while their surroundings are shrouded in gloom. And even in this the final product is not entirely satisfactory, since the painter is a poor student of light and often careless or arbitrary in his arrangement of light sources and lit edges.

In another richly painted room of VI vii 18, a room that must have been the chief reception room of the house, this painter contributed a Toilet of Hermaphroditus, the central figure remarkably like Adonis in proportions and the drawing of the hands, the three attendant figures, a man in Oriental costume with a curled beard and a couple of women, showing this painter's characteristic unfocused stare and lack of engagement with one another. One notes at once this painter's prominent lower lip in all these figures, his rounded eyes and carefully drawn, elongated, but rather vague and ineffectual hands.

Like Lucius, he seems to have been something of a specialist in garden paintings and contributed two more of some note, both showing Venus at large scale reclining on a giant scallop shell. The better preserved is in the Casa della Venere in Conchiglia, II iii 3, and shows Venus, nude except for jewelry and a billowing mantle, accompanied by two amorini, one mounted on a dolphin. Her mantle billows behind her, framing her head, and she carries a fan in one hand. She has the "melon coiffure" of the Adone Ferito Painter and his rounded, slightly haggard eyes, as does the amorino to the right. Her face is heart-shaped with prominent lower lip and chin, her torso long, and her hands are his slender, long-fingered ones of ineffectual gesture. To the left is a garden painting including a statue of a nude armed ephebe, also typical of his work; to the right a garden painting with a fountain and birds. The general effect is of a crisper style, somewhat more artificial than the pictures of the Casa di Adone Ferito.

Another version of the same subject has been in the collections of the Museo Nazionale so long that its provenience has only recently been established as the peristyle of VII vi 7. Here the face of Venus has been almost obliterated, so one can judge only its general shape. But the left hand, with which she holds her mantle that floats behind her, is nearly the duplicate of the right hand of Adonis in the Casa di Adone Ferito, and her legs and feet and the amorino who appears behind her scallop shell confirm the initial impression that this can only be the work of the Adone Ferito Painter.

At least two, and probably three, important pictures by him were found in the Casa del Citarista, I iv 5/25. One, in triclinium 19, since removed to the Museo Nazionale, shows an exhausted maenad fallen supine beside a stream. She is watched over by another barefoot maenad and a man of whom only the long legs are preserved. Her heart-shaped face and long-fingered hand with carefully articulated nails would be enough to make the attribution certain, and the profile of the maenad seated at the right, with its wedgelike nose and slanted eye, corroborate this. Another picture, from the room next to triclinium 19, room 20, shows Mars and Venus in an unusual composition; it too has been removed to the Museo Nazionale. Here the lovers sit side by side in a landscape in three-quarters profile to the left. Venus turns to put her arms around Mars's neck, while he braces himself with his left hand and with his right draws the mantle back from Venus's upper body. A woman sits sleeping at the right on a level below the lovers, while a male attendant watches from the right margin. A dog lies alert in the foreground. The drawing of Venus's head is remarkably like that of the statue of Achilles in the Casa di Adone Ferito. Mars's hand with its tapering fingers and carefully drawn nails, his elongated torso without real muscularity, and his long shin and foot confirm the impression. A third picture from the same room shows two nudes before a monarch in Oriental dress seated on a throne. This picture, although badly ruined, has been removed to the Museo Nazionale; it has been interpreted as showing Apollo and Poseidon cheated by Laomedon of their price for building the walls of Troy. Most of the faces are damaged almost beyond recognition, but those in the background to the left show well enough the Adone Ferito Painter's characteristics, and the long-torsoed, long-shinned bodies of the gods with their big, clumsy hands make it all but certain that this must be his work.

A tondo showing the head of a white-bearded poet crowned with ivy from the distyle exedra 18 of this house, now in the Museo Nazionale, is also clearly his work. The drawing of the eyes and mouth and the modeling of the forehead and left cheek are characteristic.

Actually this painter was very prolific, evidently a resident of Pompeii. Up the Via di Mercurio from the Casa di Adone Ferito he painted a floating figure of Sol/Helios in the atrium of the Casa dell'Argenteria, VI vii 20/22, now in the Museo Nazionale. And in the Casa del Centenario, IX viii 3/6, he painted a series of three pictures to decorate a large and important triclinium, an Iphigenia in Tauris, a Hermaphroditus with Silenus, and a Theseus victor over the Minotaur. In the first the authorship is obvious in almost every detail—the profiles of Orestes and Pylades, the long-shinned right leg and foot of Orestes, the left hand of Pylades with its nippled fingers. The others follow the same pattern.

In the Casa dell'Efebo, I vii 10–12, he painted the little two-figure compositions in cubiculum 12, scarcely more than sketches, an Apollo and Daphne, a Venus Piscatrix, and a Narcissus. These are negligible pieces, of value only for rounding out his *oeuvre.* They show his elongated proportions, his soft, unmuscular torso, long shin, and faulty hands. Slightly better is the Adonis Wounded he painted in I ix 3. Here the drawing of Adonis's left hand with its nails and the softness of the torso are earmarks, and the amorini are very like those in the Casa di Adone Ferito. On the strength of his way of handling his medium I am inclined to think that the portrait in the same room known from a graffito to its left as the Puer Successus is his work, but there is no proof in the forms that I can discern.

In the Casa dell'Ara Massima, VI xvi 15, the Adone Ferito Painter worked in two rooms, the exedra Stemmer calls tablinum F, where he painted an Endymion and Selene and a pair of bacchantes, one half-nude and seemingly asleep, the other apparently stepping over her, and triclinium C, next to this, where he painted four subject pictures and a series of seven busts, five of which survive in legible condition. The subject pictures are a Mars and Venus surrounded by amorini, a Bacchus discovering Ariadne, a Selene descending to Endymion, and a Hercules and Evander, the last being the picture that gives the house its name. These are all so plainly the work of our man that the case hardly needs arguing. It is interesting that he should have painted two Endymions in adjacent rooms, but that is probably to be laid to the taste of the client, since Endymion is not one of his regular subjects.

Down the Strada Stabiana from the Casa dell'Ara Massima he painted in two rooms of the Casa degli Amorini Dorati, VI xvi 7/38. In room R, north of the great axial oecus west of the peristyle, he painted a series of three subject pictures and eight tondi with busts of young women. The subject pictures are a Diana and Actaeon, a Leda, and a Venus Piscatrix. In room Q, on the other side of the oecus, he painted a set of the four seasons and the amorini that grace the remaining panels. Again the case seems not to need arguing. Considering the large heads and delicate feet of the seasons, one might be inclined to date them close to the time of the Ara Massima pictures, with which they show much in common.

In the Casa di Olconio Rufo, VIII iv 4, he painted the pictures in two important rooms. In exedra 28, south of the peristyle, he painted a Bacchus discovering Ariadne and a Hermaphroditus with Silenus and members of the thiasus, together with the decorative figures in the architectural frame. And in triclinium 29, next to this, he painted an Achilles discovered on Scyros and a Judgment of Paris. Although these are now in wretched condition, much being illegible, old photographs make the attribution certain. It is interesting that while the Hermaphroditus and Silenus follows the composition of the same subject in the Casa del Centenario fairly closely, the Achilles on Scyros is a completely new conception of that subject. All four of these pictures are rather inept, poorly conceived in composition and use of the picture field, awkward in the proportions of the figures, so that Paris would tower over the other figures if he stood up and Deidamia's lower leg is far too long. The poses and interrelationship of the figures and groups are often unpleasing (the tilt of Athena's head and helmet, the explanation for Deidamia's prone position), but there can be no doubt about their authorship.

At VII xii 23, the Casa del Camillo, he painted an Apollo and Daphne that has now faded and disappeared. Here the profile of Apollo was very like that of Paris in the Casa di Olconio Judgment of Paris, with its shadowed eye, jutting nose, and expressive mouth; the faces of both had an ardent, almost gleeful intensity. And Daphne had the horrified expression of Achilles and Deidamia in the Achilles on Scyros. There can be no doubt that these were by the same painter, and the painting of the hands strengthens the case.

In the Casa della Regina Margherita, V ii 1, this man painted a Jupiter and Danaë. Its authorship is made plain by Danaë's head and wide-eyed, gleeful expression, very close to those of Paris and Apollo just mentioned. Jupiter is less typical, but one notes the overdrawn musculature of his arm, which echoes that of Ulysses in the Achilles on Scyros.

In the Casa delle Forme di Creta, VII iv 62, in the room west of the tablinum he painted the Rape of Hylas that has now been removed to the Museo Nazionale. Here the profile of the nymph at the left side of the picture matches those of Apollo and Paris closely, while the construction of the head of the nymph facing the viewer is strongly reminiscent of that of Achilles in the Achilles discovered on Scyros in the Casa di Olconio. On the strength of this evidence I would ascribe to him very tentatively the woefully fragmentary copy of the same subject in an upper-story room (26) in the Casa del Moralista, III iv 2, and its better-preserved companion, a Satyr discovering a sleeping maenad. These are parts of a late Third Style decoration that incorporated a subject picture of considerable size in every panel of the main zone, a very unusual arrangement, and would be his earliest identified work. The fact that the style of the Rape of Hylas is clearly classic Third Style, with bright figures against a pale ground, whereas the Satyr discovering a maenad would not be out of place in the Fourth Style, is of more than passing interest.

Another group of figures that probably belongs to this painter is the Horae and amorini of oecus g of the Fullonica Stephani, I vi 7. Only one of the Horae is really well preserved, the one representing summer, but that on the north wall representing spring and the amorini accord so well with it that they must all be by the same hand. Here the wide eye, deeply shadowed, the long eyebrow drawn down at its outer end, the curl in front of the ear and prominent nose, and the svelte torso and delicate feet combine to confirm the attribution.

In the Casa dei Capitelli Colorati, VII iv 31/51, he probably painted the subject pictures in the large apsidal oecus on the east side of the smaller peristyle, a scene of sacrifice and a Leda. These are now in poor condition, but I believe that one can detect his manner of working and his characteristic forms in Leda's face and legs.

In the Casa di Cecilio Giocondo, V i 26, he painted the subject pictures of the large triclinium o, north of the peristyle, and a series of medallions in the side panels. Only one of the subject pictures has been removed to the Museo Nazionale, and it is reduced to the underpainting in most places. It shows Theseus embarking, the moment of his desertion of Ariadne. The golden brown of the underpainting of the figure of Theseus is typical of this painter, as is the drawing of his torso. Unfortunately, the head has been almost totally destroyed, and the hands are hardly typical in their drawing. The companion piece, a Judgment of Paris, still in situ, is more typical of the Adone Ferito Painter in proportions and the drawing of legs and feet, but the upper half of the picture has been reduced to a mere ghost. Somewhat better preserved are some of the busts in the side panels. They declare their authorship at once in the heart-shaped faces, the rounded, rather sad eyes, and pouting mouths with prominent lower lip. The Adone Ferito Painter also painted the similar medallions in the second cubiculum on the west side of the atrium of the Casa di Loreio Tiburtino, II ii 2, one of which is almost a duplicate of one in the Casa degli Amorini Dorati.

I believe that two portraits of boys crowned with rich garlands of leaves from the Casa del Cenacolo, V ii h, now in the Museo Nazionale, are by the Adone Ferito Painter. These are true portraits, and there is a clear effort made to give them expression and individuality, but the technique of the painter attests to their authorship, and the way of handling eyes and mouths is very much his.

I should also like to attribute to him the Narcissus picture and other figures on a wall section cut from a small room in the Casa delle Vestali, VI i 7/25. Here everything is diminutive, the floating figures and figures in the architectural frame deliberately reduced and doll-like, so that their proportions do not fit his canon. And Narcissus's left hand is not like his work. Still I think it highly likely that this is his, perhaps a work before his style had crystallized. If so, I should also have to ascribe to him the Hercules and Omphale from the Casa del Forno di Ferro, VI xiii 6. Here Hercules lies drunk, a cup tipped from his left hand, while a crowd of amorini rob him of his weapons. Of Omphale, who was seated at the upper left, only a bit of her skirt remains, but Hercules is complete, and his heart-shaped face and wide rounded eyes fit well with the Adone Ferito Painter's *oeuvre,* while the impish amorino who plays with Hercules's cup is the double of the amorino of the Casa delle Vestali Narcissus.

And in the Casa del Principe di Napoli, VI xv 7–8, the Adone Ferito Painter was responsible for the Perseus and Andromeda of triclinium k and its companion, a much ruined picture, perhaps of Venus and Adonis. These are very poor pictures, hurriedly dashed off, but very much in his manner. At much smaller scale the torso and legs of Perseus are close to those of Adonis in the Casa di Adone Ferito.

In short, this painter clearly did enormous amounts of work in Pompeii, his large compositions being his most carefully composed and highly finished work, but he never rose above the level of modest competence. He was not a good colorist; his flesh tones are flat and change without subtle shading from light to shadow; and his male figures tend to be too deeply sunburnt. He seems never to know exactly how to draw hands, and his faces register little in the way of expression or emotion. He seems to have worked mainly as an assistant, contributing floating figures, medallions, and figures in architecture. And he seems to have done a great many pictures in less important rooms, pictures that were hastily dashed off in formulaic compositions.

So ordinary a workman one would not expect to find working outside Pompeii unless it were as a member of a shop and he were assigned the less important parts of a decoration. It is therefore surprising to find that he did not only the subject pictures in the finely decorated chamber adjacent to the entrance to the Area Sacra Suburbana under the seafront of Herculaneum but also those in the Collegio degli Augustali in the heart of that city. In the room of the Area Sacra he painted a Paris and Helen and a Silenus pouring a libation, both characteristic works. In the Collegio degli Augustali he was the painter of a Hercules with Athena and Juno and a Hercules with Acheloüs and Deianira. I have not, however, been able to find any work of his at Stabiae.

→ *Works* ←

POMPEII

I iv 5/25, Casa del Citarista

Triclinium 19

• Sleeping maenad: H 566; MN 112283; HBr pl. 108; Rizzo 1929, pl. 112; *Collezioni* 1986, 61; Guillaud and Guillaud 1990, figs. 47, 246–47; *PPM* 1 (1990) 147–48, figs. 51–52.

Room 20

• Mars and Venus: H 323; MN 112282; HBr pls. 109–10; *Collezioni* 1986, 62; *PPM* 1 (1990) 153, fig. 61.

• Apollo and Poseidon before Laomedon (?): H 1401; MN 111472; HBr pl. 112; *Collezioni* 1986, 63; *PPM* 1 (1990) 151, fig. 59.

Distyle exedra 18

• Tondo of an elderly poet crowned with ivy: H 1523; MN 9073; *Collezioni* 1986, 233; Guillaud and Guillaud 1990, fig. 53; *PPM* 1 (1990) 143, fig. 44.

I vi 7, Fullonica Stephani

Oecus g

• Hora of summer: Spinazzola 1953, 2.784, fig. 772; *PPM* 1 (1990) 344, fig. 21.

• Hora of spring: Spinazzola 1953, 2.784, fig. 773; *PPM* 1 (1990) 341, fig. 14.

• Amorini: *PPM* 1 (1990) 341, fig. 15; 345, fig. 23; 346, figs. 26, 27.

I vii 10–12, Casa dell'Efebo

Cubiculum 12

• Apollo and Daphne: *PPM* 1 (1990) 662, fig. 77; *Peinture* 1993, 1, pl. 16.

• Venus Piscatrix: *PPM* 1 (1990) 663, fig. 78.

• Narcissus: *PPM* 1 (1990) 663, fig. 79; *Peinture* 1993, 1, pl. 17.

I ix 3

Room 5

• Adonis Wounded: *PPM* 1 (1990) 951, fig. 13.

• Puer Successus: Jashemski 1979, 102, fig. 160; *PPM* 1 (1990) 944–45, figs. 4–5.

II ii 2, Casa di Loreio Tiburtino

Cubiculum a

• Tondi with busts: Rizzo 1929, pl. 192.1; Spinazzola 1953, 1.377–78, figs. 425–26; *PPM* 3 (1991) 46, fig. 5.

II iii 3, Casa della Venere in Conchiglia

Peristyle

• Birth of Venus: Maiuri 1953, 7; de Franciscis 1978, fig. 70; Jashemski 1979, 62, fig. 101; Guillaud and Guillaud 1990, figs. 309–10; *PPM* 3 (1991) 140–42, figs. 45–48; *Peinture* 1993, 1, figs. 25–26.

III iv 2, Casa del Moralista

Upper-story room 26

• Rape of Hylas: Spinazzola 1953, 2.750, fig. 729; *PPM* 3 (1991) 433, fig. 45.

• Satyr discovering a sleeping maenad: *PPM* 3 (1991) 434, fig. 46.

V i 26, Casa di Cecilio Giocondo

Triclinium o

• Theseus abandoning Ariadne: S 531; MN 115396; *Collezioni* 1986, 175; *PPM* 3 (1991) 612, fig. 74.

• Judgment of Paris: S 561; *PPM* 3 (1991) 610, fig. 69.

• Tondi with busts: S 675–77; *PPM* 3 (1991) 609, 614–15, figs. 67, 77, 79.

V ii 1, Casa della Regina Margherita

Triclinium p

• Jupiter and Danaë: HBr pl. 187; *PPM* 3 (1991) 782, fig. 12.

V ii h, Casa del Cenacolo
Tablinum
• Tondi with busts of youths: MN 120620; Rizzo 1929, pl. 192.2; Guillaud and Guillaud 1990, fig. 55; *PPM* 3 (1991) 663, figs. 30, 33.

VI i 7/25, Casa delle Vestali
Room 5A (?)
• Narcissus: H 1355; MN 9701; *Collezioni* 1986, 140; Guillaud and Guillaud 1990, figs. 299–301; *PPM* 4 (1993) 47, fig. 83.

VI vii 18, Casa di Adone Ferito
Peristyle
• Adonis Wounded: H 340, 436, 1295; HBr pl. 52; Rizzo 1929, pl. 124; Jashemski 1979, 66, fig. 107 (detail); *PPM* 4 (1993) 428–32, figs. 38–44.
Oecus 11
• Toilet of Hermaphroditus: H 1369; Schefold 1962, pl. 172.4; *PPM* 4 (1993) 417, fig. 19.

VI vii 20/22, Casa dell'Argenteria
Atrium
• Sol/Helios: H 947; MN 8819; *Collezioni* 1986, 257; *PPM* 4 (1993) 450, fig. 2.

VI xiii 6, Casa del Forno di Ferro
Tablinum
• Hercules and Omphale: H 1138; MN s.n.; Schefold 1962, pl. 165; *PPM* 5 (1994) 167, fig. 15.

VI xv 7–8, Casa del Principe di Napoli
Triclinium k
• Perseus and Andromeda: Strocka 1984, fig. 140; *PPM* 5 (1994) 663, fig. 25.
• Venus and Adonis (?): Strocka 1984, fig. 141; *PPM* 5 (1994) 664, fig. 26.

VI xvi 7/38, Casa degli Amorini Dorati
Cubiculum R
• Diana and Actaeon: Seiler 1992, figs. 382–83; *PPM* 5 (1994) 839, fig. 223.
• Leda: Seiler 1992, fig. 388; *Peinture* 1993, 1, pl. 77; *PPM* 5 (1994) 839, fig. 224.
• Venus Piscatrix: Seiler 1992, fig. 389; *PPM* 5 (1994) 839, fig. 222.

- Tondi with busts: Seiler 1992, figs. 380–81, 384–87, 390–91; *Peinture* 1993, 1, pl. 76; *PPM* 5 (1994) 840–41, figs. 225–32.

Cubiculum Q

- Seasons: Seiler 1992, figs. 427, 430–31, 433; *PPM* 5 (1994) 828–29, figs. 202–5.
- Amorini: Seiler 1992, figs. 428–29, 432; *PPM* 5 (1994) 829–30, figs. 206–8.

VI xvi 15, Casa dell'Ara Massima

Tablinum F

- Endymion: Stemmer 1992, fig. 124; *PPM* 5 (1994) 869, fig. 29.
- Bacchantes: Stemmer 1992, fig. 122; *Peinture* 1993, 1, pl. 81; *PPM* 5 (1994) 865, fig. 23.

Triclinium G

- Mars and Venus: Stemmer 1992, fig. 178; *Peinture* 1993, 1, pl. 83; *PPM* 5 (1994) 872, fig. 33.
- Bacchus discovering Ariadne: Stemmer 1992, fig. 179; *PPM* 5 (1994) 877, fig. 38.
- Selene descending to Endymion: Stemmer 1992, figs. 180, 182; *Peinture* 1993, 1, pl. 80; *PPM* 5 (1994) 876, fig. 37.
- Hercules and Evander: Stemmer 1992, fig. 181; *Peinture* 1993, 1, pl. 82; *PPM* 5 (1994) 875, fig. 36.
- Tondi with busts: Stemmer 1992, figs. 183–87; *PPM* 5 (1994) 878, figs. 39–42.

VII iv 31/51, Casa dei Capitelli Colorati

Apsidal oecus east of the smaller peristyle

- Scene of sacrifice: H 1410; Schefold 1962, pl. 166.1; *Peinture* 1993, 2, fig. 248b; *PPM* 6 (1996) 1085, fig. 131.
- Leda: H 144; Schefold 1962, pl. 166.2; *Peinture* 1993, 2, fig. 248a; *PPM* 6 (1996) 1085, fig. 130.

VII iv 62, Casa delle Forme di Creta

Room west of the tablinum

- Rape of Hylas: H 1261; MN 8882; Rizzo 1929, pl. 129; *PPM* 7 (1997) 152, fig. 19.

VII vi 7

Peristyle

- Birth of Venus: H 307; MN 27704; HBr pl. 189; *PPM* 7 (1997) 178, fig. 2.

VII xii 23, Casa del Camillo

Room d, west of the atrium

- Apollo and Daphne: H 212; HBr text 1.183, fig. 53; Rizzo 1929, pl. 105.2; *PPM* 7 (1997) 556, fig. 30.

VIII iv 4, Casa di Olconio Rufo

Triclinium 29, south of the peristyle

- Judgment of Paris: H 1284; *Peinture* 1993, 2, fig. 298; *PPM* 8 (1998) 515, fig. 112.
- Achilles discovered on Scyros: H 1296; HBr text 1.189, fig. 55; Rizzo 1929, pl. 65; *PPM* 8 (1998) 513, fig. 110.

Exedra 28, south of the peristyle

- Hermaphroditus with Silenus: H 1372; Schefold 1962, pl. 171.3; *Peinture* 1993, 2, fig. 296; *PPM* 8 (1998) 499, fig. 89.
- Bacchus discovering Ariadne: H 1240; Curtius 1929, fig. 179; *PPM* 8 (1998) 505, fig. 96.

IX viii 3/6, Casa del Centenario

Triclinium 61, north of the bath suite

- Iphigenia in Tauris: S 585; HBr pl. 119; *Peinture* 1993, 1, pl. 94.
- Theseus victor over the Minotaur: S 530; *Peinture* 1993, 1, pl. 95.
- Hermaphroditus and Silenus: S 596; HBr pl. 217; *Peinture* 1993, 1, fig. 97.

HERCULANEUM

VI 21–24, Collegio degli Augustali

- Hercules with Athena and Juno: *Peinture* 1993, 1, pl. 145.
- Hercules with Acheloüs and Deianira: *Peinture* 1993, 1, pl. 144.

Area Sacra Suburbana

- Paris and Helen: Maiuri 1958, 177, fig. 144.
- Silenus pouring a libation: Maiuri 1958, 178, fig. 145.

The Casa dei Guerrieri Painter

One of the oddest painters in Pompeii is the man who worked as assistant to the Meleagro Painter in the Casa di Meleagro, VI ix 2. Here he painted figures of nymphs and satyrs in the dado, and also occasionally floating figures in side panels and upper zones, of room after room (see esp. Schefold 1962, pls. 96.2, 98; and *PPM* 4 [1993] 662–809), large figures of highly individual character, the female figures narrow-shouldered with long arms and legs and proportionately tiny oval heads, the male figures with sturdy torsos but light arms and legs and broad faces. The most distinguishing feature is their eyes, small and heavily shadowed with an anguished expression beside a wedgelike nose. In a single room, however, the yellow Corinthian oecus, the roles were reversed; he was allowed to paint the subject pictures and figures floating in the upper zone, while the Meleagro Painter did figures in the dado. The best preserved of the subject pictures is a mysterious mythological composition of a bacchante grasping an unfluted column facing a satyr who holds out to her a small snake wound around a pedum. She seems to express surprise and dismay. One other subject picture survives in this room, but in very poor state; it shows Theseus seated with the body of the Minotaur at his feet, while Ariadne stands beside him. Enough survives of the floating figures in the side panels to show that they also are his work.

The only other works of his that I have been able to identify are a series of figures in the handsome scaenae frons decoration of a room in the Casa dei Guerrieri, I iii 25, and the figures of a scaenae frons decoration of a quite different character in the Casa dell'Ara Massima, VI xvi 15. In the room in the Casa dei Guerrieri the central figures represent the contest between Venus and Hesperus judged by Apollo, the same subject that appears again in the scaenae frons decoration of the biclinial pavilion in the Casa di Apolline, VI vii 23, but these central figures are flanked by attendants who carry torches and vessels and armed and helmeted warriors. The series was sadly damaged by the theft of several figures in 1977, but the attribution is still secure. In the atrium of the Casa dell'Ara Massima there are only four figures, two women standing in doorways, one carrying vessels, the other a baetylus scepter of Venus and a thyrsus, and two larger figures shown as statues decorating the stage but in natural colors, a nude Neptune carrying a dolphin and a winged Victoria with a wreath and a palm branch.

⟢ *Works* ⟡

POMPEII

I iii 25, Casa dei Guerrieri

Oecus h

• Scaenae frons decoration including a Contest of Venus and Hesperus: Schefold 1962, pls. 90.2, 91; Eschebach 1978, fig. 181;

PPM 1 (1990) 89–100, figs. 2–4, 8–9, 14–15; *Peinture* 1993, 2, fig. 1.

VI ix 2, Casa di Meleagro

Peristyle 16

- Thetis with the armor of Achilles: H 1320; MN 8873; *PPM* 4 (1993) 719, fig. 117.

Corinthian oecus 24

- Satyr with a snake and maenad: H 541; Schefold 1962, pls. 96.1, 99; *PPM* 4 (1993) 741–42, figs. 165–66.
- Floating figures: *Peinture* 1993, 2, fig. 186b; *PPM* 4 (1993) 729–43, figs. 141, 152, 169.

Exedra 26

- Figures in dado: Schefold 1962, pl. 96.2; *PPM* 4 (1993) 749–64, figs. 182–86, 188–90, 193, 196–98, 201, 203.

Black triclinium 27

- Figures in dado: Schefold 1962, pl. 98; *Peinture* 1993, 2, fig. 187; *PPM* 4 (1993) 766–88, figs. 210, 217–19, 222, 226, 232–33, 238–39, 244.

Room 29

- Floating figures and figures in dado: *PPM* 4 (1993) 795–809, figs. 256–57, 262, 264–66, 269–75, 278–79.

VI xvi 15, Casa dell'Ara Massima

Atrium

- Figures in scaenae frons decoration: Schefold 1962, pl. 102; Stemmer 1992, figs. 78–83; *Peinture* 1993, 1, pl. 78; *PPM* 5 (1994) 855, figs. 9–11.

The Dioscuri Painter

In *Pompeii: The Casa dei Dioscuri and Its Painters* I distinguished between works attributed to a painter called the Dioscuri Painter, who painted the figures of divinities in the atrium of that house, and works attributed to a painter called the Perseus Painter, who painted the figures and pictures in the large peristyle. To the former I assigned a considerable list of works in Pompeii and Stabiae; to the latter, except for the paintings of the peristyle, I assigned only the three subject pictures of the yellow exedra (n) off the peristyle of the Casa dei Vettii, the so-called Theban Room, and the famous predelle of amorini in games and trades in the red oecus (q) of the same house, the latter with some hesitation. Over the years since then I have become convinced that these are simply different manners of the same painter, working in one case with isolated figures against a ground of solid color in a severe room and in compositions where there is little effect of chiaroscuro and in another with a rich palette and strong effects of light and chiaroscuro. Moreover, it seems clear to me that he painted the predelle in the atrium of the Casa dei Vettii, as well as those in the red oecus, all the figures in the red oecus, those in the dado and upper zone as well as the floating groups of lovers in the side panels of the main zone (which I originally ascribed to the Io Painter) and the Priapus at the entrance to the house. There is nothing that I assigned to either painter in my earlier work that I would now wish to attribute to someone else, but there are several pictures that should be added to the *oeuvre* as a whole. This painter was fairly active in both Pompeii and Stabiae and must be thought of as either a resident of Pompeii or a painter who came to the city regularly. He paints in some of the finest houses and always some of the best rooms in any house. He is sometimes assisted by the Io Painter, responsible for the less important figures in a room, whose style so much resembles his that it is tempting to think of them as master and pupil, but the Io Painter painted in more houses, and sometimes important buildings, such as the Macellum, independent of the Dioscuri Painter, so perhaps we should think of him as resident in Pompeii, while the Dioscuri Painter came only at intervals, frequent intervals, to be sure, but spaced. As he was one of the better painters, it is surprising that we do not find his work at Herculaneum; for that I can offer no satisfactory explanation. But since in the red oecus of the Casa dei Vettii he was willing to paint dado figures, while the large central pictures were on panels let into the walls that have disappeared, either salvaged by survivors or on wood that disintegrated over the course of the centuries, and so were probably prized possessions by another or other painters, he was a decorator and not an aspirant to the status of Nero's Famulus (Pliny, *HN* 35.120).

The hallmarks of this painter's style may be briefly listed. Most easily recognized are the legs and knees of his nude males. The knees, which are always carefully studied, tend to be large and overly muscled when the leg is straight and have a pronounced bulge when it is bent. The thigh is exaggeratedly short, and the muscle on the inside of the calf is almost always carefully emphasized. His heads are elongated, the face a long oval, slightly lantern-jawed but handsome. The large eyes stare intently, the upper lid commonly carefully lit above a fringe of dark lashes; the eyebrows are thin, often almost a hairline. The nose is thick and straight, the mouth very small and pursed. The chin is commonly long. The ears, set low, are often shown as a single ridge projecting from the close cap of the hair. Men's hair often has a ducktail at the nape of the neck. Torsos are elongated, waists always overemphasized; in the nude male torso there is usually a pronounced hip bulge. Arms tend to be somewhat short and light, and the artist has a number of favorite poses for hands, the hand at rest being cupped with the fingers curled in a little, while the clenched hand is almost always clenched very tight with the tip of the thumb curled out. The heel of the hand is frequently lengthened. The feet usually have an oddly muscular look and a rather thick instep.

In his women the breasts are always high and markedly hemispherical. Their arms are more muscular than is usual in Pompeian painting. Although they stare, their faces are otherwise curiously expressionless, an effect emphasized by the calmness of the mouth.

This painter usually uses a rich palette, except for individual figures in a severe decoration. The flesh of his men is usually only slightly darker than that of his women and sometimes not at all. He likes to dress his men in a rich red mantle with a shimmering blue border or lining. His women usually have gauzy clothing with cloudlike veils framing the head, and he is partial to light blue clothing for his women. Figures and objects in the foreground are emphasized by the addition of strong lights and shadows that figures in the background are not given.

→ *Works* ←

POMPEII

I iv 5/25, Casa del Citarista

Triclinium 37

- Io, Argus, and Mercury: H 137; MN 9557; Rizzo 1929, pl. 81; *Collezioni* 1986, 162; *PPM* 1 (1990) 129, fig. 21.

V iii 6

Room d

- Narcissus: *PPM* 3 (1991) 909, fig. 15; *Peinture* 1993, 2, fig. 155.

VI ix 6/7, Casa dei Dioscuri

Fauces

• Dioscuri: H 963; MN 9453, 9455; HBr pls. 120.1, 120.2; Richardson 1955, pls. 15.1, 15.2; Ragghianti 1963, pl. 29; *Collezioni* 1986, 248–49; *PPM* 4 (1993) 869–70, figs. 14–15.

Atrium

• Jupiter crowned by Victoria: H 102; MN 9551; HBr pl. 121; *Collezioni* 1986, 251; *PPM* 4 (1993) 892, fig. 62.

• Saturn: H 96; MN 8837; HBr pl. 122.2; Richardson 1955, pl. 16.2; Ragghianti 1963, 107; *Collezioni* 1986, 250; *PPM* 4 (1993) 885, fig. 53.

• Ceres: H 176; MN 9454; HBr pl. 122.1; Ragghianti 1963, pl. 30; *Collezioni* 1986, 253; *PPM* 4 (1993) 888, fig. 56.

• Bacchus and satyr: H 400; MN 9268; HBr pl. 123.2; *Collezioni* 1986, 258; *PPM* 4 (1993) 890, fig. 60.

• Apollo: H 181; London, BM; HBr text 2.30, fig. 8; *BMC* 1933, 32, pl. 13; Richardson 1955, pl. 16.1; *PPM* 4 (1993) 886, fig. 54.

Peristyle

• Perseus freeing Andromeda: H 1186; MN 8998; HBr pl. 129; Rizzo 1929, pl. 41; Richardson 1955, pl. 53; de Franciscis 1963, pl. 36; Stenico 1963, fig. 95; Seider 1968, 67; *Collezioni* 1986, 181 and p. 62; *PPM* 4 (1993) 975, fig. 224; De Caro 1994, 178.

• Medea and her children: H 1262; MN 8977; HBr pl. 130; Rizzo 1929, pl. 76; Richardson 1955, pl. 54; de Franciscis 1963, pl. 37; Ragghianti 1963, pl. 43; Stenico 1963, fig. 89; *Collezioni* 1986, 196; *PPM* 4 (1993) 975, fig. 223; De Caro 1994, 177.

• Tripods with Niobids: H 1154; MN 9302, 9304; HBr pls. 131.1, 131.2; *Collezioni* 1986, 188–89; *PPM* 4 (1993) 977, figs. 226–27.

• Floating maenad: H 481; Richardson 1955, pl. 58.1; Kraus and von Matt 1973, fig. 304; Eschebach 1978, fig. 122; *PPM* 4 (1993) 967, fig. 209.

• Armed ephebe: H 1830; Richardson 1955, pl. 58.2; *PPM* 4 (1993) 963, fig. 203.

• Ephebe with horse: H 1835; *PPM* 4 (1993) 980, fig. 232.

• Venus Pompeiana: H 295; HBr pl. 123.1.

• Seated girl: H 1886; *PPM* 4 (1993) 988, fig. 251.

• Corybant: H 1835.

• Corybant: H 1834; MN s.n; *PPM* 4 (1993) 982, fig. 237.

• Victorious girl runner: H 941b; London, BM; *BMC* 1933, 33, pl. 14; Richardson 1955, pl. 58.3; *PPM* 4 (1993) 995, fig. 262.

VI x 11, Casa del Naviglio

Atrium

• Bacchus: H 392; MN 9456; HBr pl. 1; Richardson 1955, pls. 17.1, 22.1; *Collezioni* 1986, 259; *PPM* 4 (1993) 1084, fig. 22.

• Ceres: H 175; MN 9457; Richardson 1955, pl. 17.2; *Collezioni* 1986, 252; *PPM* 4 (1993) 1085, fig. 23.

• Winged genius carrying Venus (?): H 1954a; MN 8830; Richardson 1955, pl. 22.4; Ragghianti 1963, pl. 38; *Collezioni* 1986, 213; *PPM* 4 (1993) 1082, fig. 19.

• Winged female genius carrying Diana (?): H 1954b; MN 8826; HBr pl. 222; *PPM* 4 (1993) 1086, fig. 24.

• Armed ephebe: H 1832; MN 9123; *Collezioni* 1986, 155; *PPM* 4 (1993) 1086, fig. 25.

Oecus 22, south of the peristyle

• Satyr and maenad: H 528; MN 9299; Schefold 1962, pl. 77.2; *Collezioni* 1986, 216; *PPM* 4 (1993) 1091, fig. 36.

• Satyr and maenad: H 518; MN 9299; Schefold 1962, pl. 77.1.

• Satyr with the infant Bacchus: S 154; *PPM* 4 (1993) 1090–92, figs. 35, 37.

Oecus 24, south of the peristyle

• Zephyrus and Chloris: H 974; MN 9202; Rizzo 1929, pl. 111; Richardson 1955, pl. 18; de Franciscis 1963, pl. 30; Ragghianti 1963, pl. 39; *Collezioni* 1986, 142; Guillaud and Guillaud 1990, figs. 37, 286, 289; *PPM* 4 (1993) 1094, fig. 41.

• Floating bacchante: H 480; MN 9298; de Franciscis 1963, pl. 72; Stenico 1963, fig. 85; Seider 1968, 47; *Collezioni* 1986, 129; Guillaud and Guillaud 1990, fig. 35; *PPM* 4 (1993) 1095, fig. 42.

VI xv 1/2, Casa dei Vettii

Fauces

• Priapus: Kraus and von Matt 1973, fig. 282; Grant 1975, 53; *PPM* 5 (1994) 471, fig. 2.

Atrium

• Predelle of amorini and children: HBr pls. 35.1, 35.2, 36.1, 36.2, 37.1, 37.2, 37.3; Schefold 1962, pls. 72, 74; *PPM* 5 (1994) 475–80, figs. 8–20.

White triclinium e, south of the atrium

• Cyparissus: HBr pl. 45; Rizzo 1929, pl. 107.2; Kraus and von Matt 1973, fig. 301; *PPM* 5 (1994) 487, fig. 29.

• Wrestling of Pan and Amor: HBr pl. 44; Rizzo 1929, pls. 23, 37; Schefold 1962, pl. 86; Ragghianti 1963, pl. 34; *PPM* 5 (1994) 489, fig. 32.

Peristyle

• Urania: *PPM* 5 (1994) 510, fig. 71.

• Victoria: *PPM* 5 (1994) 512, fig. 74.

• Victoria: *PPM* 5 (1994) 512, fig. 76.

• Victoria: *PPM* 5 (1994) 513, fig. 78.

• Maenad: *Peinture* 1993, 2, fig. 213; *PPM* 5 (1994) 514, fig. 80.

• Satyr: *Peinture* 1993, 2, fig. 212; *PPM* 5 (1994) 514, fig. 81.

• Victoria: *PPM* 5 (1994) 515, fig. 83.

Yellow exedra n, east of the peristyle

• Hercules strangling the serpents: HBr pl. 41; Rizzo 1929, pl. 36; Richardson 1955, pl. 57; Seider 1968, 55; Kraus and von Matt 1973, fig. 261; Eschebach 1978, fig. 151; *Peinture* 1993, 1, pl. 56; *PPM* 5 (1994) 527–28, figs. 105–6.

• Death of Pentheus: HBr pl. 42; Rizzo 1929, pl. 40; Richardson 1955, pl. 56; *Peinture* 1993, 1, pl. 57; *PPM* 5 (1994) 530, fig. 108.

• Punishment of Dirce: HBr pl. 43; Rizzo 1929, pl. 66; Richardson 1955, pl. 55; Seider 1968, 71; *PPM* 5 (1994) 532–33, figs. 110–11.

Red oecus q, north of the peristyle

• Apollo and Daphne: HBr pl. 32; Seider 1968, 53; *PPM* 5 (1994) 544, fig. 127.

• Bacchus and Ariadne: HBr pl. 31; Kraus and von Matt 1973, fig. 110; *PPM* 5 (1994) 549, fig. 136.

• Neptune and Amymone (?): HBr pl. 29; Richardson 1955, pl. 28.1; Seider 1968, 53; *PPM* 4 (1994) 564, fig. 158.

• Perseus and Andromeda: HBr pl. 30; Richardson 1955, pl. 28.2; Kraus and von Matt 1973, fig. 110; *PPM* 5 (1994) 550, fig. 138.

• Silenus and Hermaphroditus: *PPM* 5 (1994) 565, fig. 159.

• Predelle, some mythological, some of amorini and psyches: HBr pls. 2, 20.1, 20.2, 20.3, 21.1, 21.2, 21.3, 22.1, 22.2, 23.1, 23.2, 24.1, 24.2, 25.1, 25.2, 26.1, 26.2; Rizzo 1929, pls. 26–27; Seider 1968, 56–57; Picard 1970, fig. 51; Kraus and von Matt 1973, figs.

110–11, 204; Eschebach 1978, figs. 150, 152; *Peinture* 1993, 1, pls. 60–63; *PPM* 5 (1994) 545–63, figs. 128–29, 131–35, 139–49, 151–57.

• Figures in dado: HBr pls. 33.1, 33.2, 34.1, 34.2; Schefold 1962, pls. 62, 64–65; *Peinture* 1993, 1, pl. 64; *PPM* 5 (1994) 545–62, figs. 129, 150, 156.

• Figures in upper zone: HBr pls. 27.1, 27.2, 28.1, 28.2; Curtius 1929, 145–47, figs. 95–96.

VII ii 16, Casa di Gavio Rufo

Exedra o, south of the peristyle

• Theseus victor over the Minotaur: S 527; MN 9043; HBr pl. 143; Richardson 1955, pls. 21.4, 22.3; de Franciscis 1963, pl. 42; Ragghianti 1963, pl. 45; Stenico 1963, fig. 96; Seider 1968, 43; *Collezioni* 1986, 173; Guillaud and Guillaud 1990, figs. 66, 74, 285; *Peinture* 1993, 1, pl. 88; De Caro 1994, 176.

• Wedding of Perithous and Hippodamia: S 539; MN 9044; HBr pl. 144; Rizzo 1929, pl. 54; Maiuri 1953, 80; Richardson 1955, pl. 21.3; Ragghianti 1963, pl. 44; Stenico 1963, fig. 99; *Collezioni* 1986, 176; Guillaud and Guillaud 1990, fig. 279.

• Contest of Venus and Hesperus: S 164; MN 9449; HBr pl. 145; Richardson 1955, pls. 19, 21.1; de Franciscis 1963, pl. 47; Stenico 1963, fig. 117; *Collezioni* 1986, 161; *RdSP* 3 (1989) 119, fig. 6; *Peinture* 1993, 1, pl. 87.

VII iv 31/51, Casa dei Capitelli Colorati

Room c, east of the eastern andron

• Venus and the marine thiasus: H 308; HBr pl. 190; Schefold 1962, pls. 107, 163.1.

• Perseus and Andromeda: H 1196; MN 8996; Richardson 1955, pl. 20; *Collezioni* 1986, 182.

VII xii 3/4

Cubiculum east of the atrium

• Satyr and maenad: H 554; MN 27705; Schefold 1962, pl. 159.1; Grant 1975, 160; *Collezioni* 1986, 268 and p. 65.

VIII vii 28, Tempio di Iside

Triclinium 8

• Endymion or Narcissus: H 1338; MN 9379; *Pompeji: Leben und Kunst* 1973, 210; *Alla ricerca di Iside* 1992, 1.83; *PPM* 8 (1998) 847, fig. 222.

Unidentified Buildings

- Bacchus with theatrical mask, surrounded by his thiasus: H 408; MN 9050.
- Narcissus: H 1361; MN 9380; *Collezioni* 1986, 190.
- Amorino with a doe: H 795; MN 9215; Herbig 1962, pl. 1; *Collezioni* 1986, 120 (possibly from the Villa di Cicerone).

Environs, Agro Murecine, Portico dei Triclini

Triclinium A

- Jason before Pelias (?): Elia 1961, figs. 6–7; Pagano 1983, pls. 10–11.
- Floating figures: Pagano 1983, pls. 12–16.
- Floating male nude: Elia 1961, fig. 4.

Triclinium B

- Dioscurus: Elia 1961, fig. 12; Pagano 1983, pl. 17.
- Mercury: Elia 1961, fig. 11; Pagano 1983, pl. 18.
- Figures in architecture: Elia 1961, fig. 10; Pagano 1983, pls. 19–20.
- Woman with child attendant: Elia 1961, fig. 14.

Triclinium C

- Enthroned divinities: Elia 1961, figs. 8–9; Pagano 1983, pls. 21–22.
- Floating figures: Elia 1961, fig. 5; Pagano 1983, pls. 23–24.

Triclinium D

- Jupiter: Elia 1961, fig. 17; Pagano 1983, pl. 25.
- Athena: Elia 1961, fig. 16; Pagano 1983, pl. 26.
- Victorias: Elia 1961, figs. 13, 15; Pagano 1983, pls. 27–30.

STABIAE

Villa di Arianna (Villa della Venditrice di Amori, Villa di Varano)

Antechamber to great triclinium 3

- Nereid on a sea tiger: H 1036; MN 8870; HBr pl. 202; Rizzo 1929, pl. 24.2; de Franciscis 1963, pl. 73; *Pompeji: Leben und Kunst* 1973, 211; Allroggen-Bedel 1977, pl. 33.2; *Collezioni* 1986, 149; Guillaud and Guillaud 1990, fig. 38.
- Nereid on a hippocamp: H 1027; MN 8859; HBr pl. 203; Allroggen-Bedel 1977, pl. 33.4; *Collezioni* 1986, 150.
- Discobulus: H 1508; MN 9053; Allroggen-Bedel 1977, pl. 33.1; *Collezioni* 1986, 151.

The Egyptian Landscape Painter

The large panel on the east wall of the viridarium of the Casa di Ceio, I vi 15, shows a landscape in which land and water mingle, the land preponderant but enough water to show a good-sized sailboat. There are buildings scattered among patchy vegetation that includes palm trees; these buildings are of somewhat exotic architecture and include a horned altar and an open pavilion with a shallow bowed roof. Figures appear here and there, singly and in couples, seated as well as standing, most of them in long drapery but one in the right foreground wearing the hooded cucullus. They seem leisurely; such gestures as there are seem those of conversation. Spinazzola recognized that this was the work of a painter who had painted a similar landscape on the exterior of the biclinial pavilion at the northwest corner of the garden of the Casa di Apolline, VI vii 23. There the vegetation and architecture are identical with those in the Casa di Ceio picture, but the staffage figures are less numerous and include a man driving a pack mule, a Bacchic group with musical instruments, and a panther. Less water is shown, but a large ship appears in the background.

Both pictures are charming and show a painter with a clear vision of his subject and a facile brush. The bird's-eye perspective with high horizon line, the lighting, the way of painting architecture with pink roofs and delicately framed blue friezes, the drapery and grouping of figures and their proportions, all suggest that this painter also did the series of five large landscapes in the peristyle of the Casa della Fontana Piccola, VI viii 23/24 (HBr pls. 166–69; Eschebach 1978, fig. 209; *PPM* 4 [1993] 642–46, figs. 34–38, 40–41). These are very different in subject, and the appearance at regular intervals of a traveler suggests that they may be illustrations of one of the Greek romances set the Aegean world, but otherwise the atmosphere is very similar. This, then, suggests that the painter may have had a certain reputation as a landscapist, but further work by him has proved hard to find.

⇢ *Works* ⇠

POMPEII

I vi 15, Casa di Ceio

Viridarium

- Landscape: Spinazzola 1953, 1.278–79, figs. 308–10; Peters

1963, fig. 171; Michel 1990, figs. 265, 274–78, 280; *PPM* 1 (1990) 476–82, figs. 105–11; Ling 1991, 149, fig. 157.

VI vii 23, Casa di Apolline

Viridarium

• Landscape: Rizzo 1929, pl. 177; Spinazzola 1953, 1.280, fig. 311; Peters 1963, fig. 176.

The Four Divinities Painter

One of the most striking shop façades in Pompeii is that of IX vii 1, where a series of four heads painted at heroic scale, Apollo/Sol, Jupiter, Mercury, and Diana/Luna, crowns the lintel. They face symmetrically to the axis and turn their eyes upward; their expression is solemn, even lugubrious. Below them to either side of the doorway are a picture of Venus Pompeiana and Cupid flanked by floating amorini and a procession in honor of the Magna Mater in which her enthroned image is displayed on a *ferculum,* while four porters cluster around it and priests and devotees have momentarily paused. All these, despite differences in scale, are very clearly the work of a single painter. The hallmarks of his style are heavy eyebrows that sweep wide of the eyes, strong, wedgelike noses, and tight mouths that turn down at the outer corners. Chins are heavy, and the women are apt to have a single large curl in front of the ear. Men's beards drag to either side like dundrearies. Figures are broad-shouldered and tend to seem short and heavyset. The palette is somber, strong in earth colors with only touches of bright pigment; highlights are strong and tend to be sharp-edged.

The style of this painter is so individual that it is easy to locate his work elsewhere. In room n of the house at IX v 2, the Domus Uboni, he painted three large pictures illustrating the story of Achilles, Achilles discovered among the daughters of Lycomedes on Scyros, Thetis in the forge of Hephaestus, and Thetis bringing his armor to Achilles. These are all large pictures, but only the first is really carefully composed. There is little that is aesthetically pleasing about any of them. The proportions of the figures are often stubby, the facial expression vacant and without direction, the drapery harshly painted, and the finish of the whole careless.

Another room that this man painted is in the Casa della Caccia Antica, VII iv 48, where he did busts of divinities, amorini, and subject pictures of

Danaë and Leda. Danaë stands half-draped, her clothing billowing wildly about her, lifting her right hand in astonishment, while an amorino in the upper left corner pours the golden rain over her from an upturned amphora. A large thunderbolt, without logic or explanation, has been introduced at the lower right balancing the amorino. The Leda is conventional.

To these we can add the Romulus and Aeneas on the façade of the shop at IX xiii 5, a short distance down Via dell'Abbondanza from the shop of the four divinities. These are so like the figures in the procession of the Magna Mater that the case hardly needs arguing, but I have not found any other examples of this painter's work. I entertained for a while the notion that he might be Lucius in a particular vein; the fact that both worked in the Casa della Caccia Antica seemed to support it, as did the stubby proportions that Lucius occasionally gives his figures. But there are not many points of real contact, and it is the general weakness of both men's work rather than true similarity that makes them seem related. I believe the Four Divinities Painter should be one we know elsewhere in a different vein, but I cannot put my finger on him.

This painter was also identified by P. M. Allison, approaching him from a different direction in her dissertation *The Wall-Paintings of the Casa della Caccia Antica in Pompeii* (Ann Arbor: University Microfilms, 1991). She found it equally difficult to extend the list of his works beyond those offered here.

→ *Works* ←

POMPEII

VII iv 48, Casa della Caccia Antica

Cubiculum 4, west of the atrium

- Danaë: H 116; MN 9549; HBr pl. 188; Rizzo 1929, pl. 103.1; *Peinture* 1993, 2, fig. 250b.
- Leda: H 145; HBr pl. 229.2.
- Venus Piscatrix: H 346; *Peinture* 1993, 2, fig. 251.
- Tondi:
  Jupiter: H 77.
  Mercury: H 356.
  Apollo/Sol: H 946; *Peinture* 1993, 2, fig. 251.
  Diana/Luna: H 949.

IX v 2, Domus Uboni

Room n, north of the peristyle

- Achilles discovered on Scyros: S 572; MN 116085; HBr pl. 137; Rizzo 1929, pl. 58; Curtius 1929, pl. 2; Stenico 1963, fig. 93; Seider 1968, 66; *Collezioni* 1986, 206; Ling 1991, 133, fig. 138; *Peinture* 1993, 2, fig. 314b.
- Thetis bringing the armor of Achilles: S 577; HBr pl. 138; Rizzo 1929, pl. 61.
- Thetis in the forge of Hephaestus: S 576; HBr pl. 139; Rizzo 1929, pl. 59; Curtius 1929, 221, fig. 130.

IX vii 1, Taberna

Façade

- Heads of Apollo / Sol, Jupiter, Mercury, and Diana / Luna: Spinazzola 1953, 1, folding pl. 3; Ragghianti 1963, pls. 56–57.
- Venus Pompeiana: Spinazzola 1953, 1.214–15, figs. 242–43; Ragghianti 1963, pl. 53; Kraus and von Matt 1973, fig. 268; Fröhlich 1991, pl. 59.1.
- Procession of the Magna Mater: Rizzo 1929, pl. 200; Spinazzola 1953, 1.214, fig. 241, and 1.223–35, figs. 250–51, 264–65; Ragghianti 1963, pls. 54–55; Fröhlich 1991, pl. 59.2.

IX xiii 5, Taberna

Façade

- Aeneas fleeing from Troy: Rizzo 1929, pl. 194.1; Spinazzola 1953, 1.150, fig. 183.
- Romulus with the trophy of Acro: Rizzo 1929, pl. 194.2; Spinazzola 1953, 1.151, fig. 184.

The Infancy of Bacchus Painter

A painter to whom I can assign only a small group of pictures but who has a very distinctive style is perhaps best known for a square picture of medium size from Herculaneum, now in the Museo Nazionale, that shows the infant Bacchus held aloft by a seated Silenus and teased with a bunch of grapes by a maenad seated behind Silenus. Pan kneels before this group, and Mercury is seated to the right. Silenus's recumbent donkey and a panther playing with a tympanum fill the foreground, and a pair of subsidiary figures appear behind a tree in the background. The approach of the artist is very painterly; he builds his forms very directly, allowing the brushwork to show plainly, but uses a limited palette and finishes his work with a lot of black outlining and hatching that he then accents with a few touches of added light. He is also sometimes a careless draughtsman, and Mercury's petasus floats awkwardly above his head. His figures tend to be stumpy, large-headed, broad-shouldered, and short-legged. His heads are well shaped, but the mouth, which is almost always small and straight, is apt to have a set expression that, combined with staring eyes under pitched or drawn eyebrows, gives them an angry look.

Also from Herculaneum comes a floating group of Mars and Venus flanked by a pair of blonde amorini, one carrying Mars's sword, the other a bow and arrow. Venus carries a fan in her left hand; Mars puts his left hand on her left shoulder and caresses her breast with his right. The effect of this little group against its blue ground is surprisingly good. The authorship is made plain by the handling of the medium, the proportions of the figures, and the overdrawing.

Some subsidiary figures that must also be his work are the amorino and Telamon figures in a panel from the upper zone of a Third Style decoration from Herculaneum now in the Museo Nazionale. He must also be responsible for the fine tondo with heads of an ivy-crowned faun and maenad, also from Herculaneum. This is at a completely different scale, larger and more detailed, but it shows his technique in handling pigment, building his forms directly, and finishing them with overdrawing in blacks that outline the forms and add hatching. The eyes, with their sharp contrast of dark and light and elongated eyebrow of a quizzical lift, are his, as are the tight mouths. This is his best picture, and one can only regret that he did not do more at this scale.

A trio of panels from Pompeii, probably predella panels, show a group of bacchantes that includes a winged and wreathed amorino and preparations for a religious ritual led by a diminutive flute-player that include an enthroned hero, nude except for a mantle draped over his thighs, contemplated by a pensive woman heavily draped. Again the palette is limited, as one might expect in predella panels, but the brushwork and expressions of the figures reveal the authorship.

More ambitious works come from Pompeii; these are primarily genre scenes. One shows preparations for a concert, a woman seated on a couch facing the viewer who holds a lyre upright with her left hand and tunes another instrument that lies beside her with her right. Three other women in heavy drapery follow her actions attentively. In another picture, said to come from the shop I iii 18 (HBr 2.25, where the assignment is based on notes on drawings in the German Archaeological Institute in Rome; the compilers of *PPM* were unable to find any place for these pictures in this block), a group of women is assembled around a small table covered with the silver utensils for a party. One plays the double flutes, while another stands and lifts high a dipper. A pair of serving girls in the left background pull aside a curtain to watch. The companion piece shows two couples reclining on banquet couches under an awning with a small table holding cups between them. The couple in the middle of the picture is kissing. Two women, one drinking from a cup, appear at the left edge of the picture, while trees fill the space above them. These pictures declare their authorship by the drawing of the facial features, their broad brushwork in rather thick pigment, and the expressions of the faces. It is further supported by the drawing of the hands and the palette employed.

A third picture of very similar handling is the "Bride of Corinth" from cubiculum d in the Casa di Laocoonte, VI xiv 29/30, now in the Museo Nazionale. It shows a couple reclining at table interrupted in drinking by a woman attended by a small boy who seems to have entered unexpectedly and is reproachful. The drawing of faces and hands, palette, and proportions all make the attribution a certainty, and the boy attendant is a significant addition to this painter's vocabulary of forms.

Another picture that almost certainly is this painter's work is the Triumphator dedicating a trophy in the presence of Victoria from Pompeii, now in the Museo Nazionale. Dressed in armor and a great crown of golden flowers, the triumphator faces the viewer and lifts his right hand holding a vexillum toward the trophy. Victoria stands in profile on the left of the trophy and lifts her left arm as though to help affix the round shield of the trophy to its armature. Other shields rest on the ground between them. It has been suggested that the arms of the trophy are Gallic, since the helmet is horned, and that the picture represents Attalus I, but this seems doubtful. On the other hand, the painting of the picture leaves little doubt as to its authorship. The profile of Victoria is very typical of this painter, and the drawing of the features of the triumphator fits well with his repertory. The broad handling of paint here further confirms the attribution.

I believe that this painter also painted the famous Distribution of Bread from Pompeii, VII iii 30, now in the Museo Nazionale. This very interesting picture shows a magistrate in a toga seated on a suggestus surrounded by piles of loaves of bread, while three citizens in dark clothing, two adults and a child, stand before the suggestus and lift their hands to receive the donation. This is a picture that has lost much of its surface to flaking, and the drawing was originally drier and executed with finer brushes than one expects of this painter, but the painting of the figures, especially that of the young boy in the foreground, reminds one strongly of the rest of this painter's work.

Appraising his *oeuvre* as a whole, one sees that this is a painter of no exceptional talent who had a certain facility in a bold handling of his medium and liked to do genre subjects. He probably painted architectural parts and figures most of the time, and it would probably be rewarding to examine decorative frameworks of the Third and Fourth Styles for his hand with only this in mind. He was given other work only occasionally and then acquitted himself well in a limited way, but except for the interesting Infancy of Bacchus, the only mythological subject I can identify as his work is an undistinguished Europa in the Fourth Style in the Casa Sannitica in Herculaneum, a minor picture casually dashed off.

➔ *Works* ←

POMPEII

I iii 18 (?)

- Women's banquet: H 1446; MN 9016; HBr pl. 211; Ward-Perkins and Claridge 1978, 66 and 199, no. 247.
- Banquet with kissing couple: H 1445; MN 9015; HBr pl. 210; Kraus and von Matt 1973, fig. 216.

VI xiv 29/30, Casa di Laocoonte

Cubiculum d, south of the fauces

- "The Bride of Corinth": S 641; MN 111209; HBr pl. 209; Ward-Perkins and Claridge 1978, 199, no. 246; *Collezioni* 1986, 341; *PPM* 5 (1994) 357, fig. 21.

VI xiv 42, Casa dell'Imperatrice di Russia

Cubiculum 3, south of the fauces

- Genre scene with woman painting a picture: H 1444; MN 9017; *PPM* 5 (1994) 414, fig. 9.

VII iii 30, Casa del Panattiere

Tablinum

- Distribution of bread: H 1501; MN 9071; Maiuri 1953, 144; Stenico 1963, fig. 125; Kraus and von Matt 1973, fig. 235; Eschebach 1978, fig. 230; *Collezioni* 1986, 329; Ling 1991, 164, fig. 176.

Unidentified Buildings

- Preparation for a concert: H 1442; MN 9023; Rizzo 1929, pl. 143; Ragghianti 1963, pls. 74–75; Stenico 1963, fig. 115; Jashemski 1979, 99, fig. 157; *Collezioni* 1986, 107 and p. 53; Guillaud and Guillaud 1990, fig. 239; De Caro 1994, 168.
- Triumphator dedicating a trophy: H 941; MN 8843; *Collezioni* 1986, 339.
- Three predella panels of Bacchic subject: H 538, 539, 540; MN 9146, 9147, 9260; Ragghianti 1963, pls. 79.1, 79.2.

HERCULANEUM

V 1/2, Casa Sannitica

Cubiculum south of the fauces

- Europa: Maiuri 1958, 205, fig. 160; *Peinture* 1993, 2, fig. 418.

V 30, Casa dell'Atrio Corinzio

Tablinum

- Floating bacchantes: H 492; MN 8950, 8952; *KJ* 24 (1991) 40, figs. 5–6.

Unidentified Buildings

- Infancy of Bacchus: H 376; MN 9270; Rizzo 1929, pl. 107.1; Stenico 1963, fig. 107; *Collezioni* 1986, 260.
- Mars and Venus: H 328; MN 9251; *Pompeji: Leben und Kunst* 1973, no. 268.
- Tondo of faun and maenad: H 508; MN 9284; *Pompeji: Leben und Kunst* 1973, no. 238; Ward-Perkins and Claridge 1978, 68 and 169, no. 141; *Collezioni* 1986, 264.
- Panel from the upper zone of a Third Style decoration: MN 9878; *Collezioni* 1986, 47; De Caro 1994, 151.
- Four predella panels of Bacchic subject:
  - H 577; Paris, Louvre P.27; Tran Tam Tinh 1974, 52, fig. 32.
  - H 578; formerly in Munich; *RP* 118.1.
  - H 579; Paris, Louvre P.28; Tran Tam Tinh 1974, 53, fig. 34.

H 409; Tokyo, Bridgestone Gallery; Tran Tam Tinh 1974, 52, fig. 33.

- Two predella panels of Bacchic subject: H 570, 576; MN 9267, 9265; *RP* 117.5.
- Iphigenia in Tauris (predella panel): H 1334; MN 9538; *RP* 170.2.
- Apollo and Marsyas (predella panel): H 231b; MN 9539; Curtius 1929, 399, fig. 217.

The Io Painter

In *Pompeii: The Casa dei Dioscuri and Its Painters* (Richardson 1955, 124–35) I identified this painter's hand among the decorations of the atrium, the tablinum, and the black triclinium (30) of the Casa dei Dioscuri, VI ix 6/7, and was able to find other work by him in a number of buildings in Pompeii, both private and public, notably the temple of Isis, where he was responsible for the large subject pictures of the ecclesiasterion, and the Macellum, where he painted subject pictures, floating groups, and decorative figures introduced in the architectural frames. The temple of Isis pictures represent his most studied and highly finished work, the figures in architecture relatively undistinguished hackwork. I further attributed to him the figures in the scaenae frons decoration of the Casa di Pinario Ceriale, the Apollo and Daphne in the ala of the Casa dei Capitelli Colorati, figures in the white triclinium (e), the polychrome exedra (p), and the red oecus (q) of the Casa dei Vettii, a Bacchus and Silenus from Boscoreale now in the British Museum, a picture from the Casa della Caccia Nuova, and others in the Villa di Arianna at Stabiae. This considerable list of works I attempted to divide into periods, concluding that the pictures from the temple of Isis were early work marked by academic hesitancy, those of the Casa della Caccia Nuova, Boscoreale, and the Villa di Arianna late work.

As the hallmarks of his style one may cite the expression of surprise or puzzlement that appears on many of his faces, the eyebrows quizzical, often with a characteristic twist, the eyes widened, the jaw sagging, and the tight mouth slightly open. This can be seen on faces in profile as well as on those in full face. He paints hands clumsily and tends to make his hands and feet too small. There is often also an exaggerated separation between the great and second toes. The instep is commonly thick, the toes short, curling firmly down, except for the great toe, the line of the outside of the foot characteristically slightly bowed.

Most of the attributions to him made in my earlier work I continue to adhere to; only a few do I now reject: the Phrixus and Helle, which I now see as a work of the Iphigenia Painter, the figures of the polychrome exedra and the red oecus of the Casa dei Vettii, and the subject pictures in the Villa di Arianna. But I also have a number of new attributions, which greatly enlarge the Io Painter's *oeuvre* and help to define his style. He did the fine large figure of a recumbent satyr with a syrinx from a black-ground dado in an unidentified house in Pompeii (MN 8605). He was responsible for the isolated figures in the main zone of the ala of the Casa della Fontana Piccola, the medallions and miniature figures of the "sacellum" or diaeta of Isis/Diana in the Casa di Loreio Tiburtino, the Bacchic figures of the Casa del Bracciale d'Oro, VI xvii 42–44, the Apollo and Admetus and its companion medallions in I xi 15, the Arrival of Venus at Cythera in the Casa di Trittolemo, and the figures in the upper zone of the room east of the eastern andron of the Casa dei Capitelli Colorati, the Mars and Venus in the Casa di Sallustio, and the small subject pictures in two rooms of the Casa delle Pareti Rosse. It also seems very likely that this was the painter of the badly damaged Thetis in the forge of Hephaestus in the Casa degli Amorini Dorati.

He also did work at Stabiae. In the Edifizio di San Marco he was responsible for parts of the ceiling of the long loggia, supporting figures to the Planisphere of the Seasons, the famous Medusa of the ramped corridor connecting the two levels of the complex, and the figures of the main zone of the diaeta of Perseus, the Iphigenia and Perseus. And while his work is rare at Herculaneum, he certainly did the heads of Oceanus in the lower frieze of the diaeta no. 6 of the Casa del Gran Portale.

I have suggested that because we find the Io Painter so often working in conjunction with the Dioscuri Painter and so close to the him in a number of points of style, he was probably a pupil of the Dioscuri Painter. I want to reiterate that suggestion. They work together in the same room repeatedly, and when they do, the Dioscuri Painter always takes on the more important parts, which strengthens the possibility. It must be observed, however, that the Io Painter does not seem to have grown in proficiency as a draughtsman with the passage of time, and one wonders whether the Dioscuri Painter may not have been accustomed to correct his drawing when they worked together and that this is part of the reason why their work is so often so similar that one may mistake the Io Painter's work for the Dioscuri Painter's.

If I am right that the pictures of the triclinium of the Casa della Caccia Nuova are late work of the Io Painter, they show that he did grow in his proficiency as a painter, moving away from the rather heavy overpainting of his middle period, with its reliance on impasto and hatching, to a chiaroscuro with subtler luminosity and texture. But his drawing remained faulty, his hands and feet disproportionately small and poorly shaped.

→ *Works* ←

POMPEII

I vii 2/3, Casa di M. Fabio Amandione

Room l

- Tondi with busts: *PPM* 2 (1990) 575, figs. 37–38.

I xi 6/7, Casa della Venere in Bikini

Vestibulum 1

- Tondi with female busts: *PPM* 2 (1990) 527–30, figs. 1–4.

Tablinum 7

- Bacchus with a maenad: *PPM* 2 (1990) 550–51, figs. 37–38.

Cubiculum 4

- Endymion and Selene: *PPM* 2 (1990) 536, fig. 15.

I xi 15/9, Casa del Primo Piano

Upper-story room 24

- Apollo and Admetus: *PPM* 2 (1990) 650, fig. 49.

II ii 2, Casa di Loreio Tiburtino

Room f, Diaeta of Isis/Diana

- Tondi with busts, seasons, figures in architecture and in the upper zone: Spinazzola 1953, 1.387–89, figs. 438–39, 441–42; Schefold 1962, pls. 80–82; Kraus and von Matt 1973, fig. 252; *PPM* 3 (1991) 70–79, figs. 46–56; *Peinture* 1993, 1, pl. 37.

III iv 4, Casa di Pinario Ceriale (Casa di Ifigenia)

Cubiculum a (cubiculum fenestratum)

- Scaenae frons decoration with Iphigenia in Tauris, a myth of Attis (?), and other figures: Rizzo 1929, pl. 25; Spinazzola 1953, 2.695–705, figs. 661–66, 669–71; Richardson 1955, pls. 30.6, 31.1; Schefold 1962, pls. 78–79; Ragghianti 1963, pl. 35; Picard 1970, figs. 48–49; Kraus and von Matt 1973, fig. 251; Guillaud and Guillaud 1990, figs. 294, 296; *PPM* 3 (1991) 460–72, figs. 31–41; Ling 1991, 129, fig. 131.

V v 3, Casa dei Gladiatori

Peristyle pluteus, interior

- Europa and nymphs: Schefold 1962, pl. 148.2; Eschebach 1978, fig. 73; *PPM* 3 (1991) 1071, fig. 3; *Peinture* 1993, 2, fig. 164b.

VI ii 4, Casa di Sallustio

Room 34, west of the southern peristyle

- Mars and Venus: H 319; Schefold 1962, pl. 160; *Peinture* 1993, 2, fig. 168b; *PPM* 4 (1993) 142, fig. 91.

VI viii 23/24, Casa della Fontana Piccola

North ala d

- Standing and floating figures and amorini: Schefold 1962, pl. 83; *PPM* 4 (1993) 629–33, figs. 13–18; Fröhlich 1996, figs. 141–45, 147, 158, 161, 163, 165.

VI ix 6/7, Casa dei Dioscuri

Atrium

- Delusion of Pan: H 1370; MN 27700; HBr pl. 124.2; Rizzo 1929, pl. 116; Richardson 1955, pls. 23.1, 30.1; Kraus and von Matt 1973, fig. 276; Ward-Perkins and Claridge 1978, 70 and 170, no. 143; *Collezioni* 1986, 265; *PPM* 4 (1993) 889, fig. 57.

Tablinum

- Floating satyr and maenad: H 529; MN 9134; HBr pl. 126; Richardson 1955, pl. 24.1; *Collezioni* 1986, 215; *PPM* 4 (1993) 906, fig. 86.
- Floating satyr and maenad: H 522; MN 9135; HBr pl. 6; Richardson 1955, pls 24.2, 30.2; Ragghianti 1963, pl. 37; Stenico 1963, fig. 84; Ward-Perkins and Claridge 1978, 167, no. 134; *Collezioni* 1986, 214; Guillaud and Guillaud 1990, fig. 39; *PPM* 4 (1993) 910, fig. 90.
- Fragment of genre scene *(Labetrunk)*: H 1565; MN 9106; HBr pl. 124.1; Richardson 1955, pl. 23.2; Stenico 1963, fig. 122; Seider 1968, 46; Ward-Perkins and Claridge 1978, 24 and 172, no. 150; *Collezioni* 1986, 328; *PPM* 4 (1993) 907, fig. 87; De Caro 1994, 179.

Black triclinium 43, south of the tablinum

- Birth of Adonis: H 1390; HBr pl. 127; Rizzo 1929, pl. 120; Richardson 1955, pl. 25; *Peinture* 1993, 2, fig. 191b; *PPM* 4 (1993) 918, fig. 108.
- Minos and Scylla: H 1337; HBr pl. 128; *PPM* 4 (1993) 927, fig. 130.

- Figures in the upper zone: Richardson 1955, pl. 8.1; *PPM* 4 (1993) 918–19, figs. 105, 109.

VI xv 1/2, Casa dei Vettii

White triclinium (e), south of the atrium

- Figures in the upper zone, Jupiter, Danaë, Leda, dancing satyrs and maenads: HBr text 1, fig. 14 and pl. 46; Rizzo 1929, pl. 23; Schefold 1962, pl. 86; Kraus and von Matt 1973, fig. 301; *PPM* 5 (1994) 488–92, figs. 30, 31, 33, 35.

VI xvi 7/38, Casa degli Amorini Dorati

Exedra G, south of the atrium

- Thetis in the forge of Hephaestus: Schefold 1962, pls. 43, 94.1; Seiler 1992, figs. 188, 190; *PPM* 5 (1994) 786, fig. 131.

VI xvii (Ins. Occ.) 42–44, Casa di Alessandro e Rossane (Casa del Bracciale d'Oro)

Room 31

- Alexander and Roxane: Curtis 1988, 1.81–87, figs. 1–5 (A. De Caro); Zevi 1992, 259; *PPM* 6 (1996) 92, figs. 104a–c.
- Bacchus, Silenus, and a maenad: Pompeii Antiquarium P41658; Curtis 1988, 1.88, fig. 6 (A. De Caro); Zevi 1992, 258; *PPM* 6 (1996) 80–83, figs. 83–86.
- Tondo with maenad and satyr: Pompeii Antiquarium P20555.

VII ii 6, Domus Terenti Neonis

Exedra north of the atrium ("tablinum")

- Amorino embracing psyche: S 395; MN 9195; *Collezioni* 1986, 152; Guillaud and Guillaud 1990, fig. 394; *PPM* 6 (1996) 487, fig. 10.

VII iv 31/51, Casa dei Capitelli Colorati

West ala

- Apollo and Daphne: H 211; HBr pl. 133.1; Richardson 1955, pl. 27.2; *Peinture* 1993, 1, fig. 75; *PPM* 6 (1996) 1005, fig. 12.

Room c, east of eastern andron

- Figures in the upper zone:
  Danaë: H 117b; Schefold 1962, pl. 106; *PPM* 6 (1996) 1022, fig. 32.
  Concordia (Fortuna): H 945; Schefold 1962, pl. 107; *PPM* 6 (1996) 1015, fig. 25.

VII vii 5, Casa di Trittolemo

Room n, east of the peristyle

- Arrival of Venus at Cythera: S 312; HBr pl. 191.

VII ix 4–12, Macellum

West wall

- Io and Argus: H 131; HBr pl. 53; Rizzo 1929, pl. 42; Richardson 1955, pls. 27.1, 30.4; Schefold 1962, pl. 13.2; Ling 1991, 130, fig. 133; *Peinture* 1993, 2, fig. 260b; *PPM* 7 (1997) 346–47, figs. 25–26.
- Floating groups and figures in architecture: HBr text 2.35, fig. 9; Richardson 1955, pl. 30.5; Eschebach 1978, figs. 43, 56 (misidentified); *PPM* 7 (1997) 341–45, figs. 19, 21–24.

North wall

- Penelope and Ulysses: H 1332; HBr pl. 54; Rizzo 1929, pl. 52; Richardson 1955, pls. 26, 30.3, 31.4; Ragghianti 1963, pl. 42; Ling 1991, 131, fig. 136; *PPM* 7 (1997) 337–39, figs. 13–15.

VII x 3/14, Casa della Caccia Nuova

Tablinum

- Bacchus discovering Ariadne: H 1236; MN 111484; Richardson 1955, pl. 31.3 (detail); Schefold 1962, pl. 167.2; *PPM* 7 (1997) 409, fig. 50.

Triclinium s, east of the peristyle

- Busts of Bacchus and a maenad: H 385; Sommer negative 11918.

VIII vi 37, Casa delle Pareti Rosse

Room b, first room west of the atrium

- Nymph and Silenus (or Polyphemus and Galatea): Schefold 1962, pl. 118; Eschebach 1978, fig. 192; *PPM* 8 (1998) 633, fig. 26.
- Mars and Venus: Schefold 1962, pls. 5.1, 119.1; Eschebach 1978, fig. 191; *Peinture* 1993, 2, fig. 299; *PPM* 8 (1998) 626, fig. 13.

Room c, second room west of the atrium

- Punishment of Marsyas: HBr text 1.250, fig. 75; Schefold 1962, pl. 119.2; *Peinture* 1993, 2, fig. 301; *PPM* 8 (1998) 643, fig. 46.
- Apollo Citharoedus and Muse: HBr pl. 183; *Peinture* 1993, 2, figs. 300a, b; *PPM* 8 (1998) 640, fig. 39.

VIII vii 28, Tempio di Iside

Ecclesiasterion

- Io, Argus, and Mercury: H 135; MN 9548; HBr pl. 57; Rizzo 1929, pl. 80; *MdPA* 1941 (Elia), pl. A; *Alla ricerca di Iside* 1992, pl. 14; *PPM* 8 (1998) 825, fig. 188.
- Arrival of Io in Egypt: H 138; MN 9558; HBr pl. 56; Rizzo 1929, pl. 79; *MdPA* 1941 (Elia), pl. B; Richardson 1955, pls. 29,

31.2, 31.5; *Alla ricerca di Iside* 1992, pl. 10 and p. 22; De Caro 1994, 133; *PPM* 8 (1998) 837, fig. 206.

IX iii 5, Casa di Marco Lucrezio

South ala 8

- Psyches: H 835, 839, 840; MN 9346, 9345, 9344.

Unidentified Buildings

- Black-ground dado panel with recumbent satyr: MN 8605; de Franciscis 1963, pl. 29; Guillaud and Guillaud 1990, fig. 281.
- Dado panel with psyche: H 837; MN 8514; *Pompeji: Leben und Kunst* 1973, 181, no. 248; Ward-Perkins and Claridge 1978, 26 and no. 135 (companion to MN 8516, 9318).
- Dado panel with amorino: H 723; MN 8516; *Pompeji: Leben und Kunst* 1973, 180, no. 246 (companion to MN 8514, 9318).
- Dado panel with amorino with syrinx: H 722; MN 9318 (companion to MN 8514, 8516).

HERCULANEUM

V 35, Casa del Gran Portale

Diaeta 6

- Tragic masks and mask of Oceanus: *Peinture* 1993, 1, pls. 139–40.

Unidentified Buildings

- Amorino and floating figure of a woman: H 724, 1930; MN 9323; Herbig 1962, pl. 22.

STABIAE

Edifizio di San Marco

Long loggia with Planisphere of the Seasons

- Figures on the ceiling: Elia 1957, 21, 29.

Ramp connecting the two levels of the complex

- Gorgoneion: Elia 1957, 51.

Diaeta of Perseus

- Perseus: Elia 1957, 49; de Franciscis 1978, fig. 183; Guillaud and Guillaud 1990, fig. 314; *Peinture* 1993, 1, pl. 167.
- Iphigenia in Tauris: Elia 1957, pl. 18; de Franciscis 1978, fig. 183.

BOSCOREALE

Villa in Contrada Giuliana

• Bacchus and Silenus: London, BM; *BMC* 1933, 23, pl. 7; Fröhlich 1991, pl. 51.3.

The Iphigenia Painter

This painter was identified, and his style described, in *Pompeii: The Casa dei Dioscuri and Its Painters* (Richardson 1955, 145–52), where a considerable body of work was attributed to him. There was work in the Casa di Diadumeno, the Casa del Balcone Pensile, the Casa del Poeta Tragico, the Villa di Diomede, the Casa dei Dioscuri, the Casa degli Epigrammi, and the Casa del Menandro. There were also paintings in the Museo Nazionale in Naples from unidentified buildings and the suggestion that he might have done work at Stabiae. Almost all these attributions were correct; only some of the portraits and a series of busts at Stabiae seem now to call for reattribution. On the other hand, the list of his works needs to be considerably extended.

In the Casa del Menandro he painted all the subject pictures that survive, including the eccentric Punishment of Dirce. In addition to the pictures earlier ascribed to him, the three illustrations of the fall of Troy in the single ala are unquestionably his work, and so are the decorations of the semicircular exedras on the south side of the peristyle with an Actaeon and a Venus Pompeiana. The Perseus and Andromeda in the beautiful green exedra on the north side of the peristyle also is clearly by him, although it lacks the characteristic rounded solidity of his heads.

In the Casa di Marco Lucrezio Frontone he was responsible for the paintings in the cubiculum south of the tablinum, not only the Narcissus and the Micon and Pero but the busts, notably one of Mercury with an awkwardly drawn petasus set high and askew. Narcissus seems to have been a subject he was fond of, perhaps because a suitable semirecumbent figure came easy to him; one sees it elsewhere. He was also fond of Ariadne Abandoned as a subject and painted a version of this in the same room in the Casa di Diadumeno from which the pictures in the Museo Nazionale were removed and another similar to this in composition but reversed, in looking-glass image and lacking the staffage figures of the opposite side, and still another in the Villa di Diomede, where it was together with a Narcissus and a Pan uncovering a sleeping Hermaphroditus, which unfortunately is too ruined for attribution, except that the palette in the three pictures is remarkably consistent. He also painted another Apollo and Daphne following the composition of that in the Casa dei Dioscuri but somewhat simplified in the Casa di Marco Lucrezio; its companion may have been yet another Narcissus (Giulio Minervini, *BullNap* 4.80).

He was the painter of three erotic pictures in a room in the Casa del Centenario, a Hercules with amorini and two symplegmata, and he painted the erotic scene in the Casa di Cecilio Giocondo. Although the style of this picture is somewhat unusual, the woman's hand is characteristic of his work, as is the volume of her head. He also painted the *Cacator cave malum* from the caupona IX vii 21/22 and the scenes of drinking parties in the Casa degli Amanti Casti, IX xii 6/7. The lararium painting in the service atrium of the Casa dei Vettii is a highly characteristic work, and the picture of the Three Graces from an unidentified house, VI Ins. Occ. (Masseria di Cuomo), about which I had doubts in my first list of attributions, now seems to me unquestionably his work, as do its companion pieces of Phrixus and Helle and Pan uncovering a sleeping Hermaphroditus.

He painted a Mars and Venus in the Casa degli Epigrammi, now much ruined but still readily identifiable and a companion piece to the Danaë and the Fishermen. An old photograph (DAI 56.1217) shows it in much better condition. The third picture in this room has perished and is recorded only in a drawing in Presuhn (Presuhn 1878, 2, pl. 9); it was of Ariadne Abandoned, the same composition that this painter was especially fond of, almost a duplicate of MN 9047 (H 1228).

Perhaps his oddest work is the Arrival of Io in Egypt from the Casa del Duca d'Aumale. It is a very poor piece of work in every way but shows close affinities with the fall of Troy pictures in the Casa del Menandro, and the composition follows closely that of the Io Painter's treatment of the subject. It must be a very early work produced under difficult conditions on a bad day.

With such a great range of pictures in so many houses, one ought to be able to generalize about this painter's place in Pompeian artistic and economic life. First of all, he never painted in Herculaneum, so far as we know, so he was not in great demand. Second, wherever he painted he seems to have done all the figure work in a room, leaving nothing to assistants, but neither do we find him working as an assistant. He painted almost the whole of the Casa del Menandro and most of the important rooms in the Casa del Poeta Tragico, both important houses, and he painted single fine rooms in the Casa dei Dioscuri, the Casa degli Epigrammi, the Casa di Polibio, the Casa di M. Lucrezio Frontone, and the Villa di Diomede, all fine houses. His other work was in rooms of secondary importance in fine houses (Casa del Centenario) and in houses of more modest condition (Casa di Diadumeno, Casa del Balcone Pensile). He seems to have been well regarded but perhaps not admired; he was not above painting in a latrine in a caupona. It is odd to note that in the Casa del Menandro he produced admirable major efforts in the exedra of Menander and the yellow triclinium, subtle atmospheric pictures in the green exedra, and some very ordinary work in the ala and semicircular exedras of the peristyle. This discrepancy may help to define his place: he was capable but erratic. He was good at familiar compositions and tended to repeat these wherever he had the opportunity: Narcissus, Ariadne Abandoned, the Nest of Amorini. When he was called upon to do something outside his usual repertory, his work tends to be fumbling and awkward, as though he had not thought out the composition or considered the space and was simply experimenting, usually rather unsuccessfully, although the Menander portrait is an interesting accomplishment; perhaps for that he made preliminary sketches.

Thus, his finest work, the polychrome exedra (p) of the Casa dei Vettii, takes us by surprise; it hardly seems possible that it can be entirely his, although it shows a fine range of his characteristic forms. In the Daedalus and Pasiphaë we note the characteristic roundness of the heads, the clawlike hands of Daedalus and the attendant in the left background, and the way Pasiphaë's hand is posed and painted. But the statuesqueness of Pasiphaë's body marks a departure from his usual practice, as does the shimmering gauzy quality of her drapery. It is only when we consider the little Icarus intent on his carpentry in the lower left corner that we see that this must be his work. Not only is the expression of tensely focused interest a hallmark of this man's work, but he has the curiously spatulate feet and sharp heel that he likes to paint. The Punishment of Ixion, on the east wall, is his finest picture, and the bull-chested monumentality of Mercury with his broad shoulders and huge hands and feet tends to blind the viewer to the weakness of the drawing of those hands and the ineptness of the composition as a whole. The painter was clearly making an effort to show improvement in his hands and only partially succeeding, and he did not dare to make Ixion's wheel the central focus of his picture, although it ought to be, while the role of the heavily shrouded figure in yellow crouching in the foreground is obscure.

When we come to the third picture in this exedra, Bacchus discovering

Ariadne, we have less difficulty recognizing it as his work, although flaking has seriously damaged the figures of Bacchus and most of his thiasus and there may have been a general loss of overpainting that would have brought this better into harmony with the other pictures in this room. But the rounded head and sharp eye of the winged genius protecting Ariadne, the hand of Ariadne, and the amorino in the lower right corner are all in his usual manner and vocabulary of forms. Whether he painted the floating groups of satyrs and maenads in the side panels I have not been able to decide, but he certainly painted the Pan and Hermaphroditus over the door to the adjacent ala.

Group A: Early Work?

The heads tend to be large and smoothly ovoid with small and crowded features, the necks excessively short, the torsos heavy, the arms and legs short and slender, the hands and feet disproportionately large and clumsy. These proportions, although standard for this painter, are not always maintained. In a few instances the figure is drawn with almost mannerist distortion: the hips heavy, the upper torso short and light, the legs elongated and exaggerated. A case in point is the Sacrifice of Iphigenia, from which he takes his name, but in that picture different figures are drawn with different proportions.

The heads tend to be large, with long faces, broad at the corners of the jaw but tapering to the chin. In profile the skull appears somewhat longer than in full face. The crown of the head is well domed but usually not exaggerated. The eyes are distinctively small, although the brows are often excessively heavy. The line of the eyebrow closely follows the curve of the eye and is drawn down to the outer corner of the eye. To indicate expression the inner point of the brow sometimes turns up. The eyes have a narrowed look, the lower lid closing high over the ball and given a deep shadow, above which the whites seem startlingly bright and the pupils staring. In profile and three-quarters face the eye has a sharp outer corner, drawn somewhat down, sometimes exaggeratedly so. The nose is usually small and straight, narrow and tight at the nostrils, sharply pointed at the tip, but in profile it is sometimes given character by a pronounced bump high on its ridge. There is almost always a sharp, strong shadow under the tip of the nose and a distinct light along the nose. The mouth is generally very small and tight, with a somewhat pursed and sour expression. The upper lip tends to be short and in profile jutting, with the furrow from the nose well marked. The chin is almost always of exaggerated roundness, a quality frequently emphasized by a small crescent-shaped shadow under the lower lip. The cheeks are firm, sometimes slightly fleshy, especially in women and boys. The ears have a pronounced, often thickened helix, but the lobe is usually almost completely suppressed, and form is seldom indicated in the interior of the ear. Not infrequently the helix shows an unnatural deviation toward the lower point of attachment. The hair follows the shape of the skull, carefully arranged in the case of women, often a tousled mass of short locks in the case of men; men sometimes have a disheveled pompadour along the forehead.

There is little to remark about the torsos. The muscles of athletic men are usually somewhat overdrawn. The navel, when it appears, is always unusually large, indicated by a crescent-shaped shadow. In seated and bending figures the navel and belly fold are high, coming at or above the waist. The figures of youths and maidens seem almost abnormally soft, as though a layer of fat just beneath the skin covered and concealed the frame. Yet the main lines of the body, waist, breast, and linea alba, are always fairly clearly marked. When a figure leans on one arm, the shoulder is pulled in very tight to the body and the head is distinctly rounded. The breasts of the women are high and flattened; the nipples are prominent and carefully indicated in the case of both women and men.

The hands are of two distinct types, one with pointed and clawlike fingers, the other with rounded or even squarish fingertips. The structure of the hand is poorly studied in both. The passage between thumb and forefinger is always unnaturally deep, so that the palm of the hand is thick and short. Fingers and thumb are usually exaggeratedly long; the line of the thumb is generally a decided S-curve, while the fingers are only slightly curved and stiff in appearance. The painter has a peculiar trick of turning up the tips of the last two fingers; this is almost his hallmark. The least finger often sticks out oddly when the hand is closed and in these cases is pointed. The wrist is usually distinct and well understood; occasionally, when the hand is seen from the back or the inside profile, it is somewhat willowy and indistinct. In profile the heel of the hand is apt to be unnaturally soft and thick. When a figure leans on one arm, the action of the muscles in the hand is not well understood and the hand appears relaxed and weak. Similarly, when a hand grasps something, the action is never effectively conveyed; the fingers are too inert, the knuckles not given proper articulation.

The feet of these figures are as distinctive as the hands. In profile the inside of the foot has a curiously flattened heel with a sharp, almost angular turn. The great toe is short, and the next not only projects well beyond it but has a distinct bow, so that it appears unnaturally large. From the outside the foot has a spatulate look, the toes spreading and sloping down from a prominent great toe to a very flat least toe. When viewed from the front and the weight is on the foot, the ankle bone is given great prominence both inside and out and the foot spreads and flattens at the toes. In these feet the least toe often seems out of line with the rest.

The painter's command of drapery is poor, and no emphasis is ever put on it. The forms of the folds and scarves are simple and stylized. Little attempt is made to distinguish the various stuffs, and floating veils are as stiff as awnings. In long skirts the tendency is to have long reeded folds, fanning slightly. Crushed drapery is poorly handled, and there is only the vaguest approximation of locking folds.

When dealing with large scenes requiring depth of landscape or space in the background the painter is unable to convey the proper recession of space. His landscape jumps from scale to scale inconsistently or fades into opaque mist just beyond the figures. In compositions of many figures he divides the space artificially by curious boxlike architectural elements of no special logic or arrangement and groups his scene in twos and threes in this arbitrary setting. Beyond the plane of the action the background is filled with simple architecture or massed trees and sky.

The painter prefers a strong palette. Male figures are laid in in dark yellow over broad and cursive red-brown drawing, and the forms are built up by application of darks. The sunburnt hue of male figures appears in a variety of gradations, from very dark and swarthy (so Mars and soldiers) through a pale effeminacy hardly darker than the flesh of the women. The lights on swarthy flesh are strong and glistening. The final touches, outlines of forms in half-shadow, accentuation of features and expression, are carried out in black. The flesh of women has a slightly chalky quality that makes their hair, brows, and eyes seem unnaturally dark. Thus their gaze is often very intense and piercing. Neither men nor women have much color in cheeks and lips, although not infrequently their ears are startlingly pink. There is hardly any attempt to make the figures stand on a plane in front of the background by a change in palette; the one case where this seems to happen, the Sacrifice of Iphigenia, is suspect on other grounds.

The figures show firm outlines, carefully drawn even in such details as the toes. The main forms of flesh are regularly rendered in short, oblique strokes over which lights and shadows are carefully applied in longer strokes.

Thus, lights and shadows either have very sharp edges or seem hatched along their edges because of the underpainting. Eyes, ears, the tips of noses, and so on, are regularly gone over with black to make the edges crisp; this retouching is done rapidly and skillfully with medium-fine brushes and in strokes generally of some length. For the most part the drapery is laid in with large brushes and long strokes; rarely is there any sign that the painter labored over it. The backgrounds are, on the whole, casually painted but in greater detail than is usually the case in Pompeian painting. Architecture is painted in smoothly lit and shadowed planes according to formula, foliage with stippled effect to convey the shape and multiplicity of the leaves, although not the light on them, stones and water with attention to their form and surface. The shadows thrown by figures are rarely indicated and then only roughly, and the artist has difficulty with perspective in showing furniture and figures at a middle distance.

There is a wide range in the painter's use of space in this period. However, most of the figures are arranged in closely knit two- or three-figure groups that are assembled so as not to interfere with one another or overlap. The ground in front of the figures may be either shallow or relatively deep. When it is shallow, little space is left above the heads of the figures at the top of the picture unless there is a necessity to include distant views. When it is deep, considerable space is left at the top. In either case in this period the painter's individual figures are doll-like and seem to move stiffly in their attitudes and gestures. In addition, each group of figures is isolated, and there is almost no tension in the composition.

Group B: Middle Period?

The heads in this group are more nearly correct in proportion but occasionally a trifle large or a trifle small, as though the painter were aware of a tendency to err in this proportion but not always sure in his touch. The neck continues to be extremely short. The torso is generally of a good proportion, but the arms continue to be too light and ineffectual. The legs, on the other hand, are better formed than those in group A. Hands and feet are only rarely out of scale with the rest, and then not seriously.

The forms for the most part continue in the pattern established for group A, but the following particulars may be noted: The essential forms of the head continue the same; the face is perhaps a little shorter, but still broad at the corners of the jaw and tapering to the chin. The dome of the skull is still deep and well rounded. The eyes, although the form continues the same, are less emphatically pointed at the corners; the brows are not drawn down so hard at the outer corner, and the lower lid is not allowed to close too high on the ball. On the other hand, the shadow on the lower lid is still overemphasized. The forms of nose and mouth have not changed. The chin is still hard and round, the cheeks still apt to be fleshy. The ears still draw our attention, still have a heavy, fleshy helix, still suppress the lobe. The navel is still high and large, and the belly fold high. There is much less emphasis on, and exaggeration of, the musculature of male figures, but the painter's failure to understand the attachment of the arm at the shoulder continues. The hands are of the established types, although they are seldom so far out of drawing as they are in group A. The passage between thumb and forefinger is still excessively deep, and the articulation of the knuckles in hands that grasp objects, still faulty. The trick of turning up the last two fingers of a hand that gestures can be observed in several works of this group. The feet continue in the familiar forms, somewhat overdrawn, often decidedly spatulate. The enlarged and bowed second toe of feet seen from the inside is found several times. The painter's command of drapery is still poor, but it has improved. He still prefers simple heavy garments with skirts that can be rendered in reeded folds, but he now makes some attempt to distinguish between types of stuff and to render crushed and transparent drapery. His veils now seem to float, his folds to pull.

The palette changes a little in this group. The male figures are still dark and sunburnt, and the base painting of their flesh is still in dark yellow, but the finished flesh tones are somewhat warmer and ruddier than in group A. The painter is using more red in the construction and relying less on finishing the painting and giving it crispness and expression with black overdrawing. There is still overdrawing, especially around the eyes and in the hands and feet, but it is less conspicuous, more an organic part of the painting. So, too, the lights are on the whole subtler and less streaky although still frequently brilliant, especially on the faces. The women continue to seem somewhat chalky in contrast to the men, although this too seems muted. The colors are no longer predominantly browns, yellows, and whites with touches of clear green, blue, and red. Instead the background has been darkened and made mysterious with deep grayed blues and greens, while the clothing of the figures is richer in variety, and the attributes and odd bits of stage dressing, with their touches of color or natural sheen, are more carefully studied and made to count more in the finished composition.

As already observed, in this group there is less overdrawing in the Iphigenia Painter's work and the lights are better constructed. The brushwork is also smoother and more fluid, although the painter still tends to build the flesh in short oblique strokes, the finish more refined, the shadows more carefully drawn around convex surfaces. The emphasis is more on form and less on outline; the painter permits himself passages of almost true chiaroscuro. So also in his attention to differences in drapery and his attempt to translate these textures by varying his brushwork one notes his progress, however modest, as a technician.

In this period the ground before the figures is always very shallow, and the figures themselves are close to the viewer or at most in the middle distance and not so far away as they tended to be in group A. They fill the space to about four-fifths of the height of the picture, having space above them for the development of landscape or architecture, but as the painter now prefers a misty background, he is content with only the suggestion of mountain and forest. He has now abandoned the complicated compositions of many figures of group A in favor of simple groupings of two or three figures in compositional pyramids and crossed diagonals, all more or less open.

Group C: Late Work?

The heads are still large for the bodies but less frequently ovoid in outline, and the features are better spaced. The necks are still short and thick, the torsos short and sturdy, the arms short and often too slender, the legs in better proportion. The painter is fumbling in the proportions of the hands; usually they are much too small and delicate, but occasionally they are much too large. The feet are large, sometimes uncommonly large, and often emphasized.

The crown of the skull is still deeply domed and well rounded, the face large and oval or heart-shaped. The eyes continue in the character of the eyes of group A, but they are somewhat larger, and the shadow on the lower lid is rather lighter. The eyes are apt to be small, narrow, and elongated, with the lower lid closing high over the ball and given a deep shadow that makes the white seem startlingly bright and staring. The outer corner of the eye and sometimes the inner are sharply pointed; the outer corner is often drawn down, a point that is emphasized by the line of the eyebrow, which follows the arch of the eye closely and draws sharply down at the outer corner. The brows are sometimes almost a hairline, sometimes strong and thick, especially close to the nose. The space between the eyes is always wide. The nose is apt to be large, bluntly pointed at the tip, strongly marked with shadow at the nostrils. The wings of the nose are frequently emphasized with overdrawing. The mouths are small and tight, of a sour and dissatisfied expression. The upper lip is generally somewhat jutting and shadowed; the lower lip is plump, often marked with a small highlight. The chin is always short, prominent and round, emphasized by a crescent-shaped shadow below the lower lip and sometimes highlighted. The cheekbones are rather high, the cheeks distinctly fleshy, especially in women. The ears are of good size with a thick, fleshy helix but almost no lobe and no indication of form in the interior of the ear. The hair is massed evenly around the skull, generally rendered as somewhat crinkled waves with loose strands along the line of the brow.

The bodies are rectangular, broad at the shoulders and hips, only slightly narrowed at the waist. The musculature of athletic men is apt to be overdrawn. The bodies of youths and maidens, on the other hand, show a certain softness, as though the frames were covered with a layer of fat just under the skin. Only the main lines of the body, waist and linea alba, are clearly indicated. The shoulders are rounded, sometimes slightly heavy. When a figure leans on one arm, the shoulder is pulled in tight toward the base of the throat. When it is shown, the navel is always high, nearly at the waistline, and emphasized by a deep crescent-shaped shadow. When a torso is bent at the waist, there is always at least a slight belly fold.

The hands are regularly much too small but occasionally very large, as though the painter were aware of error in their proportion and erred in the other direction in his effort to correct it. The fingers are of two types still, sharply pointed and clawlike or blunt and rounded. Both types appear together in most of the paintings of this group. The passage between thumb and forefinger is almost always exaggeratedly deep, and the thumb itself turns out in a decided S-curve. The palm of the hand is apt to be thick, and when the ball is shown it is heavy. The painter has a trick of turning up or in the ends of the last two fingers of a gesturing hand that is almost a hallmark of his work. The wrist is well understood from some angles and when the hand is in certain positions, but from the back it is always poorly defined and in the inside profile it is always too thick. When a figure leans on one arm, the hand appears too relaxed; the action of the muscles of the fingers is misunderstood. So also when a hand grasps some object that action is not effectively conveyed.

The feet are very distinctive. They are large, sometimes conspicuously so, and almost always rather meticulously drawn. In inside profile the heel is curiously flattened and the turn is steep, almost angular. The great toe is short, and the second toe not only projects well beyond it but has a distinct bow, so that it seems abnormally large. From the outside the foot has a spatulate look, the toes spreading out and down from a prominent great toe. Viewed from the front, when weight is on the foot, the ankle bone is brought into prominence both inside and out, and the toes spread and flatten. In these feet the technique of foreshortening and the shape of the least toe are very characteristic.

The painter spends little study on drapery. It is arranged in broad, simple forms, and there is little attempt to differentiate the qualities of different stuffs. Three basic patterns can be distinguished in the drapery: close, reeded folds, broad, flat folds, and crushed and looped folds. But all three are stiff and unconvincing. The reeded folds are too close and regular, the flat folds too angular and with little attempt at rendering locked folds, the crushed drapery bunched and wadded rather than clinging.

The palette is almost entirely of relatively light, bright colors, a strong palette, but one not suited to effects of chiaroscuro. The figures are drawn in bright red-brown, the male figures laid in in a warm golden yellow, the characteristic color of this painter's flesh. The forms are then built up by the application of darker red, yellow, and brown, brushed rather thick in short, oblique strokes. The finished forms are accented with black outlines, especially along the shadow side, and white highlights brushed rather thin with medium-thick or thin brushes in long, crisp lines. The athletic male figures emerge a deep, ruddy, sunburnt hue, while boys and young men may have nearly the chalky flesh of women. The predominant colors are yellow, white, and brown with black accents, but the painter is fond of pale, clear green in drapery and background and occasionally uses a rich red-violet or crimson.

There is little variety in the painter's use of space in this group. The figures are arranged singly, or more commonly in close-knit groups of two or three that are then disposed so as just to overlap but not interfere with one another. The ground in front of the figures is very shallow; their feet almost touch the lower border, and almost no space is left at the sides. At the top is more space, but at most only to a depth of about one-fifth of the whole picture field, and this space is filled completely, or almost completely, with foliage or architecture. Closed tightly in this space, the figures seem stiff and doll-like, their gestures frozen and theatrical, their facial expressions a stilted caricature. The movement is artificial and formulaic, weak and without tension.

→ *Works* ←

→ *Group A: Early Work?* ←

POMPEII

I ix 1, Casa del Bell'Impluvio

Cubiculum 11

• Erotic symplegma: PPM 1 (1990) 938, fig. 31.

I x 4, Casa del Menandro

East ala

• Death of Laocoon: Maiuri 1933, pl. 4; Guillaud and Guillaud 1990, fig. 268; *PPM* 2 (1990) 285, fig. 68.

• The Trojan Horse: Maiuri 1933, pl. 5; Ragghianti 1963, pl. 69; Guillaud and Guillaud 1990, fig. 270; *PPM* 2 (1990) 281, fig. 62.

• Rape of Cassandra: Maiuri 1933, pl. 6; Ragghianti 1963, 139; Guillaud and Guillaud 1990, fig. 272; *PPM* 2 (1990) 277, fig. 56; Ling 1991, pl. 11C; *Peinture* 1993, 1, pl. 32.

• Amorini in side panels: *PPM* 2 (1990) 278–86, figs. 57, 61, 63, 66, 69.

Oecus 11, west of the tablinum

• Maenad with the infant Bacchus: *PPM* 2 (1990) 301, fig. 94.

• Perseus and Andromeda: Maiuri 1933, pl. 8; *PPM* 2 (1990) 314, fig. 114.

• Satyr with amorino: *PPM* 2 (1990) 309, fig. 106.

Triclinium 15, east of the peristyle

• Freeing of Andromeda: Maiuri 1933, fig. 77; Ragghianti 1963, pl. 71; *PPM* 2 (1990) 322, fig. 129.

• Perseus in Cepheus's palace: *PPM* 2 (1990) 320, fig. 126.

• Punishment of Dirce: Maiuri 1933, fig. 78; *PPM* 2 (1990) 327, fig. 133.

• Muses in side panels: *PPM* 2 (1990) 325–28, figs. 132, 134–36; *Peinture* 1993, 2, fig. 64b.

II ii 2, Casa di Loreio Tiburtino

Cubiculum b, west of the atrium

• Venus Piscatrix: *PPM* 3 (1991) 51, fig. 13.

• Narcissus: *PPM* 3 (1991) 55, fig. 21.

• Warrior ephebes: *PPM* 3 (1991) 50–53, figs. 11, 15, 18, 19, 22.

II iii 3, Casa della Venere in Conchiglia

Oecus 10

• Apollo and Daphne: *PPM* 3 (1991) 147, fig. 55.

• Figures in architecture: *PPM* 3 (1991) 146–50, figs. 54, 56, 58.

Oecus 14

• Leda: *PPM* 3 (1991) 166, fig. 82; *Peinture* 1993, 2, fig. 125b.

• Meleager and Atalanta: *PPM* 3 (1991) 172, fig. 90.

• Amorini in side panels: *PPM* 3 (1991) 163–71, figs. 78, 79, 84, 89.

V ii 14

• Embarcation of Helen: MN 119690; Schefold 1962, pl. 171.2; Ragghianti 1963, pl. 70; *PPM* 3 (1991) 851, fig. 3.

• Ulysses and Circe: MN 119689; Schefold 1962, pl. 171.1; *PPM* 3 (1991) 852, fig. 5.

VI ix 1, Casa del Duca d'Aumale

• Arrival of Io in Egypt: H 139; MN 9555; HBr pl. 58.2; Curtius 1929, fig. 129; de Franciscis 1963, pl. 46; Stenico 1963, fig. 106; Ward-Perkins and Claridge 1978, 179, no. 177; *Collezioni* 1986, 97.

VIII iv 4, Casa di Olconio Rufo

Ala 9

• Apollo and Daphne: H 209; *Peinture* 1993, 2, fig. 295.

IX iii 5, Casa di Marco Lucrezio

Room 21

• Apollo and Daphne: H 207; MN 9536; *Collezioni* 1986, 159.

IX vii 22

Latrine

• *Cacator cave malum:* MN 112285; Ward-Perkins and Claridge 1978, 82; *Collezioni* 1986, 324; Frölich 1991, pl. 10.1.

IX xii 6, Casa degli Amanti Casti

Triclinium

• Banquet scenes: Atti del Convegno Internazionale, *Ercolano 1738–1988: 250 anni di ricerca archeologica* (Rome 1992), pls. 157, 159, 160.1.

Environs, Via dei Sepolcri, Villa di Diomede

Unidentified room of upper story

• Narcissus: H 1351; MN 9383; Rizzo 1929, pl. 128.1.

• Ariadne Abandoned: H 1228; MN 9047; *RdSP* 2 (1988) 61, fig. 4.

➔ *Group B: Middle Period?* ⬅

POMPEII

V i 26, Casa di Cecilio Giocondo

Peristyle

- Erotic symplegma: MN 110569; Marcadé 1965, 15; Marini 1971, 91; Grant 1975, 156–57; *Collezioni* 1986, 345; Guillaud and Guillaud 1990, fig. 385; *PPM* 3 (1991) 605, fig. 59; De Caro 1994, 160.

V iv a, Casa di M. Lucrezio Frontone

Cubiculum 6

- Narcissus: Rizzo 1929, pl. 126; Kraus and von Matt 1973, fig. 257; Eschebach 1978, fig. 129; *PPM* 3 (1991) 1005, fig. 74; *Peinture* 1993, 1, pl. 45; Peters 1993, pl. 15.
- Micon and Pero: *PPM* 3 (1991) 1008, fig. 81; *Peinture* 1993, 2, fig. 159a; Peters 1993, fig. 246.
- Amorini: *PPM* 3 (1991) 1004–8, figs. 73, 75, 79, 80; Peters 1993, figs. 218–21.
- Tondi with busts: Eschebach 1978, fig. 131; Ling 1991, pl. 14A; *PPM* 3 (1991) 1001, figs. 69, 70; *Peinture* 1993, 2, fig. 158b; Peters 1993, pls. 16, 17.

VI viii 3/5, Casa del Poeta Tragico

Tablinum

- Admetus receiving the oracle: H 1158; MN 9026; HBr pl. 13; Richardson 1955, pl. 47.2; de Franciscis 1963, pl. 45; *Collezioni* 1986, 198; Ling 1991, fig. 127.

Peristyle

- Sacrifice of Iphigenia: H 1304; MN 9112; HBr pl. 15; Curtius 1929, pl. 5; Rizzo 1929, pl. 97; Richardson 1955, pl. 47.1; de Franciscis 1963, pl. 35; Ragghianti 1963, pl. 68; Stenico 1963, fig. 87; *Collezioni* 1986, 204 and p. 66; Guillaud and Guillaud 1990, figs. 291–92; Ling 1991, fig. 139; *Peinture* 1993, 1, fig. 47; *PPM* 4 (1993) 552, fig. 47; De Caro 1994, 183.

Triclinium 15, east of the peristyle

- Theseus abandoning Ariadne: H 1218; HBr pl. 16; Rizzo 1929, pl. 39; Richardson 1955, pls. 46.2, 50.3; Eschebach 1978, fig. 135; *Peinture* 1993, 1, pl. 50; *PPM* 4 (1993) 576, fig. 94.

- Nest of amorini: H 821; HBr text 1.26, fig. 5; Rizzo 1929, pls. 121–22; Richardson 1955, pls. 45.2, 50.6; *PPM* 4 (1993) 569, fig. 81.
- Aeneas and Dido (?): H 254; HBr text 1.27, fig. 6; *PPM* 4 (1993) 581, fig. 102.
- Seasons: H 977, 986, 990; *PPM* 4 (1993) 571–79, figs. 84, 88, 97, 100.

VI ix 6/7, Casa dei Dioscuri

Cubiculum 44, north of the tablinum

- Apollo and Daphne: H 208; HBr pl. 132; Rizzo 1929, pl. 106; Richardson 1955, pl. 44; *PPM* 4 (1993) 938, fig. 154.
- Silenus and the infant Bacchus: H 378; Richardson 1955, pl. 49.2; *PPM* 4 (1993) 935, fig. 148.

VI Ins. Occ., Unidentified House (Masseria di Cuomo)

- Three Graces: H 856b; MN 9231; HBr pl. 50; Curtius 1929, fig. 14; de Franciscis 1963, pl. 49; Ragghianti 1963, pl. 76; Seider 1968, 61; *Pompeji: Leben und Kunst* 1973, 271; Grant 1975, 10; *Collezioni* 1986, 99; Guillaud and Guillaud 1990, fig. 11.
- Phrixus and Helle: H 1253; MN 8889; Rizzo 1929, pl. 131; Ragghianti 1963, pl. 77; *Collezioni* 1986, 193.
- Perseus and Andromeda: H 1197; MN 8995; Rizzo 1929, pl. 132.
- Tondi with portrait busts ("Sappho" and companion): H 1420, 1422; MN 9084, 9085; Curtius 1929, pl. 11; Rizzo 1929, pls. 193.1, 193.2; Maiuri 1953, 100; Brion 1960, fig. 9; Ragghianti 1963, 131; Seider 1968, 40; Kraus and von Matt 1973, fig. 213; *Pompeji: Leben und Kunst* 1973, 270; *Collezioni* 1986, 231, 232, and p. 71; Guillaud and Guillaud 1990, figs. 52, 57; Ling 1991, fig. 169; *Peinture* 1993, 1, pl. 86; De Caro 1994, 188.

IX ii 5

Triclinium 3

- Micon and Pero: S 599; MN 115393; HBr pl. 161.

IX viii 3/6, Casa del Centenario

Cubiculum 43

- Hercules and amorini: S 498; Marcadé 1965, 7.
- Erotic symplegma: S 661; Marcadé 1965, 79; Grant 1975, 36.
- Erotic symplegma: S 661; Marcadé 1965, 126.

Unidentified Buildings

- Ariadne Abandoned: H 1228; MN 9047; *RP* 111.7; *RdSP* 2 (1988) 61.
- Ariadne Abandoned: H 1223; MN 9046; *RP* 112.2; *RdSP* 2 (1988) 67.
- Danaë on Seriphos: H 119; MN 9552; *RP* 11.2.
- Endymion: H 951; MN 9242.
- Tondo of busts of couple with infant Bacchus: H 370; MN 9281; Herbig 1962, pl. 18.
- Bust of Venus (fragment): MN 9181; Schefold 1962, pl. 158.
- Amorini: H 741, 742, 743, 745, 747, 748; MN 9203.
- Amorini: H 612, 626, 628, 626, 612; MN 9209.
- Amorino: H 730; MN 9233.
- Amorino: H 699; MN 9237; *Collezioni* 1986, 223.
- Amorini: H 642, 656, 661; MN 9238; Herbig 1962, pls. 5–7; *Collezioni* 1986, 119.
- Standing figure with Bacchic attributes (companion to MN 9273): MN 9272.
- Maenad (companion to MN 9272): H 463; MN 9273.

⇾ *Group C: Late Works?* ⇽

POMPEII

I x 4, Casa del Menandro

Peristyle, south wing

- Menander: Maiuri 1933, pl. 12; Richardson 1955, pls. 48.2, 50.5; Eschebach 1978, fig. 200; Guillaud and Guillaud 1990, fig. 273; *PPM* 2 (1990) 367, fig. 204; Ling 1991, pl. 14B; *Peinture* 1993, 1, pl. 33.
- Diana and Actaeon: Maiuri 1933, fig. 43; Guillaud and Guillaud 1990, fig. 274; *PPM* 2 (1990) 364, fig. 199.
- Venus Pompeiana: Maiuri 1933, fig. 45; *PPM* 2 (1990) 369, fig. 207; *Peinture* 1993, 1, pl. 35.

Yellow triclinium 19

- Satyr and maenad: Maiuri 1933, pl. 15; Richardson 1955, pl. 48.1; *PPM* 2 (1990) 360, fig. 194.
- Maenad with tragic mask: Maiuri 1933, fig. 84; *PPM* 2 (1990) 355, fig. 187.

I x 10/11, Casa degli Amanti

Triclinium 8

- Ceiling medallions: *PPM* 2 (1990) 479, fig. 58.

V i 18, Casa degli Epigrammi

Exedra o

- Danaë on Seriphos: S 77; MN 111212; Rizzo 1929, pl. 68; Richardson 1955, pls. 49.1, 50.2; Brion 1960, fig. 130; de Franciscis 1963, pl. 50; *Collezioni* 1986, 180; *PPM* 3 (1991) 557, fig. 37.
- Mars and Venus: S 139; *PPM* 3 (1991) 556, fig. 34.

V ii 1, Casa della Regina Margherita

Triclinium r

- Narcissus or Adonis: HBr pl. 233; *PPM* 3 (1991) 792, fig. 30; *Peinture* 1993, 2, fig. 152b.

VI vii 20/22, Casa dell'Argenteria

Tablinum

- Endymion: H 958 (= H 953); MN 9241; HBr pl. 135; *PPM* 4 (1993) 456, fig. 13.
- Narcissus: H 1363 (= H 1365); MN 9388; *Collezioni* 1986, 191; *PPM* 4 (1993) 455, fig. 11.

VI xv 1/2, Casa dei Vettii

Atriolum

- Lararium: HBr pl. 48; Rizzo 1929, pl. 199.2; Seider 1968, 54; Eschebach 1978, fig. 147; Fröhlich 1991, pl. 7; *Peinture* 1993, 1, pl. 59; *PPM* 5 (1994) 571, fig. 167.

Triclinium (polychrome exedra) p, east of the peristyle

- Daedalus and Pasiphaë: HBr pl. 38; Rizzo 1929, pl. 34; Ragghianti 1963, 124; Seider 1968, 63; Picard 1970, 78, fig. 52; Kraus and von Matt 1973, fig. 285; *Peinture* 1993, 1, fig. 70; *PPM* 5 (1994) 536, figs. 114–15.
- Punishment of Ixion: HBr pl. 39; Rizzo 1929, pl. 35; Ragghianti 1963, 123; Kraus and von Matt 1973, fig. 109; Eschebach 1978, fig. 149; *Peinture* 1993, 1, fig. 71; *PPM* 5 (1994) 538–39, figs. 118–19.
- Bacchus discovering Ariadne: HBr pl. 40; Curtius 1929, fig. 178; *PPM* 5 (1994) 540, fig. 120.
- Pan and Hermaphroditus: *PPM* 5 (1994) 542, figs. 123–24.

VII i 40, Casa di Cesio Blando

Atrium

- Tondo with busts (Hippolytus and Phaedra?): H 1247; HBr text 2.56, fig. 18; Schefold 1962, pl. 180.2; *PPM* 6 (1996) 391, fig. 24.

VII xii 26/27, Casa di Diadumeno

Room h, west of the atrium

- Aeneas and Dido (?): H 253; MN 111441; HBr pl. 18; Curtius 1929, fig. 29; Richardson 1955, pl. 46.1; *Collezioni* 1986, 164; *PPM* 7 (1997) 580, fig. 26.
- Nest of amorini: H 823; MN 111437; HBr pl. 17; Curtius 1929, fig. 28; Rizzo 1929, pl. 123; Richardson 1955, pls. 45.1, 50.1, 50.4; *Collezioni* 1986, 192; *PPM* 7 (1997) 576, fig. 17.
- Theseus abandoning Ariadne: H 1231; *RdSP* 2 (1988) 62, fig . 5; *PPM* 7 (1997) 571–72, figs. 10, 13.
- Tondo with head of a satyr: HBr text 1.117, fig. 30; Rizzo 1929, pl. 190.
- Tondi with busts: *PPM* 7 (1997) 571–72, figs. 10, 12.

VII xii 28, Casa del Balcone Pensile

Tablinum k

- Admetus receiving the oracle: H 1161.

VII xv 1/2, Casa del Marinaio

Tablinum t

- Narcissus: Pompeii Antiquarium; *PPM* 7 (1997) 736, fig. 64.

VIII ii 38/39, Casa di Giuseppe II

Unidentified room

- Leda: H 147; MN 9550; *RP* 17.6; *PPM* 8 (1998) 353, fig. 87.

STABIAE

Villa di Arianna (Villa della Venditrice di Amori, Villa di Varano)

Room 7, next to the antechamber to great triclinium 3

- Seated youth: H 1823; MN 9093; Allroggen-Bedel 1977, pl. 20.1.
- Seated girl with looking glass: H 1898; MN 9088; Allroggen-Bedel 1977, pl. 20.2; *Collezioni* 1986, 154 and p. 53.
- Seated woman ("Penelope"): H 1885; MN 9097; Allroggen-Bedel 1977, pl. 20.3; *Collezioni* 1986, 153.
- Seated elderly man: H 1525c; MN 9142; Allroggen-Bedel 1977, pl. 20.4.

Lucius

It is well known that the only artist's signature that has so far been found in Pompeii is the enigmatic *Lucius pinxit* written in rather carelessly formed characters on one of the stuccoed masonry couches on the euripus of the Casa di Loreio Tiburtino, II ii 2 (Spinazzola 1953, 1.404, fig. 460), where it is not clear whether the reference is to the couch itself or to the poor picture of Pyramus and Thisbe on the wall above it. The picture is so dreadfully badly drawn that Thisbe, who is shown plunging the sword into her breast over the corpse of Pyramus, seems to be wearing a great fur cap over her hair and swimming through the air, while Pyramus watches, one leg cocked, anything but corpselike. The companion picture, of Narcissus, is a little better, but not a great deal better, his gaze abstracted and directed upward, while his foreshortened reflection in the pool before him is more Medusa-like than seductive. Hands and feet are large and poorly drawn in both; the palette is limited, the forms without plasticity or chiaroscuro; even the rocks are clumsy and unconvincing. It is hard to imagine why anyone would want to claim responsibility for such incompetence. The secret lies in the landscape, where in the Pyramus and Thisbe we see the lion responsible for the tragedy bounding off to the left, its very long tail stretching out sinuously behind it, and the little tree on which is hung the bloody garment, a gnarled trunk forking in a series of short zigzags against foliage brushed in quick, broad scribbles and daubs. Such animals with exaggerated tails are characteristic of the man who painted many of the big hunt panels (or *paradeisos*) in Pompeian gardens, and his landscapes are vistas of bleak rocks and desert slashed by sharp-edged cracks and gullies and relieved by this sort of meager and misshapen vegetation.

Maria Theresa Andreae in her study of a range of the better-preserved hunt panels of Pompeii objected to Wilhelmina Jashemski's assertion that Lucius must have been the painter of most such pictures in Pompeii (*RdSP* 4 [1990] 45–124, esp. 62 and 94). She held that the grounds for such attribution were based on similarities of subject and motif, features that lent themselves to copying and imitation, whereas the only valid basis for attribution is brushwork and the forms of details, the method brilliantly developed by Morelli in the last century. Consequently, she distinguished different manners within large panels and thought she could identify painters of different sections and find painters of background who were distinct from painters of animals. She concluded that no single painter was responsible for any large number of these hunts. But Morelli's method so applied works best when one is dealing with copies, imitations, forgeries, or pictures produced in large ateliers, where the work of an apprentice may be mistaken for the work of the master. And in Pompeii one has only to consider the enormous differences in the various versions of a single composition, Achilles discovered on Scyros or Perseus showing the head of Medusa to Andromeda, to see that the Pompeian painter was never trying to approximate an original; rather, he was using the composition as the basis for display of his own pictorial style. Consequently, in any room in Pompeii the subject pictures are almost always by a single painter and make a harmonious decoration; when they are not, as, for example, in exedra G, south of the atrium of the Casa degli Amorini Dorati, VI xvi 7/38, one painter has made no effort to imitate the style of the other, and the contrast is obvious and startling. Therefore, in attempting to attribute Pompeian pictures one should look, not for niceties of brushwork, for the picture surface is seldom what it would have been in antiquity and the loss of overpainting will vary greatly within a relatively small picture, but rather to the vocabulary of forms and their syntax, on which point Morelli was particularly emphatic. Despite the care and patience with which Andreae worked, it is a classic case of the forest and the trees.

Lucius must have painted the whole of the upper terrace of the Casa di Loreio Tiburtino, not only the Pyramus and Thisbe and Narcissus but the Diana and Actaeon at the opposite end of the euripus, work easily identified as his, and also the long wall with its ruined Orpheus and Birth of Venus flanking the door to the oecus of Hercules, the long hunt panel that covered the east end of the wall, and the Calydonian Boar Hunt on the south wall of the Diaeta of Isis/Diana.

The best preserved of Lucius's work today is the large hunt panel in the Casa di Ceio, I vi 15, where a lion chasing a bull across his typically gashed terrain occupies the foreground, while a tree of his characteristic zigzag form grows to the left. A pair of boars, one of them attacked by a brace of huge dogs, occupies the middle ground, and other animals appear left and right. The lion and the bull in the foreground have the exaggerated long, streaming tails that are his hallmark, and the bull points his deeply cleft hooves as he races away and wears a peculiarly mournful expression that one finds repeatedly in Lucius's bulls, alternating with one of supercilious nonchalance. Here he did not paint the Egyptianizing landscape on the adjacent east wall, but the pygmy landscape on the west wall is in his typical palette, and its foreground is slashed by his crisp-edged cracks and gullies. The landscape here is made exotic by the addition of swamp vegetation and a crocodile and hippopotamus, but we have no difficulty recognizing his style. He is likely also to have painted the frames with their fountains supported by sphinxes and figures shown as relief panels.

A series of hunt scenes that is reasonably well preserved in the garden of the Casa di M. Lucrezio Frontone, V iv a, is also clearly Lucius's work. Here the tails are sometimes almost absurdly long, and the pointing of the hooves is marked in gazelles and antelopes, as well as bulls. There is his usual gashed foreground, but the vegetation, although sparse, is lusher and more varied than is customary in his work. In this house, in a room on the garden described as a triclinium aestivum, is another, much smaller representation of Pyramus and Thisbe, which I believe is also his work; it is a better version than that in the Casa di Loreio Tiburtino but still inept, and the brushwork, the awkwardness of Thisbe's pose, and the character of the lion's tail suggest that it is by Lucius.

Another hunt panel that is certainly by him is that in the Casa di Romolo e Remo, now faded to a faint fragment, but his characteristic tails, postures, and landscape are proof of his authorship. Adjacent to this is a large garden painting with statues of nymphs and fountains and a long-legged peacock, but this is probably not his work. Other hunt panels that are his work, however, can be found in the Casa della Caccia Antica, the Casa delle Quadrighe, the Casa della Caccia Nuova, the Casa del Centenario, and the Casa dell'Efebo. The reader may now be tempted to ask whether there is any large animal painting in Pompeii that I would not identify as his work. In answer, he did not paint the animals on the pluteus of the peristyle of the Casa dei Gladiatori nor those on the pluteus of the peristyle of the Casa del Menandro. Nor did he paint the large Orpheus surrounded by animals in the Casa di Orfeo, VI xiv 20.

Although his painting of the whole of the walls around the upper euripus of the Casa di Loreio Tiburtino would amply justify his having signed his name there, there was a further reason, for he painted the larger frieze in the oecus of Hercules and probably the smaller one as well. The large feet of Hercules and Telamon, with their long toes and slender ankles, are like those of Narcissus and Actaeon. The weakly drawn hands with large rubbery fingers and prominent thumbs, almost absurd in the figure of Priam supplicating Achilles, are marks of his work. And in both friezes one notes the elongation of the heads of the Trojans and the similarity in the conception and draping of their turbans. That this is right and Lucius fancied himself as a figure painter as well as a specialist in animals is further proved in the Casa della Caccia Antica, where in addition to the big hunt panel in the peristyle, he painted the subject pictures in the big oecus opening east off the peristyle, an Apollo and Admetus still in situ, where the mournful expression of the cow in the background is as good as a signature, a Diana and Actaeon, and a Polyphemus and Galatea, the last now in the Museo Nazionale. The first is a poor performance, the squat and lumpy proportions of the figures unpleasing, but the Polyphemus and Galatea is charming. Here he has avoided showing the faces of his protagonists, and the delicacy of the gesture is nicely rendered. Were it not for the presence of the companion pictures and a similarity in palette and brushwork, one might think that this was by a better artist.

Moreover, since he painted the large exotic landscape peopled with round-headed, spindle-shanked dwarves in the Casa di Ceio, we can attribute to him a small group of Nilotic landscapes similarly populated, notably three from the Casa del Medico, VIII v 24, including the famous "Judgment of Solomon," and three in the Casa dei Pigmei, IX v 9. Not only are the proportions of figures and the treatment of landscapes strikingly similar, but the animals repeat with remarkable fidelity, a hump-backed crocodile, a snub-nosed hippopotamus, and an ibis with raised wings, arched neck, and crooked legs. Nilotic scenes and dwarves were not his specialty, but they were very popular in Pompeii.

With so much work in a range of subjects to his credit in Pompeii, one might expect to find this painter in demand in Herculaneum and Stabiae and for subject pictures as well as hunt scenes. That this is not the case might be laid to his having been a loner and to there being an abundance of work available in Pompeii. It is more likely that few buildings at either site called for the sort of large-scale panel at which he so excelled, and his figure painting was not of an order to be in demand otherwise. He was never more than a marginally competent journeyman.

✣ *Works* ✣

POMPEII

I vi 15, Casa di Ceio

Viridarium

• Animal chase: Spinazzola 1953, 1.276, fig. 306; Eschebach 1978, fig. 171; Jashemski 1979, 69, figs. 111–12; Michel 1990, figs. 256–

57, 268, 271; *PPM* 1 (1990) 473–75, figs. 100–103; *RdSP* 4 (1990) 49–53, figs. 2–11; *Peinture* 1993, 1, pl. 11.

• Nilotic landscape with dwarves: Spinazzola 1953, 1.276, fig. 305; Michel 1990, figs. 263, 284–85; *PPM* 1 (1990) 471–72, figs. 97–99.

I vii 11/12, Casa dell'Efebo

Viridarium

• Animal chase: *PPM* 1 (1990) 708–9, figs. 158–59.

II ii 2, Casa di Loreio Tiburtino

Garden, upper euripus terrace

• Narcissus: Spinazzola 1953, 1.402, fig. 458; Brion 1960, fig. 110; Picard 1970, fig. 54; *PPM* 3 (1991) 104, fig. 93.

• Pyramus and Thisbe: Spinazzola 1953, 1.402, fig. 458; Picard 1970, fig. 54; *PPM* 3 (1991) 105, fig. 94.

• Diana and Actaeon: Spinazzola 1953, 1.392–93, figs. 446–47; *PPM* 3 (1991) 100–101, figs. 87–88.

• Orpheus: *PPM* 3 (1991) 102, fig. 89.

• Birth of Venus: *PPM* 3 (1991) 102, fig. 90.

• Calydonian Boar Hunt: Spinazzola 1953, 1.391, figs. 444–45.

Oecus h, east of the peristyle (oecus of Hercules)

• Frieze of the Labors of Hercules: Picard 1970, 80–81, pl. 55; *PPM* 3 (1991) 84–91, figs. 64–65, 68–69, 72; *Peinture* 1993, 1, pls. 38–41.

• Frieze of the *Iliad:* Spinazzola 1953, 2.974–1007, figs. 989–1051; Picard 1970, 80–81, pl. 55; *PPM* 3 (1991) 86–98, figs. 68–84; *Peinture* 1993, 1, pls. 38–41.

II iv 3, Praedia Iuliae Felicis

Triclinium/nymphaeum, west of the peristyle

• Nilotic landscape with dwarves: *PPM* 3 (1991) 265–67, figs. 139–41.

V i 7, Casa del Torello di Bronzo

Atrium

• Frieze with panels of dwarves between masks: H 1546; *PPM* 3 (1991) 487, figs 9–11.

V i 18, Casa degli Epigrammi

Peristyle

• Silenus and animal chase: S 170, 698; Spinazzola 1928, pl. 162; *PPM* 3 (1991) 549, fig. 21.

V iv a, Casa di M. Lucrezio Frontone

Peristyle

• Animal chases: Schefold 1962, pls. 150.1, 150.2, 151.1; Jashemski 1979, 71, fig. 115b; *RdSP* 4 (1990) 64–69, figs. 19–31; *PPM* 3 (1991) 1021–24, figs. 99, 101, 103, 105–8; Peters 1993, 341–46, figs. 248–53.

Summer triclinium r

• Pyramus and Thisbe: HBr pl. 162.1; Rizzo 1929, pl. 134.1; *PPM* 3 (1991) 1028–29, figs. 115a, b; Peters 1993, pl. 21.

VI ii 4, Casa di Sallustio

Small peristyle south of the atrium

• Diana and Actaeon: H 249b; *Peinture* 1993, 2, fig. 169; *PPM* 4 (1993) 131–32, figs. 76–79.

VII ii 25, Casa delle Quadrighe

Viridarium

• Animal chase: H 1586; *RdSP* 4 (1990) 77, figs. 43–44, and 95, fig. 61; *PPM* 6 (1996) 703–4, figs. 36–39.

VII iv 48, Casa della Caccia Antica

Peristyle

• Animal hunt: H 1520; Jashemski 1979, 71, fig. 115c (= *MB* 13.18–19); Zahn 3.5.

Oecus 15, east of the peristyle

• Apollo and Admetus: H 221; HBr pl. 184; *PPM* 7 (1997) 37, fig. 52.

• Diana and Actaeon: H 250; *Peinture* 1993, 2, fig. 254; *PPM* 7 (1997) 41, fig. 57.

• Polyphemus and Galatea: H 1052; MN 27687; Kraus and von Matt 1973, fig. 275; Grant 1975, 152; *Collezioni* 1986, 168; *PPM* 7 (1997) 39, fig. 54.

VII vii 10, Casa di Romolo e Remo

Peristyle

• Animal chase: S 703; Schefold 1962, pl. 151.2; Jashemski 1979, 70, fig. 115a; *PPM* 7 (1997) 266–70, figs. 16–20, 23–24.

VII x 3/14, Casa della Caccia Nuova

Peristyle

• Animal chase: H 1583–84.

VIII v 24, Casa del Medico

Peristyle

• Nilotic hunt with dwarves: MN 113195; Spinazzola 1928, pl.

160; Rizzo 1929, pl. 151.1; Maiuri 1953, 111 (detail); Picard 1970, 82, pl. 56; Kraus and von Matt 1973, fig. 306; *Collezioni* 1986, 354; *PPM* 8 (1998) 606, fig. 4.

• Alfresco banquet of dwarves: MN 113196; Schefold 1962, pl. 144.2; Marcadé 1965, 36; Marini 1971, 24–25; *PPM* 8 (1998) 606, fig. 5.

• "Judgment of Solomon": MN 113197; Rizzo 1929, pl. 151.2; Maiuri 1953, 110 (detail); Schefold 1962, pl. 144.1; Kraus and von Matt 1973, fig. 305; *Collezioni* 1986, 352; *PPM* 8 (1998) 606, fig. 3.

IX v 9, Casa dei Pigmei

Oecus north of the peristyle

• Panorama of the Nile flood with dwarves: S 689; Schefold 1962, pls. 146–47; Zevi 1992, 278–79; *Peinture* 1993, 1, pls. 90–92, and 2, figs. 317–18.

IX v 14/16

Triclinium o

• Pyramus and Thisbe: S 600; MN 111483; HBr pl. 162.2; Rizzo 1929, pl. 134.2.

• Pair of men before an enthroned queen (Aeneas before Dido?): S 626; MN 111480; HBr pl. 185.

• Bacchus and Ariadne with thiasus: S 168; MN 111481; HBr pl. 51.

IX viii 3/6, Casa del Centenario

Viridarium south of the great oecus

• Animal chase: Spinazzola 1928, pl. 157; Guillaud and Guillaud 1990, fig. 293 (misidentified); *RdSP* 4 (1990) 83–89, figs. 47–59.

Environs, Via Marina, Terme Suburbane, Exterior

• Nilotic landscape with dwarves: Zevi 1992, 174.

The Marco Lucrezio Painter

One of the more elusive painters of Pompeii is the Fourth Style painter responsible for a number of rather small pictures in the atrium complex of the Casa di Marco Lucrezio, IX iii 5. These are for the most part two-figure compositions, especially representations of theatrical and genre subjects combined with amorini or ephebes in single figures in the side panels, but there is also a good range of mythological subjects: Narcissus, Pan discovering a bacchante, Mars and Venus, and similar subjects. These tend to be rather simple pictures in small, square, or nearly square, panels, the figures in the side panels also small but not miniature. The most interesting pictures are those from the south ala, which have been removed to the Museo Nazionale. One shows a poet, half-nude, seated beside a *scrinium* in earnest conversation with a young man who bends toward him wearing a soft cap and carrying a pedum, presumably an actor in comedy. This is a well-preserved picture and gives us fair knowledge of the way this painter's work was finished. The companion piece to this, also in the Museo Nazionale, has been interpreted as showing a poet with a Muse. The poet sits at the left, again beside a *scrinium,* again half-nude, while the Muse sits with crossed legs at the right and turns toward him, leaning forward and bracing herself with both hands. Her expression is earnest and pleading. Although this is less well preserved than its companion, there can be no doubt about its authorship; with their uniformity in scheme and aesthetic there is a prima-facie case for their being by the same hand, and this is confirmed by study of the structure of the figures.

This is a competent but not superior workman on the order of the Adone Ferito Painter. His figures tend to be well proportioned, somewhat light in build, with high breasts and slender arms and legs. Wrists are often unarticulated or poorly articulated, and hands and feet are exaggeratedly delicate but seldom well drawn. The painter seems to have avoided painting hands whenever he could hide them. Heads tend to be rather narrow with an oval face, often childish in appearance, and hair in a cloud of tousled tufts and loose ringlets surrounding and standing out from the head. Men's hair may also be a shiny cap that blouses over the forehead. Eyes are small, set wide under low brows, and usually have an intensity of gaze that amounts to a slight frown. Noses are large, not infrequently unbecomingly so, men's noses occasionally aquiline or even irregular in profile. Mouths are small and tend to seem slightly open, while cheeks are shaded in underpainting and sometimes look unshaved. Drapery is on the whole well handled and relatively simple, falling into formulaic shapes for cloaks and skirts. Backgrounds are neutral, almost never developed.

Figures are built by drawing with brushes of medium width, laying in color, and modifying by overpainting, first in broad areas and then in a general retouching of the whole with small brushes to add detail. Lights and edges are soft, but there is no chiaroscuro.

A good example of this man's work elsewhere is the well-known Judgment of Paris from V ii 15, now in the Museo Nazionale. It shows Paris in Phrygian shepherd's dress seated at the right, his head bent pensively over his lifted right hand, while Mercury, behind him with petasus and caduceus, looks upward and off to the right. The three rival goddesses stand in a row in the foreground, Juno to the left with diadem and scepter, Venus in the middle, almost nude, silhouetted against a mantle that billows out behind her, Athena to the right, helmeted, with spear and shield decorated with a gorgoneion. The picture is of only mediocre quality and has lost much of its overpainting, so that it appears rather heavily drawn, but Mercury's head gives us some indication that the original finish was finer. Of the goddesses Venus is the best preserved, and she provides a canon of this painter's female nudes.

This painter was responsible for a very similar nude in room t of the Casa di Cecilio Giocondo, V i 26, in a picture of Hermaphroditus and Silenus now in the Museo Nazionale. Hermaphroditus is nude except for a cloak draped behind him and caught over his elbows. He holds a long, slender torch and turns a little in a gentle S-curve toward Silenus, who stands in profile facing right and lifts a large tympanum with his left hand, about to strike it with his right. At the same time he turns his head back to look at Hermaphroditus. He wears a wreath of leaves and a mantle kilted about his fat belly.

The characteristic frown is missing from Hermaphroditus's face, but he has the loose, curling hair typical of this painter. Most of all it is his hands and feet that identify this painter, who was responsible for another picture from the same room, a Mars and Venus in a familiar composition, she seated leaning back against his chest, one arm lifted above her head, while he pulls back her (or his own) drapery. An amorino to the right holds Mars's shield and spear; another to the left offers Venus a box, presumably of jewelry. Mars rather incongruously wears his helmet. The surface of the picture is badly rubbed, and the features of the divinities are barely distinguishable, but Venus has the characteristics of Venus in the Judgment of Paris, the loose, curled hair and delicate hands and feet, and Mars fits well with Mercury and Paris.

It seems quite possible that this painter produced a near copy of the Hermaphroditus and Silenus in the triclinium aestivum (12) of the Casa di M. Lucrezio Frontone. The only difference seems to have been that here Silenus has a cithara instead of a tympanum. Unfortunately, the painting has deteriorated, so that the upper half is now barely legible, but the forms seem to hold true. Another picture in the same apartment is too far gone for one to make out the subject (*PPM* 3 [1991] 1027, fig. 113), but a third shows Thisbe stabbing herself over the body of Pyramus. This was never a good picture, and today it is little more than a ghost (*PPM* 3 [1991] 1028–29, figs. 115a, b). One would hate to have to attribute it to even a mediocre painter, and the tail of the lion disappearing off to the right in the background suggests that it is the work of Lucius, who painted the panels of animal chases on the garden wall of the peristyle.

Another room that seems to have been decorated by the Marco Lucrezio Painter is the black exedra (y) of the Casa della Parete Nera, VII iv 59, the room that gives the house its name. Here there are three small, squarish pictures showing groups of amorini and psyches engaged in religious rituals. The amorini all have archaistically curled wings, the psyches double butterfly wings. The pictures show a peacock and the attributes of Juno before a round base surmounted by a statuette of Victoria; preparation to sacrifice a young kid (?) to Athena, with a small round altar before a base on which are mounted a round shield decorated with a snake and a spear and helmet; and preparation to make offerings in a rustic shrine containing a statuette of Priapus. In all these pictures the foreground is enlivened with religious paraphernalia, while the background is neutral except for a sketched tree that emphasizes the picture's axis. The second is the best preserved, and its authorship is revealed by the way the medium is handled and the addition of the loose curls that are this painter's hallmark. Despite the unusualness of the subjects and the artificiality of the archaizing, there is no question about the authorship.

Finally, a group of four floating figures from the fauces of the Casa di Olconio Rufo, VIII iv 4, now in the Museo Nazionale, seem to be his work. They show wreathed young women, half-nude or in diaphanous drapery, one carrying a wreath of ivy, one carrying the baetylus scepter of Venus, one carrying a calathus, and a fourth, carrying a looking glass, who seems to have been lost. They declare their authorship by their narrow oval faces with prominent noses, the drawing of their small, slender hands and feet, and the way their drapery is handled and lit.

I believe this painter must have been regularly the assistant to someone else, used to doing subsidiary parts of a decoration, still life, architecture, vistas, and the like, fairly regularly entrusted with the execution of amorini, floating figures, Muses, and Horae, but seldom commissioned to do a subject picture and never, or almost never, a large one. The rooms in which we find his work are not showplaces, and most of his compositions are simple ones of few figures. The Judgment of Paris seems to have been his most ambitious work. Yet he was not without merit and shows a considerable facility with his medium.

⇢ *Works* ⇠

POMPEII

V i 26, Casa di Cecilio Giocondo

Room t, at the south end of the west portico of the peristyle

- Hermaphroditus and Silenus: S 594; MN 111213; *PPM* 3 (1991) 618, fig. 89.
- Mars and Venus: S 138; MN 111214; *PPM* 3 (1991) 618, fig. 91.

V ii 15

Triclinium l, between atrium and peristyle

- Judgment of Paris: MN 119691; Schefold 1962, pl. 172.2; *PPM* 3 (1991) 859, fig. 9.

V iv a, Casa di M. Lucrezio Frontone

Triclinium aestivum, south of the peristyle

- Hermaphroditus and Silenus: *PPM* 3 (1991) 1025, fig. 110; Peters 1993, pl. 20.

VII iv 59, Casa della Parete Nera

Exedra f, south of the peristyle

- Sacrifice to Juno: H 776; Brogi negative 6552; Curtius 1929, 396, fig. 215.
- Sacrifice to Athena: H 773; Brogi negative 6551.
- Sacrifice to Priapus: H 775; Brogi negative 6553; Spinazzola 1928, pl. 136; Curtius 1929, 397, fig. 216; *Peinture* 1993, 2, fig. 256b.

VIII iv 4, Casa di Olconio Rufo

Fauces

- Floating figure with wreath: H 1909; MN 9149; Schefold 1962, pl. 161.1.
- Floating figure with baetylus scepter: H 1920; MN 9300; Schefold 1962, pl. 161.2; *Collezioni* 1986, 211.
- Floating figure with calathus: H 1913; MN 9144; Schefold 1962, pl. 162.1.
- Floating figure with looking glass: H 1942.

IX iii 5, Casa di Marco Lucrezio
South ala 8
- Poet and actor of comedy: H 1455; MN 9038; HBr pl. 66.
- Poet and Muse: H 1458; MN 9030; HBr pl. 67.

Cubiculum 6, north of the atrium
- Pan discovering a bacchante: H 562.
- Narcissus: H 1354; MN 9381; HBr pl. 230.2.

Cubiculum 7, north of the atrium
- Polyphemus with the letter of Galatea: H 1049; *Peinture* 1993, 2, fig. 310.
- Phrixus and Helle: H 1253; MN 8896.
- Mars and Venus: H 269, 277.

Cubiculum 4, south of the atrium
- Chiron and Achilles: H 1294; *Peinture* 1993, 2, fig. 307.
- Endymion: H 950.

Cubiculum 5, south of the atrium
- Cyparissus: H 219; *Peinture* 1993, 2, fig. 308b.

The Meleagro Painter

The style of this painter is described, and a number of pictures by him are listed, in *Pompeii: The Casa dei Dioscuri and Its Painters* (Richardson 1955, 139–45). His salient characteristics are a highly painterly technique uncommon in Campanian painting, an original sketch being executed in rather broad, short strokes of black, over which the forms are built in successive layers of color in a palette heavy with deep greens, blues, and violets touched with dull, silvery lights, warm ruddy flesh for the men and rosy cheeks for both men and women. His emphasis is on chiaroscuro and dark, mysterious backgrounds. There is little overdrawing of the finished forms, only occasional picking out of facial features and locks of hair.

The range of his subjects is relatively wide but confined to relatively simple compositions in which the figures stand well apart. When figures overlap or there is a complicated recession of space he is clearly in technical difficulties. His figures seem to stand in a single plane. He is also awkward at conveying relationships among figures by expressive glance and gesture; the gaze of a figure is apt to slide past another on whom it should focus. Few of the compositions might be considered in any sense his own, for while some of the more complicated are known in no other copy, the fumbling way in which they all are handled, especially in regard to the alignment of figures, argues that he is not sure how to develop them and would be happier with simpler groups, and his simpler groups are simply figures in stock poses chosen from various sources and provided with identifying attributes. In most rooms where he worked he seems to have painted all the figures as well as the subject pictures, and in the figures cut from decorations and preserved in the Museo Nazionale in Naples his range embraces amorini, figures from architecture, figures of divinities that must have come from the upper zones of decorations, and figures that may have come from side panels.

The ready earmarks of this painter extend to every part of the human body, every form of drapery, nearly every object. Perhaps the most conspicuous are certain forms of the hand. His favorite hand is lifted, plucking at the shoulder of a garment, and twisted to expose the palm with the little finger crooked. The hand is almost always absurdly small with a strongly triangular palm and tapering fingers. The fingers are apt to be unnaturally spread and clawlike. The eye is frequently marked by a quizzical lift of the eyebrow toward the outer corner of the eye, and the mouth by an excessively short, full upper lip. In nudes there is usually a little double fold of flesh at the navel, which is set high. The arms of figures tend to be very short; the thighs of seated figures are exaggeratedly short and conical and taper to small knees. The feet are small and rather thick at the instep with an exaggerated great toe, which is usually distinctly turned up, while the other toes are set back from the great toe steeply, so the outer line of the foot becomes much too short.

In my earlier work I attributed to him a single picture of Endymion from the Casa dei Dioscuri and all the subject pictures of the Casa di Meleagro except the figures of nymphs and satyrs in the dadoes and the subject pictures of the Corinthian oecus, but nothing else from Pompeii except possibly three pictures in a large oecus of the Casa di Sirico, the Arrival of Venus at Cythera in the Casa di Trittolemo, and a Perseus and Andromeda from the Insula Occidentalis of Regio VI. On the other hand, I attributed to him a few pictures from Herculaneum: a Phaedra and Hippolytus, figures of Apollo and Bacchus, and with some hesitation Polyphemus receiving the letter of Galatea and a Leda.

The attributions from the Casa dei Dioscuri and the Casa di Meleagro still seem correct, and so are all the attributions of pictures from Herculaneum. But I have abandoned the attribution of the pictures in the Casa di Sirico, the Casa di Trittolemo, and the Insula Occidentalis. In fact, the Arrival of Venus at Cythera in the Casa di Trittolemo now seems to me very clearly a work of the Io Painter. On the other hand, I have now a good many new attributions to add to this painter's *oeuvre.* In the Casa di Fabio Rufo he painted the pictures in the black triclinium, especially a Contest of Venus and Hesperus. In the Casa del Labirinto he painted a Paris and Oenone. In IX ii 5 he painted a Micon and Pero now in the Museo Nazionale. In the Casa di Giulio Polibio he painted the unfortunately fragmentary Pasiphaë. He seems to have been as much at home in Pompeii as at Herculaneum.

He was, in fact, one of the more productive painters of Campania, so much so that he must be regarded as resident in the neighborhood. He does not seem to have worked consistently with anyone else. The fact that he seems to have painted in only one room of the Casa dei Dioscuri and one picture in the Casa dell'Ara Massima suggests that he was very much a journeyman, given small commissions whenever there was work to be done and glad to get them. But that he painted so much, some of it his most finished product, in the Casa di Meleagro and the Casa dei Cervi, both large and sumptuous houses, shows that his style was admired, although his draughtsmanship was always faulty, especially in proportions, and his handling of space was seldom imaginative. Still, his command of his medium was proficient, his use of light and texture, especially in soft shadows and the development of chiaroscuro, very skillful, and the building up of his forms in successive layers or glazes so that the finished picture is soft and luminous is highly successful. One must place him high among the painters of the second rank.

⇢ *Works* ⇠

POMPEII

I xi 1, Caupona

- Bacchus and Venus: *PPM* 2 (1990) 514, fig. 12.

VI ix 2, Casa di Meleagro

Fauces

- Ceres and Mercury: H 362; Schefold 1962, pl. 169.2; *Peinture* 1993, 2, fig. 184; *PPM* 4 (1993) 667, fig. 18.
- Meleager and Atalanta: H 1163; Schefold 1962, pl. 169.1; *PPM* 4 (1993) 663, fig. 6.

Atrium

- Dido Abandoned: H 113c; MN 8898; HBr pl. 214; Rizzo 1929, pl. 83; Richardson 1955, pl. 41; *Collezioni* 1986, 210; *Peinture* 1993, 1, fig. 50; *PPM* 4 (1993) 677, fig. 42; De Caro 1994, 185.
- Thetis in the forge of Hephaestus: H 1317; MN 9528; *PPM* 4 (1993) 675, fig. 39.
- Dressing of a lyre-player: H 1386b; MN 9543; Richardson 1955, pl. 42; *PPM* 4 (1993) 679, fig. 45.

Tablinum

- Mars and Venus: H 318; MN 9256; Richardson 1955, pl. 40.1; *PPM* 4 (1993) 682, fig. 51.
- Io and Argus: H 132; MN 9556; Richardson 1955, pl. 40.2; *Collezioni* 1986, 163; *PPM* 4 (1993) 681, fig. 50.
- Painted figures in stucco relief settings:

  MN 9595; Spinazzola 1928, pl. 175; Elia 1932, fig. 48; Kraus and von Matt 1973, fig. 303; *Collezioni* 1986, 143 and p. 59; Guillaud and Guillaud 1990, figs. 303, 305; *PPM* 4 (1993) 685, fig. 55.

  MN 9596; Spinazzola 1928, pl. 173; *Collezioni* 1986, 144; Guillaud and Guillaud 1990, figs. 304, 306; *PPM* 4 (1993) 684, fig. 53.

  MN 9625; Spinazzola 1928, pl. 174; *Collezioni* 1986, 145; Guillaud and Guillaud 1990, fig. 307; *PPM* 4 (1993) 684, fig. 54; De Caro 1994, 174.

Cubiculum 12, south of the atrium

- Ganymede: H 154; MN 9547; HBr pl. 242.1; Rizzo 1929, pl. 105.1; *Pompeji: Leben und Kunst* 1973, 160, no. 215; *PPM* 4 (1993) 688, fig. 60.
- Youth and girl at dinner: H 1448b; MN 9254; *PPM* 4 (1993) 689, fig. 61.

Cubiculum 13, south of the atrium

- Hermaphroditus and Pan: H 1371; MN 9264; Schefold 1962, pl. 167.1; *PPM* 4 (1993) 692, fig. 65.

Peristyle

- Wrestling of Pan and Amor: H 406; MN 9124; *PPM* 4 (1993) 718, fig. 114.
- Hymenaeus: H 1227; MN 9320; *PPM* 4 (1993) 718, fig. 115.

• Ariadne Abandoned: H 1227; MN 9051; Rizzo 1929, pl. 109.1; *RdSP* 2 (1988) 59, fig. 2; *PPM* 4 (1993) 719, fig. 116.

• Perseus and Andromeda: H 1201 (= H 1202); MN s.n.

• Apollo and Daphne: H 214; MN 9534; *PPM* 4 (1993) 720, fig . 118.

Black triclinium 27, northeast of the peristyle

• Judgment of Paris: H 1285; HBr pl. 215; *PPM* 4 (1993) 772–73, figs. 214–15.

• Hector and Paris: H 1313; Schefold 1962, pl. 170.1; *PPM* 4 (1993) 786, fig. 240.

Location uncertain, possibly from the peristyle

• Seated woman with amorino: H 1168; MN 8897; Schefold 1962, pl. 170.2; *PPM* 4 (1993) 817, fig. 293.

• Mars and Venus: H 314; MN 9250; Schefold 1962, pl. 169.4; Guillaud and Guillaud 1990, fig. 284; *PPM* 4 (1993) 816, fig. 292.

VI ix 6/7, Casa dei Dioscuri

White triclinium 38, northwest of the atrium

• Endymion: H 960; MN 9240; HBr pl. 134; Rizzo 1929, pl. 126.1; Richardson 1955, pl. 39; Ragghianti 1963, 129 (detail); *PPM* 4 (1993) 894, fig. 65.

VI xi 8–10, Casa del Labirinto

Room 29

• Paris and Oenone (?): H 1287; Schefold 1962, pl. 170.4; Strocka 1991, fig. 160; *PPM* 5 (1994) 20, fig. 35.

VI xvi 15–17, Casa dell'Ara Massima

Pseudo-tablinum D

• Narcissus: Rizzo 1929, pl. 127; Stemmer 1992, fig. 200; *Peinture* 1993, 1, pl. 79; *PPM* 5 (1994) 881, fig. 45.

VII iv 10, Casa di Bacco

Cubiculum north of the atrium

• Micon and Pero: H 1376; MN 9040.

VII Ins. Occ. 17–19, Casa di Fabio Rufo

Apsidal room 62 (black triclinium) in the lower story

• Contest of Venus and Hesperus: Kraus and von Matt 1973, fig. 302; *Pompei 1748–1980,* 25, fig. 5; *RdSP* 3 (1991) 121, fig. 7; *Peinture* 1993, 2, fig. 276b; *PPM* 7 (1997) 1088, fig. 279.

• Muses: *Pompei 1748–1980,* 26, fig. 6; *PPM* 7 (1997) 1084, fig. 271, and 1086, fig. 275.

IX ii 5

Triclinium c

- Micon and Pero: S 599; MN 115398; HBr pl. 161; Rizzo 1929, pl. 53; *Collezioni* 1986, 199.

IX xiii 1/3, Casa di Giulio Polibio

Cubiculum in the upper story

- Pasiphaë: *Peinture* 1993, 1, pl. 100.

Unidentified Buildings

- Androsiren: H 898; MN 8664.
- Satyr and maenad: H 553; MN 27693; Marcadé 1965, 14; Marini 1971, 51; Grant 1975, 158; *Collezioni* 1986, 269.
- Wall including a banquet scene: H 1452; MN 9731 (companion to H 1450).
- Banquet scene: H 1450; MN s.n. (companion to H 1452, MN 9731).
- Amorino: H 712; MN 9324 (= MN 9321).
- Psyche: H 829; MN 9316.
- Sacrificant: H 1812; MN 8930.

HERCULANEUM

III 3, Casa dello Scheletro

Cubiculum at the south corner

- Two amorini.

IV 3/4, Casa dell'Alcova

Oecus 8

- Ariadne Abandoned: Maiuri 1958, 390, fig. 325.

Biclinium 19

- Figures of divinities in the upper zone.

IV 21, Casa dei Cervi

Cryptoporticus

- Amorini with thrones for divinities: H 769, 771; MN 9210; Rizzo 1929, pl. 139.1; *Collezioni* 1986, 225; *Peinture* 1993, 2, figs. 415a, b.
- Amorini at games and as musicians: H 761, 762, 764, 765; MN 9176; Rizzo 1929, pl. 140.1; Jashemski 1979, 98 fig. 156; *Collezioni* 1986, 226; *Peinture* 1993, 2, figs. 415c, d, e, f.
- Amorini at games and trades: H 754, 799, 1640; MN 9177; Rizzo 1929, pl. 140.2; *Collezioni* 1986, 227; *Peinture* 1993, 2, figs. 415g, h, i.

• Amorini at games: H 755, 782, 784, 763; MN 9178; Rizzo 1929, pl. 140.3; *Collezioni* 1986, 228 and p. 65 with H 763; *Peinture* 1993, 2, figs. 415k, l, m, n.

• Amorini at games and trades: H 753, 804, 805, 806; MN 9179; Rizzo 1929, pl. 139.2; *Collezioni* 1986, 229; *Peinture* 1993, 2, figs. 415o, p, q, r; De Caro 1994, 260–61.

• Amorini as armorers: Maiuri 1958, 316, fig. 252; *Peinture* 1993, 2, fig. 413.

• Amorini with throne: Maiuri 1958, 315, fig. 249.

Tablinum/oecus 15

• Woman fleeing from a bearded king: Maiuri 1958, 318, fig. 253.

V 6/7, Casa del Mosaico di Nettuno e Anfitrite

Room north of the tablinum

• Reclining nymph and two figures in architecture.

Environs, Villa dei Papiri

• Amorino with a cantharus: H 664; MN 9319; *Collezioni* 1986, 220.

Unidentified Buildings

• Endymion: H 955; MN 9246 bis (= MN 9245); HBr pl. 136; Rizzo 1929, pl. 125; *Collezioni* 1986, 169.

• Harpocrates, *Genius huius loci montis:* H 81; MN 8848; *Pompeji: Leben und Kunst* 1973, 198, no. 279.

• Leda: H 148; MN 27695; Rizzo 1929, pl. 103.2; *Pompeji: Leben und Kunst* 1973, 190, no. 264; Grant 1975, 146.

• Phaedra and Hippolytus: H 1244; MN 9041; HBr pl. 235; Richardson 1955, pl. 43; *Pompeji: Leben und Kunst* 1973, 69, no. 263; Ward-Perkins and Claridge 1978, 69, no. 152; *Collezioni* 1986, 195.

• Polyphemus receiving the letter of Galatea: H 1048; MN 8984; Spinazzola 1928, pl. 128; Rizzo 1929, pl. 133; *Collezioni* 1986, 167.

• Banquet scene: H 1448; MN 9024; Kraus and von Matt 1973, fig. 226; *Pompeji: Leben und Kunst* 1973, 81, no. 266; *Collezioni* 1986, 340 and p. 65.

• Three divinities:

Apollo Citharoedus: H 180; MN 9542; HBr pl. 218.1; *Collezioni* 1986, 256.

Bacchus: H 387; MN 9277; HBr pl. 218.2.

Venus: H 1869; MN 8947; HBr pl. 218.3; *Collezioni* 1986, 254.

- Concordia Augusta: H 944; MN 9451.
- Hermaphroditus: H 1368; MN 9224; Herbig 1962, pl. 21; *Collezioni* 1986, 115.
- Amorino and goat: H 734; MN 9321.
- Three amorini: MN 9185, 9212, 9321 bis.
- Sacrificant: MN 8827.
- Sacrificant: MN 8932.
- Sacrificant: MN 9651.
- Lampadophorus: H 1792; MN 8904; Herbig 1962, pl. 19; *Collezioni* 1986, 116.
- Sacrificant with tympanum and salver: MN 9143; *Pompeji: Leben und Kunst* 1973, 174, no. 235.
- Three sacrificants: H 1790; MN 8899, 8906, 9369; HBr pl. 243; *Collezioni* 1986, 148.
- Athena, nude warriors, and sacrificants: H 260, 1804, 1839; MN 9516, 9517.
- Busts of members of the Bacchic thiasus: H 414, 425, 459, 1499; MN 9081, 9129; Elia 1932, fig. 39.

STABIAE

Unidentified Buildings

- Five amorini: H 740b; MN 9192.

UNCERTAIN CAMPANIAN PROVENIENCE

- Bust of a girl with a comic mask: MN 8833; Herbig 1962, pl. 30.

The Nozze di Ercole Painter

One of the more eccentric painters of Pompeii is the artist who painted the frieze in the upper zone of a large oecus on the north side of the peristyle of the Casa di Marte e Venere, also known as the Casa delle Nozze di Ercole, VII ix 47/65. This frieze shows Hebe descending the stair of a tetrastyle temple to be received by Hercules. In the temple stands Venus Pompeiana flanked by Amor and a diminutive Priapus. To either side of this central composition stretch parts of a procession bearing *fercula* on which are mounted models of the tree of the golden apples, a small prostyle temple, a thing or things no longer legible, and a draped throne decked out with a crown. There are also sacrificial animals, including a bull or cow, and a priestess of Isis with a sistrum. The central figures are of good size, the others small and somewhat sketchily painted.

The painter is also the man who did the subject pictures in the little suite of reception rooms with its own diminutive peristyle north of the main peristyle of the Casa dei Vettii, a Hercules and Auge and an Achilles discovered on Scyros. The identifying similarities are the rather oddly shaped faces of Hebe and the winged figure behind Auge, with their deep, rounded jaw, large eyes under long eyebrows, and curiously beatific expression; the feet of Auge and Hebe, which seem almost detachable, oddly out of drawing, flaccid and flipperlike with elongated toes; and the curious way many of the heads are cocked to one side. In the Achilles discovered on Scyros, Ulysses (or perhaps Diomedes, since he is beardless) has the same sort of foot, as does one of the daughters of Lycomedes in the background. The graceful floating figures of women carrying garlands of flowers and metal vessels that occupy medallions in the side panels also are clearly by the same painter.

Another series of floating figures for which the Nozze di Ercole Painter is responsible are the six surviving Victorias in the Armamentarium (also called the Schola Iuventutis), III iii 6. These carry a spear or sword and shield in a variety of shapes and poses, but their authorship is plain in the painting of the feet and faces. And he painted at least one subject picture in a room of the Casa del Centenario, a Selene and Endymion, but he certainly did not paint its companion, commonly identified as Cassandra (S 628, HBr pl. 82). He also painted the floating figures of nymphs in the side panels of this room. In the temple of Isis he painted the panel showing Harpocrates in his shrine against the east wall of the precinct and the figures of priests of Isis in the portico surrounding the temple.

The only other works that are readily identifiable as his are the large figures of priests and priestesses (or acolytes) from Stabiae now in the Museo Nazionale, thought to have come from the apse at the end of the great peristyle of the Edifizio di San Marco. However, since this painter seems to have been skilled at rendering floating figures but clumsy with more complicated compositions, it may be that he was an assistant to one of the painters in greater demand and that his work therefore will be found in the figures in architecture and in side panels and upper zones that have been largely passed over in the present study. The notion that this small group of works might be an aberrant part of the work of Lucius, suggested by the odd painting of the foreground of the Hercules and Auge, has been pondered and dismissed.

⇢ *Works* ⇠

POMPEII

III iii 6, Armamentarium (Schola Iuventutis)

- Winged Victorias: *PPM* 3 (1991) 398–405, figs. 6, 8, 9, 10, 13, 15, 18.

VI xv 1/2, Casa dei Vettii

Triclinium t, east of the small peristyle

- Hercules and Auge: HBr pl. 47; Rizzo 1929, pl. 70; Schefold 1962, pl. 127; *Peinture* 1993, 1, pl. 70; *PPM* 5 (1994) 568, fig. 164.
- Achilles discovered on Scyros: *Peinture* 1993, 2, fig. 297 (misidentified).
- Floating figures: Schefold 1962, pls. 128–29; *PPM* 5 (1994) 569–70, figs. 165–66.

VII ix 47/65, Casa di Marte e Venere (Casa delle Nozze di Ercole)

Oecus north of the peristyle

- Procession with Hercules and Hebe: H 1479; HBr pl. 234; *PPM* 7 (1997) 374–75, figs. 34–36.

VIII vii 28, Tempio di Iside

Shrine of Harpocrates, against the east wall of the precinct

- Harpocrates: H 1; MN 8975; *MdPA* 1941 (Elia), 7–8, figs. 6–7; *Alla ricerca di Iside* 1992, 1.5; *PPM* 8 (1998) 758, fig. 40.

Portico surrounding the temple of Isis

- Priest of Isis: H 1099; MN 8921; *MdPA* 1941 (Elia), 14, fig. 16; *Collezioni* 1986, 275; *Alla ricerca di Iside* 1992, 1.6; *PPM* 8 (1998) 759, fig. 41.
- Priest of Isis: H 1099; MN 8922; *MdPA* 1941 (Elia), 14, fig. 17; *Collezioni* 1986, 272; *Alla ricerca di Iside* 1992, 1.8; *PPM* 8 (1998) 762, fig. 48.
- Priestess of Isis: H 1103; MN 8923; *MdPA* 1941 (Elia), 17–19; *Collezioni* 1986, 278; *Alla ricerca di Iside* 1992, 1.21; *PPM* 8 (1998) 772, fig. 62.

• Acolyte of Isis: H 1097; MN 8918; *MdPA* 1941 (Elia), 16, fig. 20; Maiuri 1953, 87; *Collezioni* 1986, 277; *Alla ricerca di Iside* 1992, 1.26; *PPM* 8 (1998) 775, fig. 68.
• Priest of Isis: H 1099; MN 8969; *MdPA* 1941 (Elia), 14; *Collezioni* 1986, 274; *Alla ricerca di Iside* 1992, 1.30; *PPM* 8 (1998) 779, fig. 75.
• Anubis figure: H 1960; MN 8920; *MdPA* 1941 (Elia), 14, fig. 19; *Collezioni* 1986, 276; *Alla ricerca di Iside* 1992, 1.36; *PPM* 8 (1998) 784, fig. 84.
• Priest of Isis: H 1099; MN 8925; *MdPA* 1941 (Elia), 14, fig. 18; *Collezioni* 1986, 273; *Alla ricerca di Iside* 1992, 1.46; *PPM* 8 (1998) 745, fig. 48.

IX viii 3/6, Casa del Centenario

Room 42, north of triclinium 61

• Selene and Endymion: S 457; Spinazzola 1953, 1.544, fig. 602.
• Venus Piscatrix: S 145; *Peinture* 1993, 2, fig. 330.
• Floating nymphs: S 225; Schefold 1962, pls. 125, 162.2.

STABIAE

Edifizio di San Marco

Apse at the end of the great peristyle

• Sacrificants or acolytes: H 1783, 1797; MN 8890; Elia 1957, 47; *Collezioni* 1986, 279.
• Sacrificants or acolytes: H 1786, 1794; MN 8891; Elia 1957, 46; *Collezioni* 1986, 280; Guillaud and Guillaud 1990, fig. 59.

The Panthera Painter

This painter seems to have painted only a few pictures in Pompeii and none in Herculaneum or Stabiae, but those he painted are of exceptionally high and consistent quality. In the Casa di Panthera, IX ii 16, from which he receives his name, he painted a group of the Three Graces, a charming picture of the three nude sisters in the customary ring composition, their hands on one another's shoulders. Their hands and feet are impossibly tiny, and their heads therefore seem too large, but the soft tones of the forms, carefully built up in diagonal stippling and touched with black accents in the faces and hair against a luminous, almost shimmering mist of grayed blue-green, make a highly effective picture. The pose is easy and graceful, the contrapposto well understood. Unfortunately, this is the only picture surviving from this room, and even the scheme of the decoration of the room, a tablinum-like room open at both ends, cannot be reconstructed.

In the Casa dei Capitelli Colorati this painter did the subject pictures in one of the reception rooms west of the smaller peristyle, an Ariadne discovered by Bacchus and a fragmentary picture of divinities of light, possibly a composition similar to that of the more familiar picture from the Casa di Gavio Rufo showing the Contest of Venus and Hesperus (S 164; MN 9449). Both have been removed to the Museo Nazionale, and while neither is in good condition, the Ariadne Discovered having lost most of its overpainting of the figure of Bacchus and the upper half of the picture, the lower corners with groups of Ariadne and Somnus (?) and Silenus and a satyr are well preserved, and what survives of the other picture, perhaps a third, is in good condition. The composition of the Ariadne Discovered is masterly, a triangle developed in depth, so that the viewer's eye travels from the group of Ariadne and Somnus across to Silenus and the satyr, who pulls the old fellow up the slope and then up to the calm vertical of Bacchus with his thyrsus flanked by bacchantes. And the painting, wherever it is preserved, is superior, especially in the figure of Somnus, with his great gray wing framing the sleeping form of Ariadne and his calm, watchful expression. The structure of forms and the picking out of detail in black, the palette and atmosphere of this picture and its companion, immediately associate them with the picture of the Three Graces.

In the triclinium fenestratum of the Casa di Marco Lucrezio, IX iii 5, where the main pictures were three very large panels of Bacchic subject painted by the Achilles Painter, the Panthera Painter painted a series of small, square pictures in the side panels showing companies of amorini and psyches at parties and entertainments of various sorts. These are unique and show a lively invention as well as masterly handling of the medium. The amorini are clever little scapegraces, the psyches both pert and coy. Without having an obvious relationship with the large pictures, they complemented them very nicely. The palette of soft shimmering colors, the use of stippling, and the technique of random overdrawing with touches of black to bring out expression identify the painter.

One more picture is certainly this artist's work, a Narcissus in the Museo Nazionale said to come from a villa at Torre Annunziata. In this the boyish youth stands on a rock in a pool beside a votive column surmounted by a bronze basket with flaring sides and a high, arched handle. He lifts his half-closed right hand toward this, leans on a slender staff held in his left, and gazes down at a pool in which a kneeling amorino seems about to immerse a torch while looking up toward the youth. In the left background above masses of cloudlike rocks appears the anxious face of a woman who lifts her left hand to a barlike object, possibly a flute, across her throat. The whole conception of the picture is unusual and accomplished, the composition simple and subtle, and the structure of the body forms with stippling emphasized by overdrawing with fine black lines in the features and the hair clearly declares the authorship.

Ragghianti would assign the Three Graces to his "Maestro degli Scorci" (p. 66), the Ariadne Discovered of the Casa dei Capitelli Colorati to his "Maestro Colorista" (p. 67) or a man related to him (p. 161, legend), and the Narcissus to his "Maestro Bucolico" (p. 82). Since he says nothing in support of these assignments, there is little point in arguing against them, but we may be grateful for his providing a color plate of the Narcissus and another fine detail of the Ariadne Discovered, since these are seldom reproduced.

With only a small group of attributions scattered among four locations, two of them only very poorly documented in their decoration and contents, it is impossible to speak with authority about this artist's activity in Pompeii. It seems clear that he was a foreigner to the city, very likely brought in to help decorate the villa at Torre Annunziata from which the Narcissus comes and then persuaded one way or another to do a little work elsewhere nearby. His appearance in the Casa dei Capitelli Colorati, moreover, is suggestive since that house shows many signs of having been a gallery of different styles of Fourth Style decoration and different hands, like the Casa dei Dioscuri and the Casa del Citarista. The room in which he worked was a large room for receptions, one of the largest rooms in the house; it is significant that he should have been given so important an apartment.

➛ *Works* ➛

POMPEII

VII iv 31/51, Casa dei Capitelli Colorati

Room i, the fourth room on the west side of the smaller peristyle

- Ariadne discovered by Bacchus: H 1237; MN 9278; Rizzo 1929, pl. 109.2; Ragghianti 1963, 127 (detail).

• Divinities of Light ("Apollo and Rhodos"): H 969; MN 9537; Elia 1932, 83, fig. 26.

IX ii 16, Casa di Panthera

Room k

• Three Graces: H 856; MN 9236; HBr pl. 49; Rizzo 1929, pl. 137; Brion 1960, fig. 37; Stenico 1963, pl. 111; Ward-Perkins and Claridge 1978, 15 and 172, no. 153; *Collezioni* 1986, 100; Guillaud and Guillaud 1990, fig. 10; De Caro 1994, 164.

IX iii 5, Casa di Marco Lucrezio

Triclinium fenestratum 16

• Amorini feasting: H 757; MN 9255; HBr pl. 65.1; Rizzo 1929, pl. 141.2.

• Amorini feasting: H 759; MN 9207; HBr pl. 64.2; Rizzo 1929, pl. 141.1; Jashemski 1979, 97, fig. 153; *Collezioni* 1986, 267.

• Amorini feasting: H 760; MN 9208; HBr pl. 65.2.

• Amorini feasting: H 766; MN 9206; HBr pl. 64.1.

• Amorini feasting: H 767; MN 9193; HBr text 1.83, fig. 22.

• Amorini feasting: H 768; MN 9191; HBr text 1.82, fig. 21.

Environs, Villa at Torre Annunziata

• Narcissus: H 1358; MN 9385; HBr pl. 231; Rizzo 1929, pl. 128.2; Ragghianti 1963, 147.

The Telephus Painter

Comparatively few works by this painter, one of the most gifted and most consistently painstaking, survive, and it seems unlikely that he was a resident of either Pompeii or Herculaneum. In Herculaneum he may have worked in only a single building, the "Basilica," where he was responsible for most of the important subject pictures. In Pompeii his work appears in private houses but is confined to a single room in each, in one case a single picture. The evidence suggests that he came from a distance, perhaps brought on commission to decorate the "Basilica" of Herculaneum, and spent a comparatively short time in the Campanian cities. His repertory seems to have been large and includes several unusual compositions, most notably perhaps the Telephus, but none of these seems to have been his own invention. At least half his subjects are stock for Pompeii, and on one occasion he employs essentially contrasting compositions for counterparts, the Telephus and the

Theseus Victor, which may be indication that he was dependent on a restricted number of models. For the atrium of the Casa del Poeta Tragico he seems to have been able to provide certain unusual illustrations for Homer but had then to eke these out with other subjects. Of course, in both cases the taste of the patron is an imponderable factor that must not be ignored, and certainly this painter's repertory is richer and more varied than those of all but a very few of the best painters. He likes complex compositions, which he understands and reproduces with care and accuracy, although sometimes somewhat mechanically.

The easiest of his characteristics to recognize are the large, well-shaped eyes with startling whites and great staring pupils of rather haggard expression with which he endowed nearly all his figures. Only a little less noticeable are the deep, small creases that regularly appear at the corners of the small mouth, the shelving, poorly shaped upper lip, and the lower lip of sucked-in appearance. In his hands the metacarpus is usually distinctly elongated and the fingers exaggeratedly slender and spidery, but without distinct articulation of the knuckles.

His figures are well proportioned, rather statuesque. They show only a slight concession to Flavian mannerism in the heavy limbs and slender, sometimes small hands and feet. The women's breasts are fashionably small. The proportions of children are rather better understood than is usual in Campanian painting.

The heads usually are given a very regular ovoid shape with a well-rounded skull and a bluntly pointed chin. The hair often tends to appear thin and grows in loose short ringlets. The eyes are regularly exaggeratedly large, the white dramatized, the iris nearly a complete circle. The shape of the eye is well studied and carefully drawn, the inner corner set low, the outer elongated. The lower lid sometimes tends to close a little high over the ball, an effect emphasized by shadow. The brows sweep in a low arc from high at the bridge of the nose wide of the outer corner of the eye nearly to the hair; they generally seem raised and questioning. The nose is apt to be long, straight, and slightly thick with a broad bridge and sharp point. The mouth is almost always very small, with deep creases painted in at the corners. The upper lip is heavily shadowed; the lower is less carefully delineated. Chin and cheeks are smooth and full. Ears, when they are shown, are neat and well placed with a distinct lobe. The throat is apt to be slightly heavy.

The torso is generally slightly long with heavy, smoothly rounded shoulders. The male torso has a deep rib cage with a high clavicle, carefully drawn deltoid, distinct but not overly muscular breasts with small nipples and a deep linea alba. The female torso is apt to have a narrow rib cage in proportion to the shoulders, small breasts with large nipples, and very soft, subdued musculature. The female waist is slender, softly marked, the hips heavy, the navel low and large. In male figures the hip bulge is not strongly pronounced.

Women's arms are remarkably smooth, with rather sharp elbows, well-shaped forearms, and heavy, smooth wrists. The hands of both male and female figures are remarkably long and slender with an elongated metacarpus and almost spidery fingers that are without sharply marked knuckles. When carefully drawn the tips of the fingers are rounded and have large, spatulate nails. When the fingers are in play, they curl in S-curves.

The thighs are smooth and taper regularly. Knees are correctly understood but without detailed modeling. The ankles are heavy and soft, like the wrists, without conspicuous modeling or prominent bones. Feet are small and neat with rather long toes.

The artist attempts a variety of draperies, usually several in a single picture, with varying success. Heavy wool pulls in broad panels and half-cylinders dragging away from shoulder or knee, folded in overlapping planes that are sometimes too crisp and facile in execution. Transparent veils are cleverly rendered with crisp white edges of light along the spines of folds. The folds are usually slightly nervous, angular and calligraphic. The painter is fond of transparent drapery and of fur, which he paints boldly with coarse brushes and rapid, cursive strokes. His metal is of a rich, dark hue with very brightly gleaming lights and edges; once identified, it is not easily mistaken.

The palette of the Telephus Painter is heavy, full of dark, somber blues and greens, deepened by graying and overdrawing in black and brown, and accented with frequent overbrilliant, rather spotty lights. The highlighting tends to give a picture a slightly eerie quality that is reinforced by dully glowing, misty backgrounds and passages of chiaroscuro. The drawing and underpainting are in warm earth colors, especially warm rosy browns; the finished picture was retouched with black and white to sharpen edges and lights. Large forms and drapery are laid in with large brushes and broad strokes; flesh is developed with fine brushes and nervous scribbling and hatched strokes, layer upon layer, the transitions between forms blurred and feathered, so that an effect of impasto is procured. Highlights and sharp edges, both dark and light, were added in final touches. The technique is extremely unusual and produces a slightly rough texture that is characteristic of this painter.

→ *Works* ←

POMPEII

VI viii 3/5, Casa del Poeta Tragico

Atrium

• Zeus and Hera on Mount Ida *(Dios apate):* H 114; MN 9559; HBr pl. 11; Curtius 1929, 33, fig. 22; Rizzo 1929, pl. 64; Elia 1932, fig. 6; Brion 1960, fig. 53; de Franciscis 1963, pl. 38; *Collezioni* 1986, 156; Guillaud and Guillaud 1990, figs. 49, 50, 290; *PPM* 4 (1993) 538, fig. 20a; De Caro 1994, 181.

• Achilles' surrender of Briseis: H 1309; MN 9105; HBr pl. 10; Curtius 1929, 35–37, figs. 23–25; Rizzo 1929, pls. 62 and A; Elia 1932, fig. 4 and pl. 2; Brion 1960, fig. 62; de Franciscis 1963, pl. 39; Stenico 1963, pls. 91–92; Seider 1968, 74; *Collezioni* 1986, 207 and p. 64; Guillaud and Guillaud 1990, figs. 51, 287; *Peinture* 1993, 1, fig. 46, and 2, fig. 181a; *PPM* 4 (1993) 540, fig. 22; De Caro 1994, 182.

• Embarcation of Helen: H 1308; MN 9108; HBr pl. 12; Rizzo 1929, pl. 63; *Collezioni* 1986, 203; *Peinture* 1993, 1, fig. 45, and 2, fig. 181b; *PPM* 4 (1993) 540, fig. 21.

VII ix 47/65, Casa di Marte e Venere (Casa delle Nozze di Ercole)

Tablinum

• Mars and Venus: H 320; MN 9248; HBr pl. 4; Rizzo 1929, pl. 104; Curtius 1929, 252, fig. 149 and pl. 1; Elia 1932, fig. 21; de Franciscis 1963, pl. 40; Ragghianti 1963, 121; Stenico 1963, pl. 104; Seider 1968, 58; Kraus and von Matt 1973, fig. 269; *Collezioni* 1986, 157; Guillaud and Guillaud 1990, fig. 282; *Peinture* 1993, 1, pl. 89, and 2, fig. 261; De Caro, 1994, 175; *PPM* 7 (1997) 370, fig. 27.

HERCULANEUM

"Basilica"

• Hercules discovering Telephus: H 1143; MN 9008; HBr pls. 79–80; Curtius 1929, 3–8, figs. 2–5; Rizzo 1929, pl. 69; Elia 1932, pl. 1; de Franciscis 1963, pl. 32; Stenico 1963, pl. 86; Seider

1968, 68; Kraus and von Matt 1973, fig. 160; *Collezioni* 1986, 187 and p. 61; Guillaud and Guillaud 1990, figs. 325–26, 329; *Peinture* 1993, 1, fig. 122, and 2, fig. 451.

- Theseus victor over the Minotaur: H 1214; MN 9049; HBr pls. 80–81; Curtius 1929, 10–11, figs. 7–8; Maiuri 1953, 67; de Franciscis 1963, pl. 33; Ragghianti 1963, 83; Stenico 1963, pl. 94; Seider 1968, 69; *Collezioni* 1986, 174 and p. 53; Guillaud and Guillaud 1990, figs. 330–31; *Peinture* 1993, 1, fig. 123, and 2, fig. 452.
- Chiron and Achilles: H 1291; MN 9109; HBr pl. 82; Curtius 1929, 13, fig. 9; Elia 1932, fig. 5; de Franciscis 1963, pl. 34; Stenico 1963, pl. 80; Kraus and von Matt 1973, fig. 159; *Collezioni* 1986, 177 and p. 60; Guillaud and Guillaud 1990, figs. 61, 327–28; *Peinture* 1993, 1, fig. 124, and 2, fig. 453.
- Marsyas and Olympus: H 226; MN 9151; HBr pl. 87.1; *Collezioni* 1986, 178.

Unidentified Buildings (almost certainly the "Basilica")

- Jupiter reclining among clouds: H 113; MN 9553; HBr pl. 186; Rizzo 1929, pl. 102; *Pompeji: Leben und Kunst* 1973, 212; *Peinture* 1993, 1, fig. 156.
- Medea: H 1264; MN 8976; HBr pl. 7; Curtius 1929, 305, fig. 175 and pl. 8; Ragghianti 1963, 84; Stenico 1963, pl. 88; *Collezioni* 1986, 194; Guillaud and Guillaud 1990, fig. 332; *Peinture* 1993, 1, fig. 157.
- Sacrificant: H 1802; MN 8949; Herbig 1962, pl. 32; Ragghianti 1963, pl. 28.
- Sacrificant: H 468; MN 8946; Elia 1932, fig. 30; Ragghianti 1963, pl. 27; *Pompeji: Leben und Kunst* 1973, 249; Ward-Perkins and Claridge 1978, 19 and 123, no. 19; *Collezioni* 1986, 235.

The Triclinio Painter

At V ii 4, the Casa del Triclinio, a simple house of modest size with atrium and peristyle, the single large room on the peristyle, a broad rectangle, produced three square pictures showing late phases of rather disheveled drinking parties alternating with floating figures of the seasons in the side panels. These pictures have been removed to the Museo Nazionale. That from the north wall shows a triclinium arrangement in which two reclining couples flank a single seated man under an awning. A small round table set with drinking vessels stands in the middle, while a servant boy stands attentively at the right, and a girl, behind the couch at the left. The representation is explained by an inscription in large letters above the participants: *FACITE VOBIS SVAVITER EGO CANTO*, and after a space, *EST ITA VALEAS*. The painting has lost much of the overpainting, and flaking has destroyed some of the center, but the character of the drawing and a certain amount of detail remain. One notes the light frames of the figures and the rather pinched noses and mouths, in contrast to their wide eyes, sometimes with strongly arched eyebrows, their puny arms of only slight modeling with hands in which the long slender fingers stand well apart, and the awkwardness of the perspective.

One sees these same qualities in a better-preserved companion piece from the west wall showing the breaking up of a party attended only by men. There are six men present and four servant boys. The table has been removed, and one servant is putting his master's shoes on, while another supports a guest so far gone in drink that he is limp. One has covered his head with his garment and appears about to leave. Over their heads are the words *SCIO* and *BIBO*. Here we get a fair range of this painter's forms. His heads have a deep skull, sometimes exaggeratedly so in the case of the servants, covered with a close cap of hair that sometimes breaks into a characteristic cowlick over the forehead. In profile the hair bulges over the forehead, which itself is apt to bulge slightly, and is often ducktailed at the nape of the neck. The nose breaks from the forehead and is sharply pointed. The mouth is small, often with a slightly pursed look. The chin is very short and shallow. Both hands and feet are exaggeratedly small, but the hands have a strikingly long, straight thumb. In full face the eyes are sometimes heavily shadowed between the lid and eyebrow and especially at the inner corner of the eye. The ear is small but rather conspicuous, set low. Our general impression is of an artist given to drawing rather than painting. Some of the servants seem to be almost scrawny dwarves, and the guests look more like boys than men.

The third picture from the east wall has suffered most; one can only make out that it shows a woman dancer accompanied by two flute-players performing for a party of eight diners, evidently four couples, who are so far advanced in drinking that one has fallen asleep. A statue at the right seems to serve to carry a tray with drinking vessels. One can see that the general character of the picture is consonant with its companions; the proportions of the figures, the shape of the heads, the faulty perspective, and the palette are the same.

This man painted the lararial panel over the thermopolium in I viii 8, a long rectangle showing the genius, togate, flanked by a pair of Lares, symmetrically posed, who carry situla and rhyton, and these in turn flanked by Mercury with caduceus and purse and Bacchus with long scepter and panther, to which he pours wine from a cantharus. A garland is looped over their heads and hangs to frame the panel on either side. The profile of Mercury is immediately in every way strikingly like that of the guest having his shoes put on in the second picture, and the hands of the genius and Bacchus have this painter's long thumb. One also notes the artist's tendency to draw rather than paint.

Another picture by the Triclinio Painter is the Slaughter of the Niobids from the Casa del Marinaio, VII xv 1/2, now in the Museo Nazionale. In this panorama all of his hallmarks are in evidence: the deep skull, sharp nose, and short chin, the heavily shadowed eyes and odd long thumb, and the tendency to draw rather than paint. It is unfortunate that this is the only one of four panoramas in this room that has survived in reasonably good condition. Another fragmentary Slaughter of the Niobids, from VII vi 28 (HBr text 1.208, fig. 60), is certainly not his work.

One other picture that I can positively identify as this painter's work is the procession of woodworkers carrying a *ferculum* from VI vii 8/9, now in the Museo Nazionale. This was a façade picture, more an advertisement for the shop behind than an artistic effort, but it betrays its authorship by the shape of the skulls, the sharp-nosed and short-chinned profiles, the conspicuous ears, and the excessively small hands and feet. I also believe that the picture of a potter working at his wheel from II iii 7, now in the Antiquarium of Pompeii, is probably by him, but its state of preservation prevents positive attribution.

One may ask whether this man may not have been especially a sign painter, possibly even one of the *scriptores* who painted the elegant electoral programmata of Pompeii, who was occasionally given decorative work. The inscriptions in these pictures are finely lettered, although not in rustic capitals.

⇢ *Works* ⇠

POMPEII

I viii 8

Thermopolium, south wall

- Lararial picture: de Franciscis 1978, fig. 88; Eschebach 1978, fig. 225; *PPM* 1 (1990) 805, figs. 3a, b; Fröhlich 1991, pl. 2.1; *Peinture* 1993, 2, fig. 40.

II iii 7

Façade at the southwest corner

- Vulcan and potter: Pompeii Antiquarium 21631,F19 (= 2193–4); Kraus and von Matt 1973, fig. 196; Ward-Perkins and Claridge 1978, 204, no. 281; Fröhlich 1991, pl. 16.1; *PPM* 3 (1991) 182–83, figs. 1–2; *Peinture* 1993, 1, fig. 27.

V ii 4, Casa del Triclinio

Triclinium r, northwest of the peristyle

- *Facite vobis suaviter:* MN 120031; HBr pl. 212.2; Ward-Perkins and Claridge 1978, 198, no. 245; Fröhlich 1991, pl. 21.2; *PPM* 3 (1991) 813, fig. 38; *Peinture* 1993, 1, fig. 36.
- End of the party: MN 120029; HBr pl. 212.1; Rizzo 1929, pl. 197.2; Ward-Perkins and Claridge 1978, 198, no. 244; *Collezioni* 1986, 342; Fröhlich 1991, pl. 20.2; *PPM* 3 (1991) 815, fig. 41.
- Party with dancer: MN 120030; HBr text 2.22, fig. 1; Fröhlich 1991, pl. 21.1; *PPM* 3 (1991) 818, fig. 47.

VI vii 8/9

Façade

- Procession of woodworkers: H 1480; MN 8991; Eschebach 1978, fig. 235; *Collezioni* 1986, 327; Fröhlich 1991, pl. 57.1; *Peinture* 1993, 1, pl. 47, and 2, fig. 171; *PPM* 4 (1993) 391, fig. 1b.

VII xv 1/2, Casa del Marinaio

Exedra of the bath complex

- Slaughter of the Niobids: S 505; MN 111479; HBr pl. 151; Peters 1963, fig. 59; *Collezioni* 1986, 93; *Peinture* 1993, 1, fig. 80; *PPM* 7 (1997) 749, fig. 88.

Afterword

The chief result of this study is the catalog itself. To these lists other students of antiquity will be able to add other paintings as they are unearthed or as a skilled eye finds telltale characteristics in some of the many paintings that have not been included here. I have preferred to limit the lists to pictures of whose authorship I am reasonably sure rather than blur the focus with possibilities. And I have limited my discussion of each painter's *oeuvre* to essentials, persuaded that speculation about the relative chronology of works and their importance, or lack thereof, in a man's career belongs elsewhere. Only after a painter's identity has been well established and understood can other questions about him be properly addressed.

Certain phenomena of general interest, however, do emerge. The Boscotrecase Painter, the Adone Ferito Painter, the Io Painter, the Iphigenia Painter, Lucius, and the Meleagro Painter were almost certainly residents of the area, and the only figure painters that we can be reasonably sure were. None of these is a first- or even second-rate workman, yet the Adone Ferito Painter and the Io Painter worked at all three ancient sites, and the Meleagro Painter seems to have been more popular at Herculaneum than at Pompeii. Lucius was in demand for garden decorations at large scale but seldom asked to do other figurative work. The Iphigenia Painter seems to have worked only at Pompeii but produced a vast amount of work there in a wide range of houses.

No accomplished workman did more than a small amount of work in Pompeii, but none worked in only one house or building. On the other hand, many inferior workmen did only a small amount of work at these three sites. The best workmen, the Amore Punito Painter, the Centauro Painter, the Cecilio Giocondo Painter, the Telephus Painter, the Achilles Painter, and the Panthera Painter, worked in only a very few buildings, all important, and evidently commanded a substantial fee. The painters of the next rank, the Giasone Painter, the Principe di Montenegro Painter, the Triptolemus Painter, the Dioscuri Painter, the Nozze di Ercole Painter, and their ilk, seem sometimes to have worked in a few other places, but only a few, and in many cases no other places at all. The evidence suggests strongly that most figure painters were itinerant and went from town to town looking for commissions.

In no house or building in Pompeii, Herculaneum, or Stabiae are all the figure paintings of consistently high quality. A few, such as the Casa del Menandro and the Casa di Meleagro, have numerous figure paintings that are the work of only one or two painters, but these are not painters of the first rank. Most large houses showed a wide range of figure paintings by several hands, although none seems to have been conceived as a gallery of art. The main reception room of a house, be it the tablinum or a particular oecus or triclinium, seems to have been decorated with special elaboration, and the subject pictures executed with extra care, either by superior artists or with special effort by less accomplished workmen, but there is almost never more than one such room in a house. The Casa dei Vettii and the Casa dei Dioscuri seem to be the only real exceptions to this rule. Pompeian painting was, indeed, furnishing rather than art, intended to embellish and populate the space it enclosed more or less richly, as the occasion and function of that space might require, full of allusion to poetry and drama but seldom programmatic and never to be studied, simply a background for other activity.

Indexes

Topographical Index

Sites in Campania.

Museum Inventory Number Index

Inventory numbers in the Museo Nazionale Archeologico, Naples.

Picture Subject Index

Library of Congress Cataloging-in-Publication Data

Richardson, Lawrence.
A catalog of identifiable figure painters of ancient Pompeii, Herculaneum, and Stabiae / L. Richardson, jr.
p. cm.
Includes indexes.
ISBN 0-8018-6235-3 (alk. paper)
1. Mural painting and decoration, Roman—Expertising—Italy. 2. Mural painting and decoration, Roman—Italy—Themes, motives Catalogs. 3. Human figure in art Catalogs. 4. Pompeii (Extinct city) 5. Herculaneum (Extinct city) 6. Stabiae (Extinct city) I. Title.
ND2575.R53 2000
759.937′7—dc21 99-33031
CIP